Partnerships and New Roles in the 21st-Century Academic Library

Creating the 21st-Century Academic Library

About the Series

Creating the 21st-Century Academic Library provides both conceptual information and practical guidance on the full spectrum of innovative changes now underway in academic libraries. Each volume in the series is carefully crafted to be a hallmark of professional practice and thus:

- Focuses on one narrowly defined aspect of academic librarianship.
- Features an introductory chapter, surveying the content to follow and highlighting lessons to be learned.
- Shares the experiences of librarians who have recently overseen significant changes in their library to better position it to provide 21st-century services to students, faculty, and researchers.

About the Series Editor

Bradford Lee Eden is one of librarianship's most experienced and knowledgeable editors. Dr. Eden is dean of library services at Valparaiso University. Previous positions include associate university librarian for technical services and scholarly communication at the University of California, Santa Barbara; head of web and digitization services and head of bibliographic and metadata services for the University of Nevada, Las Vegas Libraries. He is editor of *OCLC Systems & Services: International Digital Library Perspectives* and *The Bottom Line: Managing Library Finances*, and he is on the editorial boards of *Library Hi Tech* and the *Journal of Film Music*. He is currently the editor of *Library Leadership & Management*, the journal of the Library Leadership and Management Association (LLAMA) within ALA.

Titles in the Series

1. *Leading the 21st-Century Academic Library: Successful Strategies for Envisioning and Realizing Preferred Futures*
2. *Enhancing Teaching and Learning in the 21st-Century Academic Library: Successful Innovations That Make a Difference*
3. *Cutting-Edge Research in Developing the Library of the Future*
4. *Creating Research Infrastructures in the 21st-Century Academic Library*
5. *Partnerships and New Roles in the 21st-Century Academic Library: Collaborating, Embedding, and Cross-Training for the Future*

Partnerships and New Roles in the 21st-Century Academic Library

Collaborating, Embedding, and Cross-Training for the Future

Edited by
Bradford Lee Eden

ROWMAN & LITTLEFIELD
Lanham • Boulder • New York • London

Published by Rowman & Littlefield
A wholly owned subsidiary of The Rowman & Littlefield Publishing Group, Inc.
4501 Forbes Boulevard, Suite 200, Lanham, Maryland 20706
www.rowman.com

Unit A, Whitacre Mews, 26-34 Stannary Street, London SE11 4AB

British Library Cataloguing in Publication Information Available

Library of Congress Cataloging-in-Publication Data

Partnerships and new roles in the 21st-century academic library : collaborating, embedding, and cross-training for the future / edited by Bradford Lee Eden.
pages cm. – (Creating the 21st-century academic library)
Includes bibliographical references and index.
ISBN 978-1-4422-5539-5 (cloth : alk. paper) – ISBN 978-1-4422-5540-1 (pbk. : alk. paper) – ISBN 978-1-4422-5541-8 (ebook)
1. Academic libraries–Relations with faculty and curriculum. 2. Academic librarians–Professional relationships. 3. Academic libraries–Effect of technological innovations on. 4. Academic librarians–In-service training. 5. Libraries and colleges. I. Eden, Bradford Lee, editor.
Z675.U5P342 2015
027.7–dc23
2015019700

Printed in the United States of America

Contents

Introduction

Partnerships and New Roles in the 21st-Century Academic Library

The fifth volume in this series focuses on partnerships and new roles for libraries in the 21st century. Topics such as consulting, coaching, assessment and engagement partnerships, university commercialization, adult student support, librarian-faculty partnerships, information commons, MOOCs, digital badging, cross-training, global librarianship, shared services between and among libraries, and research support are brought together in this volume.

Kelly Evans begins this volume by discussing the role of librarians, particularly business librarians, in the provision of services and research support to students similar to a consulting model. She provides a case study of both consultant-to-client and librarian-to-consultant models, along with helpful hints.

Todd Bruns, Steve Brantley, and Kirstin Duffin follow with the importance of infusing coaching and scholarly communication into library liaison roles. They describe this in relation to their institutional repository, STEM scholars, and assisting faculty at their particular institution, and examine some of the current coaching models, such as Oregon State University's "Rights Well Workshop," the University of Colorado Boulder's Training Needs Assessment program, the University of British Columbia's disciplinary scans and embedded services approach, and the University of Minnesota's systems approach.

Katy Mathuews documents the library's data management program at Shawnee State University in Ohio and how a partnership with the institution's Office of Institutional Effectiveness assisted in gaining a better understanding of library users and the nonuser population, as well as the library's impact on student success as defined by GPA and graduation rates. The assessment and results of this partnership have been informed by library and institutional strategic planning, and it is an excellent model for other libraries to emulate and experiment with.

Jason Dewland and Cynthia M. Elliott describe an interesting new role at the University of Arizona, that of academic commercialization librarian, whose job is to actively engage and collaborate with faculty, researchers, and institutional offices focused on commercialization efforts related to research. Some interesting partnerships and workflows are mentioned, along with challenges and recommendations for those wishing to explore this new librarian role within the academy.

Jessica Alverson and Susan Shultz discuss an important and challenging new focus for many academic librarians: e-learners and adult learners. They provide a select analysis of key theories and frameworks around these types of learners, and describe their own work with the School for New Learning at DePaul University. They provide many tips, best practices, and guidelines for establishing rapport, creating a supportive environment, developing instructional content, and assessment and feedback surrounding e-learners and adult learners.

Troy Davis and Ann Marie Stock detail their partnership at the College of William and Mary, illustrating how a librarian and a professor of Hispanic studies/film and media studies have worked together over a number of years on courses and workshops that are highly collaborative and student-focused. This partnership has resulted in unique field trips and access to important political and artistic personages. They provide a pilot model for the future of librarian/faculty partnerships, where each partner is an equal player in course creation and in the teaching endeavor.

In a chapter focused on teamwork, John Weed and his colleagues at the University of Texas Health Science Center at San Antonio discuss many of the physical, instructional, curricular, and technological changes and directions they have led and participated in for the last few years. Many of the workflow, planning, and change management details are provided, showing how they have become leaders in partnering and collaborating with their colleagues across their institution.

Joseph Fennewald writes about the challenges and opportunities that the library commons model presents for academic libraries, and he examines recent job postings for managers of library, information, and knowledge commons to find both similarities and differences in duties and responsibilities. His research informs his own current job, and assists anyone else who is considering applying for and working within this learning continuum.

Marissa Ball and Patricia Pereira-Pujol then describe a unique evolution of the information commons model at the Hub at Florida International University, where student assessment activities have helped to transform and fund new and continuing library services and resources, and to inform campus administration of the needs and desires of the student body.

JJ Pionke provides a useful background of embedded librarianship, MOOCs, and digital badging, along with helpful hints and suggestions for success with both patrons and faculty in implementation, participation, and questions.

Ashley Krenelka Chase relates her library's story of cross-training, teams, and rotating duties at the Stetson University College of Law Libraries. Her library has become very adept at change management and cross-training, having gone through the loss of library personnel numerous times in the last six years. Sound familiar? Read about how this particular library addressed this issue.

Global librarianship provides unique opportunities for partnerships, and Apollo Abungu and Margaret Law detail the development and building of a public library and community center in the village of Ndwara, Kenya. The partnership involves a librarian from the Kenyan village, along with a Canadian librarian with rural public library development experience. Their success is based on an understanding of project management, fundraising, flexibility, and teamwork.

Emily Lin describes the history and process of the Next-Generation Technical Services (NGTS) initiative in the University of California (UC) Libraries system from 2009 through the present. The UC Libraries have a long history of shared services and collaboration, and this partnership was tested and expanded during the recent economic recession. Lin describes the various phases of NGTS, providing details on its collaborative yet time-sensitive nature, in a uniquely visual and concise manner (this editor was also a major participant in the NGTS initiative, leading one of the three phase 2 committees).

Finally, Linda O'Brien and Joanna Richardson encapsulate the importance of research support and infrastructure through partnerships in and through institutions of higher education. Their background in this area centers around the Australian higher education landscape, and they provide a unique perspective on what has happened and is currently happening in Australia to supply the resources and people necessary to support research.

It is hoped that this volume, and the series in general, will be a valuable and exciting addition to the discussions and planning surrounding the future directions, services, and careers in the 21st-century academic library.

Chapter One

From Consultant to Client

Using a Business-Centered Approach in Classroom Instruction

Kelly Evans

Helping business students understand the competitive nature of the global economy is not just the purview of business faculty any longer; it is a role that business librarians can be proactive in stepping into. Business librarians can take a role in the classroom that business students will understand and recognize as meaningful: the role of consulting librarian. Consulting librarianship is not a new concept and does tie into the model of being "embedded" in the classroom. This chapter will discuss a business librarian's approach to providing research and resources to students as a consultant would to a client and how this model can be effectively incorporated into any instructional setting.

OVERVIEW OF CONSULTANT ROLE

Consulting librarianship has been perceived as a role that fits into corporate librarianship and/or information centers. With the growth of embedded librarianship in academic settings, consulting librarians fit into a model of being proactive, creative, and mobile. Consulting librarians as described by David Shumaker are "specialized role players with a unique expertise—in this case, information analysis and management—that the client needs in order to achieve certain objectives" (2012, p. 16).

The clients in the academic setting are students, usually in teams, and their information analysis would involve an assigned business or marketing plan based on a real-life business or start-up. Shumaker describes the role of

1

consultants in relation to their clients as "able to spot information problems that others on the team may not recognize. They are in the position to come up with solutions crafted to the special needs of the team" (2012, p. 16). The consulting model of librarianship does take the librarian role further by going beyond the provision of information resources to actually giving the clients the answers to their queries. In academia, giving the students the answers is frowned upon, yet the consulting role can be modified in teaching students to critically think about their information query and come up with their own solutions by utilizing library resources and tools.

Business librarians have unique opportunities to embed with business coursework, in particular marketing classes. Marketing classes are mainly project-based and team-oriented. Students are given either a mock business plan or a real company business plan. They are assigned a team to work on, creating a marketing strategy plan for a business. Business librarians can partner with the professor of the marketing course by offering to be a resource for these student teams and an information consultant for the students' research. It is up to the students to utilize the information consultant as a resource, yet the business librarian can promote his or her research support by providing initial instruction on how to access library resources, supplying contact hours and info in the course syllabi, and sending email reminders to students.

For an experienced business librarian, embedding with new business classes is not as daunting. The most challenging aspect is the time commitment. When teams are required to utilize their business librarian, there may be a lot of meetings with students and longer consultation times. The most vital piece in the success of the librarian/consultant partnership with the students/clients is emphasizing that, in the real world, time with a consultant costs quite a bit of money. The time the students have with their librarian costs them no capital, and is their opportunity to receive pertinent research tools they can apply to their future careers. Being available and flexible to meet with students at their point of need is essential for a successful partnership.

CONSULTANT TO CLIENT

In the past year, a collaborative consultant-client partnership took place during a semester in a Sales Force Marketing class. Sales Force Marketing is an upper-level marketing course requiring students to work with a local business in the creation of a marketing and advertising plan. The professor assigns businesses to teams of five to six students. The students are required to make initial contact with the business owner and arrange a meeting to find out the specifics of the company mission and financials. Then the students have to spend time researching the industry into which their company would fall. This is the most challenging part of the process for most students. Some of the companies do not fall into a clear-cut industry category. For example, one of the teams was assigned a local marijuana store. The recreational pot industry is relatively new. Within NAICS (North American Industry Classification System) headings, marijuana or pot is listed as medical, not recreational. Another category frequently used is hydroponics stores. The role of the business librarian as a consultant is to help students figure out which industry category would apply to their company, by delving into the industry description and then providing the appropriate information to the students.

From the beginning of the term, the students were aware of their consultant/librarian because the contact information was listed in the course syllabus. The professor explained to the students on the first day of class the research expectations for their project, and that it was required that they make contact with their librarian at least once. The students received a library instruction session during their third week. They were asked to share their assigned companies during the session. It gave them an advantage in having their librarian show them examples of how to locate company and industry information. The professor stressed that their librarian would not give all the answers during the session, just one example per team. It was up to the team to utilize the rest of the research. An overview of the research tools was thoroughly demonstrated during the session. The tools demonstrated were linked on a LibGuide course page created specifically for this class. The LibGuide was linked in the course management system as well.

The marketing plan was not a semester-long project. The professor gave the students a deadline for completion, based on how a real-world business would operate. The students would feel the pressure of having a limited amount of time to produce a marketing plan for their companies, as they would experience in their future careers. The components of their research were the following: locating comparative companies in the area, industry analyses including trends and segmentation, financial information by industry and comparative sales volume, and market research including articles from journals and trade publications. The databases that were compiled on the LibGuide were a mix of industry, company, and article databases. The library had just acquired three pertinent databases for market research. One was a local business directory resource where students could look up comparable companies to their assigned companies. The other two databases were industry market report resources. Students could search by industry category or NAICS heading, and locate a report that would demonstrate trends and analysis that would help in formulating a marketing plan for their company.

For many of these students, this was their first foray into a real-world project and working in a team setting with their classmates. The students were also not used to projects with very tight deadlines. Thus they would need their consultant/librarian to help them save time. The librarian's role after leading a detailed instruction session was to be available to meet with student teams or provide help via email or even chat. Some of the students preferred email communication, while others wanted to meet in person and spend the time being shown the steps to locating the information.

Another challenging aspect of the research process for the students was locating articles related to their company. The pot industry, for example, yielded few articles in trade publications. With the legalization of pot in Colorado and Washington as a recent event, articles involving retail stores selling pot were almost nonexistent. It was essential, then, for the librarian to help students find other sources, such as regional newspaper articles and authentic website research, to fill the gap.

Academic librarians normally assist students in focusing their topic searches and locating articles. They will teach students how to use specific database tools. It is becoming more common for librarians to ask to view the final results of a student's paper or a "works cited" page; however, it is still not common practice for academic librarians to be involved throughout the entire project or paper process in a particular class. Business students are tasked with assignments where they are asked to come up with real solutions for a company, whether it be a business plan or a new product/service. The challenge for these students is to apply critical thinking, problem solving, and research skills to the information they are gathering, in addition to the teamwork. Having their business librarian fulfill an information consultant role ties in to the type of work the students are completing.

As a consultant working with the Sales Force Marketing class, another piece of the collaboration was to meet with student teams and vet their market proposals. The students would arrange a meeting when they needed more in-depth marketing research, and when they were struggling with connecting their topic to the information search. In the first part of the meeting, the students would describe their company and the type of market scenario they were investigating. The librarian would proceed with a standard reference interview, inquiring about what resources they found, the topics they were using, and the gaps they needed to fill in their search for information. Once the students felt satisfied that they were on the right track with the needed resources, they would receive critical feedback about the content gaps in their proposals.

For example, one of the teams was working with a local company similar to a major ride-share company. The students knew about the growing trend of ride sharing and could find basic information about the industry as a whole; however, they were missing the critical-thinking piece of the information-gathering process. Key questions:

- What does the company you are working with need in order to compete and succeed?
- How can you as their marketing team help them in promoting and furthermore establishing their company so in the end they are a success story?
- Does the company have all the demographic and consumer data they need for marketing purposes?

These students assume that their librarian has all the answers to locating research. What the students don't expect is for their librarian to engage in their topic, and then delve into the challenges the students may face in coming up with an original proposal for a real-world client. When these students graduate, most of them could work in a business setting where their company employs consultants in order to support informed financial decision making. It was important for the students to understand that the information consultant role of their librarian was preparing them for the critical business decision-making process that they will face in their careers.

Being embedded in this course meant an invitation to the final presentations each team would make. The teams would have to present their proposals and be ready to answer a multitude of questions as to the feasibility of their marketing plans. It was the professor, their classmates, and the librarian who questioned the students on the various facets of the proposals. Since there was no formal assessment of the course at that time other than an instruction feedback survey, the only assessment piece was the opportunity to view the presentations. Overall observations: the students engaged with various facets of the research and were able to interpret how this research would apply to helping their company partners succeed.

LIBRARIAN TO CONSULTANT

So how do academic librarians transition to a consultant role and embed this framework with selected courses? For one, there needs to already be a robust and creative information literacy instruction program in place. In terms of creativity, librarians should be pursuing embedded classroom opportunities as well as incorporating active learning strategies with students. Librarians have to align themselves closely with liaison faculty by creating successful teaching partnerships, where the liaison faculty member is open to further librarian involvement in the coursework. Furthermore, librarians have to be interested in building their own knowledge base in the coursework. As a business librarian with very little business background, learning the business planning steps and terminology was a key to being successful in a consultant role.

It is essential to have library administration buy into the work that you are creating. Reaching out and creating new instructional opportunities requires a huge commitment, and support from the organization is vital to making the partnerships a success for all parties. Conducting a scan of your organizational culture will help in assessing whether your library is ready for a new approach to working with students in the classroom.

Once you have evaluated the readiness of your organization or colleagues for the consultant role, the next step is to identify classes where a consultant librarian could fit right in. Not every class will be viable for embedding, nor will all liaison faculty be receptive to this idea. Speaking from experience, instructors and assistant professors are more willing to invite a librarian to partner with them in the classroom. For a lot of faculty, fitting in the time will be their greatest concern, and for some courses if there is no project or paper then there is no purpose in being embedded. The classes that seem to be the best fit for embedding a librarian as a consultant are those with a real client project or even a service learning aspect. Service learning covers many subject disciplines and projects in which students work in helping community organizations, and it has grown significantly across many colleges and universities. When students are assigned creative learning experiences, it is more applicable to have a person with a wide range of research experience present to support the critical inquiry challenges the students may face. A decision on the part of the faculty that the librarian is the person to fulfill that role in the classroom speaks to how the librarian is viewed as an equal colleague contributing to the mission of higher education student achievement.

So what do you do once you are officially embedded in the course? For starters, your contact information and office hours should be displayed in the course syllabus. The students need to know from day one your role in the course, and the many ways they can reach out to you. Before the course has started, it is important to have met with the professor to hash out the project requirements, as well as how often you will visit the class for instruction time and what the time commitment will be from all parties. The greatest challenge for any librarian embedding in one course is that there are always many other instructional opportunities prioritized in the beginning of the term. Having the course framework and how you will be involved set up ahead of time is the best way to lock in the time commitment to the course.

So how to impress upon your students your consultant role? It may be difficult for non-business majors to grasp the term "consultant." Coming up with a more creative title can help in making students relate better to what you are selling. Students hear from librarians that information literacy will empower them in life. For a lot of students who are overwhelmed with a lot of coursework, however, they may not be thinking as much about all the critical inquiry pieces in their information-gathering process. This is what librarians can sell to them at no cost, the critical inquiry steps that will help empower students to see different facets of an issue.

So how do you know your consultant role is making a difference in the course? The key word is "assessment." There are a lot of current studies published in library science publications involving assessment of information literacy instruction. Assessment can be done in many different ways: pre- and post-test, through survey feedback, and even through student feedback. Having students write a brief feedback paper about the librarian involvement in the course is helpful, if the students can list what they gained from the experience and apply that to how they completed their projects. If your colleagues are also embedding in courses, then assessing as a whole can be highly beneficial in obtaining data on the success and challenges of this type of venture.

HELPFUL HINTS

The following are helpful hints for succeeding in a consultant role:

- Attend departmental faculty meetings and market yourself as a valuable information expert.
- Be flexible and adaptable to new ways of engaging with students in the classroom.
- Encourage your colleagues to embed as consultants with their liaison areas (the more the merrier, and it creates opportunities for cross-pollination of ideas).
- Meet with students at their point of need. Working with student teams involves a lot of consultation hours; however, some students prefer to communicate through email or even chat. Not every student can meet face-to-face depending on their busy schedules, and they may just want to pop in to chat about a couple of questions.
- Attend student presentations and get copies of the final papers. It is impor- tant to see the end results of what the students gained from working closely with their consultant librarian. Papers can also be used for assess- ment purposes.
- Become conversant with the topic and research by asking for copies of previous paper assignments and by working through the steps of the re- search process. Having a firm grasp of what the assignment entails will be beneficial when students are meeting with you.
- Promote what you do to other departmental faculty across campus, and definitely keep your administration informed of any successes.
- Look for grant opportunities. Grants are a good way to help in funding your own research study into the viability and successes of the instruction-

al partnerships. If students are surveyed in detail about their experiences, then institutional review board approval will be needed from your institution in order to proceed with a research study.

REFERENCE

Shumaker, David. (2012). *The Embedded Librarian: Innovative Strategies for Taking Knowledge Where It's Needed*. New Jersey: Information Today.

Chapter Two

Scholarly Communication Coaching

Liaison Librarians' Shifting Roles

Todd Bruns, Steve Brantley, and Kirstin Duffin

Two and a half decades into the open access (OA) movement, rapid changes in scholarly communication are creating significant demands on scholars. Today's scholars must wrestle with meeting funder mandates for providing public access to their research, managing and preserving raw data, establishing/publishing open access journals, understanding the difference between "green OA" and "gold OA," navigating the complicated issues around copyright and intellectual property, avoiding potentially predatory publishers, adapting their tenure plans to OA, and discovering increasing amounts of OA resources for their research and their curricular materials. These demands present an opportunity and a need for librarians to step in and assist scholars with the scholarly communication process.

Along with a rapidly shifting scholarly communication field, two important areas of librarianship have been undergoing changes in the past fifteen years. Institutional repositories (IR) continue to proliferate in academia, in tandem with the growth of discipline repositories such as arXiv and scholars' commons such as Research Gate and Academia.edu. In spite of increasing numbers of repositories, institutional repositories have not yet achieved status as an embedded technology central to the research enterprise of the institution. Although enthusiastically embraced by librarians, institutional repositories are still unknown to significant numbers of faculty, or viewed by discipline scholars as primarily a purview of the library and not integral to their research life (Creaser, 2010, p. 9; Cullen and Chawner, 2010, p. 133; Hahn and Wyatt, 2014, p. 93; Dutta and Paul, 2014, p. 295).

The second important area, the duties of subject liaisons, has been impacted by the continuation of the serials crisis, now coupled with devastating losses in library collection budgets due to the Great Recession (Prottsman, 2011, p. 107). T. S. Plutchak (2012, p. 11) argues that more scholars now tend to view their research processes as largely "outside the library," even as scholarly communication proliferates and changes in publishing increase the needs of scholars for librarians' skills.

These increasing needs are requiring a commitment to scholarly communication support among libraries that goes beyond a staff member or two dedicated to managing an IR or being responsible for scholarly communications issues. In this chapter, four different methods of training subject liaisons to be "scholarly communication coaches" (the authors' term) are explored, and an integrated method of training subject liaisons at a master's-granting university library is suggested. "Scholarly communication coach" is defined here as a subject liaison, trained to understand copyright, authors' rights, and the use of various scholarly communication tools (e.g., the copyright-checking online database Sherpa/RoMEO), then embedded in his or her academic department to partner with the department faculty and assist with scholarly communication demands throughout the research process. By putting scholars' needs at the center of liaison efforts, librarians would be addressing critical needs of the research community, reasserting the librarian role as central to connecting scholars with knowledge, and perhaps establishing the institutional repository as an embedded technology central to the research life of the university (Kenney, 2014, p. 3; Kirchner, 2009, p. 23; Malenfant, 2010, p. 64; Mullen, 2011, p. 2).

It should be noted that this chapter describes partnering subject liaisons with the institutional repository librarian and the head of reference services at a specific master's-granting university in the development of an "engagement-centric" model (Kenney, 2014, p. 3) to support academic scholars' scholarly communication and publication needs. At other institutions, the more appropriate partnership may be an institutional repository or scholarly communications librarian with the head of collection development. An engagement-centric model is consistent with the service approach described by the University of Nebraska–Lincoln's Paul Royster at the 2014 Open Repositories Conference, and with cross-collaboration (Bruns et al., 2014, p. 244) as beneficial for creating a robust institutional repository.

GEARING LIBRARY SERVICES TO SUPPORT SCHOLARLY COMMUNICATION

Although the rapid adoption and growth of institutional repositories in academic libraries can be seen as an indicator of success of the open access initiative, faculty often perceive the repository as being something "the library does" and not integral to their research process. As pointed out by Peter

Suber, one of the challenges that institutional repositories face is that scholars generally do not comprehend that depositing in a repository and publishing in a subscription journal are both compatible and comparable. In order to address this resistance, some advocates of open access, such as Steve Harnad, have suggested the implementation of institutional mandates. A similar concept was suggested at the 2012 Budapest Open Access Initiative, with a proposal that institutions with repositories require deposit for attainment of tenure and promotion. Presenting the repository as part of a service demonstrates potential for integrating the repository into the research life of the campus in a way that makes more sense for discipline scholars' workflows (Neugebauer and Murray, 2013, p. 91; Royster, 2014). As Tomasz Neugebauer and Annie Murray note, if there is no compelling reason from the scholars' perspective to participate in a repository, getting them to do so is challenging (2013, p. 90). Depositing into a repository has to make sense in the context of the scholar's academic career.

For the institution, success of the repository is imperative. Institutions face increasing competition for diminishing resources and students seeking the greatest educational return on investment, making the public profile of the university and the institution's prestige increasingly important. The repository enables open access to the published intellectual output of the institution, increasing the likelihood that prospective students can discover research being performed in their areas of interest. The success of the repository is also essential for the continuing evolution of scholarly publishing. The shift to the open access model of scholarly publishing has been significantly slowed by the failure of faculty—through ignorance or indifference more often than from a philosophical opposition—to actively participate in depositing their work into institutional repositories. Positioning the repository into the research life cycle of the institution is essential to creating sustainable growth of the repository.

The actual work of raising the relevance of the repository in the estimation of the university faculty requires a concerted, dedicated, and collective effort by the library professionals most closely associated with the research life cycle: the IR librarian, digital initiatives or scholarly communication point person, and subject liaisons. Liaisons need to focus on both collection development and the provision of services to their departments. Liaison support of the repository, both in promoting its use and in assisting with deposits (content collection) into it, is just one aspect of scholarly communication support. Other aspects of their roles as scholarly communication support specialists include authors' rights support, data management, and data curation, expanded access to unknown collections and consultations on the state of the publishing landscape of the discipline being some of the other products of a subject liaisonship. Clearly, when one begins to elaborate the set of needs the contemporary scholar must face to thrive in an intensely competitive and complex research and publication environment, it is plain that a single professional or small group is insufficient to manage the task. To successfully address the current needs of a forward-thinking faculty, the academic library needs to place scholarly communication competencies in the toolkit of every librarian who has a role interacting with subject faculty.

SCIENCE, TECHNOLOGY, ENGINEERING, AND MATHEMATICS (STEM) SCHOLARS

The disciplines in science, technology, engineering, and mathematics (STEM) have generally led the trend toward open access and often have the most advanced needs. One of the first open access repositories, arXiv, was developed in the early 1990s as a means for the rapid sharing of research preprints among researchers. The field of mathematics has shifted its entire scholarly publishing model to open access. Funder mandates, initiated by the National Institutes of Health (NIH) and since embraced by other organiza- tions, necessitate the public access of research supported by public funds. For scholars working to get grants from NIH and other sources, providing public access to the published scholarship and planning for data management have become central to the research process.

Science faculty at the authors' institution put teaching at the center of their professional focus, although research is also very important to most of these scholars. Journal prestige and appropriateness of the publication plat- form for the research is of tantamount importance to these scholars. While scholars are becoming increasingly aware of open access publishing, they may not be able to distinguish between an OA journal and a subscription- based journal (Thorn et al., 2009, p. 43; Xia, 2010, p. 620). According to Sue Thorn et al., self-archiving in a subject or institutional repository is supported by a minority of researchers (2009, p. 44). Publishing in an OA journal, along with making access to research available through the IR, is perceived by some as less esteemed, similar to findings at other institutions (Davis and Connolly, 2007; Harley et al., 2010, p. 226; Laughtin-Dunker, 2014, p. 9).

At the authors' institution, participation in the IR varies by department. In the sciences, only faculty in the biological sciences department have em- braced adding their works to the IR (92% participation), whereas faculty in chemistry (26%), physics (16%), and geology/geography (13%) have been slower to contribute. Suzanne Bell et al. discovered that low participation by faculty is due to a lack of understanding of the role of the IR (2005, p. 286). Lack of confidence in the IR concept (Davis and Connolly, 2007; Kim, 2011, p. 248) and concerns of violating copyright (Davis and Connolly, 2007; Kim, 2011, p. 247; Dutta and Paul, 2014, p. 293) are other factors demotivating faculty participation. Understanding these scholars' hesitations associated with the IR will help guide the training of subject liaisons as scholarly communication coaches.

In terms of conducting literature research, finding and accessing articles is the goal for science scholars. Bell et al. point out that faculty rarely care how research articles are made available to them (2005, p. 287). It may not be clear to faculty who use Google Scholar that some articles they are accessing come from IRs (St. Jean et al., 2011, p. 35). In addition, while some scientists at the authors' institution, particularly biologists and chemists, are relatively heavy users of interlibrary loan (Tolppanen and Derr, 2010, p. 311), immediate access to articles is preferred. For these scholars, the sharing of preprints is less daunting than in other disciplines. Librarians can grease the wheels of IR participation if they are able to communicate to these scholars that IRs improve access to the research they need; providing data will clarify this message.

With library budgets still shrinking and journal prices still skyrocketing, maintaining subscriptions to desired scientific journals may now be a luxury. Michael Taylor et al. (2008, p. 19) and Stephen Bosch and Kittle Henderson (2014, p. 32) note the existence of a gap at many institutions between scholar information needs (i.e., access) and the modern evolution of scholarly publishing. Well-populated IRs can help sustain the instantaneous access to published research that scientists desire. To achieve this, particularly in a sustainable fashion, subject liaisons trained to offer scholarly communication coaching in the STEM areas can both assist their faculty with access and promote open access collection development into the IR.

LITERATURE REVIEW: SCHOLARLY COMMUNICATION SERVICES

A review of the scholarly communication literature reveals a wide range of scholarship on a number of issues, including managing institutional repositories (Armstrong, 2014, p. 43; Bruns et al., 2014, p. 244; Bull and Eden, 2014, p. 263; Burns et al., 2013; Royster, 2014; Sterman, 2014, p. 360), authors' rights (Wirth and Chadwell, 2010, p. 337), open access (Harnad, 2010, p. 68; Linlin, 2014, p. 3), citation rates (Gargouri et al., 2010; Suber, 2012, p. 15), library publishing (Allen, 2008, p. 59; Park and Shim, 2011, p. 76), metrics (Bruns and Inefuku, 2015; Gordon, 2012, p. 198; Inefuku, 2013; Konkiel and Scherer, 2013, p. 22), and faculty engagement (Tewell, 2014, p. 80; Wiegand, 2013, p. 335). The transformation of liaison librarians into scholarly communication supporters is a recent phenomenon in the literature.

Plutchak has described what he refers to as the upcoming "great age of librarians" (2012, p. 10). In his address to the 111th annual meeting of the Medical Library Association in 2011, Plutchak took the position that, as user habits take a digital turn, the library as place and public services in the form of reference, collection development, and organization of library resources for use all have diminishing value to researchers. The library is perceived as less central to their research process, decreasing its relevance. Conversely, information and newly created knowledge continue to proliferate. This fact, combined with research that crosses disciplinary boundaries, confounding efforts to classify it, is making librarians more relevant and necessary than ever (Plutchak, 2012, p. 10).

Laura Bowering Mullen (2011, p. 3) reports that as recently as 2011, Association of College and Research Libraries standards for libraries in higher education had still not emphasized scholarly communication or open access as a core competency. She suggests also that reference librarians and subject liaisons may be more confident and comfortable using traditional library resources rather than open access sources or the institutional repository. Nevertheless, rapid changes in scholarly communication continue to increase both the support needs of discipline scholars and calls for the inclusion of scholarly communication skills as a core librarian competency (Bailey, 2005, p. 259; Bonn, 2014, p. 132; Bresnahan and Johnson, 2013, p. 413; Kenney, 2014; Kirchner, 2009, p. 22; Thomas, 2013, p. 167; Neugebauer and Murray, 2013, p. 84; Wirth, 2011, p. 197). Subject liaison librarians, already connected to academic departments, are key to the "engagement-centric" model of embedding librarianship into the research enterprise of the institution and in the support of scholarly communication needs (Kenney, 2014; Malenfant, 2010, p. 63; Neugebauer and Murray, 2013, p. 84; Plutchak, 2012, p. 10; Thomas, 2013, p. 167).

A shift to an engagement-centered practice means that subject liaisons focus on indicators of research value that their departments and their institution consider important and not what the library considers important. By doing so, subject liaisons are better positioned to provide scholarly communication coaching to faculty at targeted points of need. William Joseph Thomas (2013, p. 170) proposes a three-level system of scholarly communication support: open access support in the form of assisting scholars with the variety of publishing models and with making their work open access; copyright and intellectual property support in the form of consultations about copyright transfer agreements (CTAs) and the fair use of copyrighted work; and research support in the form of enabling scholars to successfully evaluate open access sources and to meet funder mandates. As libraries investigate shifting liaison librarians to these new roles, a variety of methods are being employed.

IMPLEMENTATIONS OF "SCHOLARLY COMMUNICATION COACHING"

Oregon State University's "Rights Well Workshop"

Andrea Wirth and Faye Chadwell describe the creation of a Rights Well Workshop at Oregon State University Libraries that provides focus to the complexity of scholarly communication by training subject liaisons to better understand authors' rights and CTAs (2010, p. 337). In this perspective, authors' rights are a key component of scholarly communication, and assisting faculty with better management of their copyrights and their intellectual property would provide fundamental advancements to more scholarship being open access.

The Rights Well Workshop is first conducted for librarians. Wirth and Chadwell note that not only do librarians need to be trained to better serve the scholarly communication needs of the faculty with whom they liaise, but librarians like any other authors need to understand and exercise their own authors' rights (2010, p. 341). Additionally, librarians who will be supporting scholarly communication and especially the depositing of open access work in repositories need to be self-archiving their work. Responding to Doug Way's 2010 study on the limited (27%) open access availability of library and information studies articles, Wirth and Chadwell state, "There is no reason that librarian authors should not be self-archiving their articles in significant numbers while simultaneously working to inform authors in other disciplines to do the same" (2010, p. 342).

In the Rights Well Workshop, discipline-specific key journals are determined. This can be done through a variety of methods and sources: creating or reviewing reports of faculty publications at the home institution, checking the *Web of Science* Journal Citation Reports for a ranking of impact factor and the calculation of the *Eigenfactor* score, or consulting a recent review of the literature of the field if one is available (Wirth and Chadwell, 2010, p. 342). The next step is to identify the publishers of the journal and get their CTAs, followed by checking their copyright policies via the Sherpa/RoMEO online database (http://www.sherpa.ac.uk/romeo) and the CTA statement. This preparation is vital to understanding the discipline under review, and essential for speaking *with* faculty about the journals they are very familiar with as opposed to *at* them with broad generalities.

Wirth and Chadwell report that the workshop itself is divided into six sections (2010, p. 351). A brief introduction and discussion of outcomes are followed by some background discussion of the importance of authors' rights and explanation of terminology such as CTAs. This is followed by fifteen minutes of discussion on publishers and journals in the discipline, and thirty minutes of small-group reviews of CTAs, which are reported back to the larger group. Sections on amending CTAs, reviewing author addenda such as the Scholarly Publishing and Academic Resources Coalition (SPARC) addendum (http://www.sparc.arl.org/resources/authors/addendum), and listing resources to help in this analysis, followed by a short period for questions, conclude the workshop.

Wirth and Chadwell argue that this method of deploying subject liaisons prevents scholarly communication services from being limited to a one-person or one-unit "silo" (2010, p. 345). Competency in scholarly communication skills and specialized knowledge of the publishing landscape of a discipline or subdiscipline, combined with an adapted Rights Well Workshop, demonstrate the best of what "embedded librarianship" is supposed to be: working alongside and in support of scholars through the process of creating new knowledge.

Critics of authors' rights instruction argue that author addenda are suspect and perhaps unenforceable (Royster, 2014). Anxiety over tenure and promotion also contributes to scholar hesitation on pushing publishing rights addenda. Scholars may have discomfort advocating for authors' rights if they see it as potentially risking a rejection. No amount of knowledge of one's rights can resolve the issues surrounding the pressure to maintain the status quo under the current system. Neugebauer and Murray maintain that until scholars have a compelling reason to alter their publication habits, getting scholars in the disciplines to assert their own authors' rights could remain a significant hurdle (2013, p. 93).

University of Colorado Boulder: Training Needs Assessment

The approach taken at the University of Colorado to create awareness of the need for scholarly communication support services was to survey the librarians for knowledge deficits via training needs assessment. Involvement in the design process of the training program led to increased receptivity to the new skills training by participants (Bresnahan and Johnson, 2013, p. 426). Scholarly communication issues were rated in a Likert scale of "Strongly Disagree" (-2) to "Strongly Agree" (2). The survey asked for knowledge and anxiety levels about authors' rights, copyright, data analysis and manipulation, data citation, data life cycles, data management plan consultation, data sharing, data preservation, finding data, funder mandates and policies, institutional and disciplinary repositories, metadata and data description, and open access. In order to prioritize the needs once identified, the survey included questions that allowed the trainees to design the training: "What should the institution be doing? What is not being done at the institution? Why is the institution not doing what should be done?" (Bresnahan and Johnson, 2013, p. 417).

Perhaps not surprisingly, the concepts having to do with data (the exception being the finding of data) received higher anxiety and need-for-training marks than non-data concepts like authors' rights, open access, institutional repositories, copyright, and funder mandates (Bresnahan and Johnson, 2013, p. 424). Also noted were specific concerns communicated by the subject liaisons, including a need for practical, hands-on training, and anxiety that librarians would be "unwelcome" to converse with scholars on these issues.

Participants expressed concern about potential disciplinary differences among researchers, although no disciplinary breakdowns were provided in the survey to ascertain whether subject liaisons to particular fields anticipated higher data management knowledge requirements than in other fields. While this approach is effective for engaging subject liaisons in a new scholarly communication training program, Megan Bresnahan and Andrew Johnson noted the limitations of their own survey in that it addressed librarian perceptions and not those of disciplinary scholars (2013, p. 426).

University of British Columbia: Disciplinary Scans and Embedding Services

At the University of British Columbia (UBC), subject liaisons were identified not only as appropriate support personnel for assisting discipline faculty with scholarly communication, but also as rich sources of feedback to the library regarding changes in the scholarly communication environment of disciplines (Kirchner, 2009, p. 25). The strategy at UBC was to insert the subject liaison at the discipline level: besides having a basic understanding of scholarly communication, subject liaisons would develop greater confidence in their own knowledge of the trends, issues, and models of scholarship in their discipline. The UBC method of disciplinary scans and embedding services also requires deeper levels of involvement in the discipline and the workings of its faculty.

Prior to the creation of the scholarly communication training program, the institutional repository librarian and the digital initiatives librarian (responsible for helping faculty launch open access journals using the Open Journal Systems platform) had both worked with subject liaisons on the launch of their institutional repository and a journal hosting program (Kirchner, 2009, p. 24). This experience and familiarity proved valuable for setting the tone of the scholarly communication training. The earlier projects had already adapted the subject liaisons to thinking about their particular discipline's needs.

Lee Van Orsdel's *Faculty Activism in Scholarly Communications: Opportunity Assessment Instrument* (http://www.arl.org/storage/documents/ publications/scprog-fac-activism-assessment.pdf) was adapted into a tool for subject liaisons and renamed "Delving into Your Discipline" (Kirchner,

2009, p. 24). Liaisons used the tool to conduct environmental scans of the scholarly communication milieu in their discipline. The scan was followed up with interviews with disciplinary scholars. The interviews by liaisons proved to be an extremely valuable method that led to greatly increased understanding of the research needs and habits of the faculty they supported. Additionally, liaisons established connections with the campus Office of Research Services so that liaisons might partner with grant managers to assist faculty in meeting funder mandates. The interviews also helped create connections with journal editors for the purpose of assisting their journal's transition to an open access publishing model.

With the assistance of the institutional repository librarian and the digital initiatives librarian, Joy Kirchner reported, subject liaisons were able to better assess and understand the scholarly communication systems of their particular disciplines (2009, p. 25). This accomplished two of the project's primary goals: sustaining library relevance and impact on the campus research community, and bringing subject liaisons further into the scholarly communication heart of their particular disciplines (Kirchner, 2009, p. 27).

University of Minnesota: A Systems Approach

Although scholarly communication skills are increasingly seen as a core competency, resistance to doing "one more thing" by already overworked librarians can be a potential issue. Librarians also report lack of confidence and comfort in some areas of scholarly communication support, as seen previously with the needs assessment training exercise. The importance of "mainstreaming" scholarly communication support skills into the daily work lives of subject liaisons, to "fully own" them, led to the creation of the University of Minnesota Libraries' new Academic Programs department, led by Karen Williams (Malenfant, 2010, p. 64).

Karen Williams employed a systems approach as a conceptual framework, a method that "recognizes the innate networks, the interconnectedness, interdependency, and collaboration among people in organizations" (Malenfant, 2010, p. 64). The thinking at Minnesota was that scholarly communication was shifting rapidly and required significant alteration of the service model. Malenfant writes of four key steps taken at the University of Minnesota Libraries. The first step was to establish a support system for subject liaisons. This took the form of a "Scholarly Communications Collaborative," a method of educating subject liaisons via workshops, and creating resources and learning tools (Malenfant, 2010, p. 67). This reinforced the idea that the librarians were not just learning new skills but an intrinsic change of perception was taking place: subject liaisons should not only understand scholarly communication issues but also be of the mind-set that they were to actively seek opportunities to promote open access.

Development of support tools in the first round of step 1 included a video on authors' rights, a PowerPoint template, and talking points for an open access "elevator speech" (Malenfant, 2010, p. 67). An environmental scan exercise (similar to that conducted by the University of British Columbia) ascertained the existence of any discipline repositories and the positions taken on open access by major societies in the field.

As a result of the environmental scan, and with the use of the developed tools, subject liaisons were able to engage their faculty in discipline-specific terms. This set the stage for the second round of step 1: identifying influential faculty across campus who serve as journal editors or officers in their societies and who might champion the subject liaisons to their colleagues and help communicate the liaisons' role in supporting scholarly communication in their discipline (Malenfant, 2010, p. 68).

Inherent to a systems approach is the formalization of new skills and duties. The second step of the process involved rewriting subject liaison responsibilities. This allowed the new standardized responsibilities to include scholarly communication support as specific duties (Malenfant, 2010, p. 68). After the rewrite, subject liaisons were expected to educate their faculty on scholarly communication issues; advocate for open access and sustainable scholarly communication; work with faculty to help them understand changes to the scholarly communication workflows; promote the institutional repository as a resource for the faculty; and use the repository as a new collection development activity by working to incorporate their faculty's scholarship into the repository.

Step 3 was an assessment exercise. Malenfant describes a survey given to liaisons to ascertain their new skill levels in a number of areas: an understanding of the unique aspects of scholarly communication in their discipline, a basic understanding of the publishing models available, understanding of the tenure pressures in their discipline (such as journal impact factors), a self-assessment of their advocacy of open access, and their activities advising faculty on authors' rights (2010, p. 69). By taking part in this exercise, subject liaisons were receiving the message that scholarly communication skills were inherent to their work as liaisons, not something additional.

Step 4 of this systems approach was meeting a performance goal. This involved the subject liaison discussing authors' rights with faculty, in a format of the liaison's choosing (Malenfant, 2010, p. 70). They could give a presentation, meet individually with faculty in consultations, send an email, or give an entire seminar. Having a performance goal emphasized the importance of the new scholarly communication services duties, and liaisons were released from previously required responsibilities such as reference desk duties, managing departmental libraries, and collection development in order to "re-direct scarce resources—their time" to their new duties (Malenfant, 2010, p. 70).

One value of the systems approach is that it lays bare areas of resistance. Such a wholesale alteration of duties is intended to make scholarly communication support a core competency of what it means to be a subject liaison, yet Kara J. Malenfant writes that post-project reports indicate that some subject liaisons still felt that minimal knowledge about scholarly communication was acceptable, an attitude that would be unheard of in other areas of liaison competency such as a discipline subject index (2010, p. 71). Despite those few discouraging reports, the project positions the library in a leadership role on campus on a number of issues, including authors' rights and the efforts to meet funder mandate requirements. This approach to subject liaison training demonstrates that liaisons are learning new knowledge and skills in advocacy and persuasion, and new methods of interacting with their faculty.

CASE STUDY: SCHOLARLY COMMUNICATION COACHES

At a library serving a medium-sized comprehensive master's-granting university, librarianship requires collaboration, informal communication, and a diverse skill set. The faculty librarians at Eastern Illinois University (EIU) number fewer than twenty and represent all areas of operation in the library. All but three also share collection development and single or multiple department liaison responsibilities. Acquiring new knowledge and skills surrounding scholarly communication is one of many hats they wear. The librarians are used to performing a variety of roles and the addition of new skills does not represent a threat; however, achieving a level of true comfort with the intricacies of scholarly communication in one or more disciplines might appear daunting.

At Eastern Illinois University the institutional repository librarian, the head of reference services, and the dean of library services initiated the transition of subject liaisons from collection development librarians to scholarly communication librarians in response to growing campus needs for scholarly communication support. The institutional repository librarian, regularly fielding questions from faculty regarding authors' rights, copyright, depositing into the repository, contacts from questionable publishers, repository embargoes, and content quality, noted increasing numbers of questions related to these issues.

The head of reference services, who was pursuing a modernization of the reference service workflow, also recognized the growing need for the generalist and specialist librarian to have some understanding of the shifting landscape of scholarly communication. The collaborative nature of service at the library meant that all the reference librarians were also subject liaisons, and other librarians whose primary duties were not reference nonetheless performed some reference assistance. From a public service perspective, it made sense for all librarians who had responsibilities providing reference service to also have an understanding of how new knowledge is disseminated, and how that model is changing. In addition, every librarian performing reference assistance also had a department or departments to whom they were responsible for collections and library instruction, and as liaison to the faculty.

For the dean of library services, establishing stronger ties between the subject liaisons and their respective departments was part of a major initiative to reassert the library as central to research on campus.

Added to this was a series of library materials budget cuts that necessitated a higher-than-usual frequency of meetings of subject liaisons for collection development purposes, meetings that included advocating for more open access scholarly sources to balance necessary journal cancelations. These three leadership perspectives and the collection development situation created something of a "perfect storm" in which to implement the training to be a scholarly communication coach.

The institutional repository librarian and head of reference began to design a program with a literature review to try to see if this kind of program had been implemented at an institution of a similar size. They also needed to decide if there were areas of scholarly communication that were not appropriate for the faculty population. Previous consultations with the campus Research Services Office had determined that data management needs for the campus research community were not likely to be intensive; therefore, the training will not apply to data services beyond helping with data management plans. The scholarly communication coach program will focus more on authors' rights, an environmental scan of departments, and providing liaisons with a "toolkit" of resources with which to perform "scholarly communication coaching"—some examples being checking copyright permissions, describing a data management plan for a grant proposal, and avoidance of potentially predatory publishers. In the rare cases in which extensive data services are required, the institutional repository librarian working with the head of library technology will handle extensive data management. In keeping with the collaborative and informal environment of the library, a systems approach of formally revising job descriptions was considered to be unnecessary.

Initial Steps: Authors' Rights and Environmental Scans

An authors' rights workshop similar to that conducted at Oregon State University, combined with discipline-area environmental scans and discussions with faculty, as done at the University of Minnesota and the University of British Columbia, is planned for the "foundation" course in subject liaison training. These two activities will give subject liaisons the best initial core competency knowledge for understanding the scholarly communication environment in their respective fields. Armed with this knowledge, each liaison will be established as a resource for faculty support surrounding scholarly communication issues.

At Open Repositories 2014 in Helsinki, Paul Royster advocated for the institutional repository as a service (2014, p. 1). Royster's service orientation goes far beyond mediated depositing in the IR and includes copyright clearance, typesetting, metadata, scanning, uploading, usage reporting, and other services. Not all libraries have the ability to provide this *carte blanche* service model, but by applying Royster's service orientation the subject liaisons, who include the institutional repository librarian and the head of reference among their ranks, will establish core areas of scholarly communication need based on a specific discipline. Liaisons then will know where they need to develop competencies if there is a deficit in their knowledge, and hence what services they can develop, offer, support, and promote. The core areas will each fall somewhere along the timeline of the research life cycle, from the literature search and data gathering to data curation (where necessary) and archiving of the OA version of the scholarly product. Understanding the research process will help liaisons communicate with faculty about their needs and identify areas that need additional service development.

Core Areas and Tools of Scholarly Communication Coaching

OA Resources for Faculty Research

The ongoing library serials crisis and the diminishment of state allocations made available to public institutions of higher education as evidenced in Eric Kelderman (2014, p. A6) has forced many college and university libraries to cancel journal after journal after journal. The reduction in the number of subscriptions equates to a reduction in the research immediately available to a faculty member at an institution. Knowing this, one area of faculty support will be targeted during the initial research stage. For this competency, subject liaisons are expected to understand the scholarly communication environment in their discipline, and in particular be aware of open access resources for research. Tools and sources available to develop this competency include the Directory of Open Access Journals, the Digital Commons Network, the Registry of Open Access Repositories, pertinent discipline repositories, and scholars' networks or scholars' commons appropriate to the discipline (see the list of suggested scholarly communication coaching tools in the appendix to this chapter).

The institutional repository librarian and the head of reference will conduct instruction workshops to introduce the subject liaisons to these resources. To demonstrate competency, subject liaisons in turn will lead the other liaisons in workshops on open access resources specific to a discipline.

These sessions serve to educate the liaisons in other areas but also as a self-assessment of one's level of competence. The internal library sessions will be important for establishing liaison confidence levels and comfort with the resources, but are ultimately meant to introduce discipline faculty to open access research as source materials. In addition to adding to the faculty members' knowledge of research resources, the sessions may serve as a remedy to a common faculty misperception about open access not being peer-reviewed or high-quality research (Nicholas et al., 2014, p. 129).

Managing Data

Although this area is not intensive at a medium-sized master's-granting university, it is still important to offer the possibility of support as service. Service development in data management and curation can be an educational tool for both the librarians and the faculty who are introduced to the idea. Funder mandates requiring public access to published research, and to the research data informing the published work, are in place and are increasing. As such, scholars are frequently being tasked with describing data management plans in their grant proposals.

The established competency here is familiarity with the DMPTool (https://dmptool.org/), developed by a consortium of research institutions to assist scholars with developing data management plans specific to their institutions' policies and to the grants they are writing for. Training exercises will include completion of the DMPTool webinar series (http://blog.dmptool.org/webinar-series/), through which free recordings, slides, and bibliographies are available. Despite the current low demand for these needs, subject liaison knowledge of this area, particularly in the STEM fields, is an important feature of scholarly communication support and will likely grow in relevance to many fields.

Publishing Options

Once research has culminated in a manuscript, the author seeking a publisher has several alternatives. Acceptance in the author's journal of choice could mean no open access at all, publication fees for making the manuscript freely available for the user ("gold OA"), an OA journal that requires author processing fees, or deposit of a peer-reviewed manuscript or publisher PDF in a repository ("green OA"). At this point in the research life cycle, the role of the subject liaison is to assist the faculty with navigating a variety of publishing opportunities. Also important in this area is the avoidance of potentially "predatory publishers" that lack editorial boards and an established peer-review process and demand payment after manuscript "acceptance." As Zhao Linlin describes in her investigation of scholarly publishing literacy, the continually shifting sands of academic publishing in the era of open access and subscription-based access to scholarly communication are a source of confusion for scholars (2014, p. 3). The liaison librarian, working in partnership with the publishing scholar, can identify appropriate publication avenues. If by virtue of the liaison's support the author retains rights over their intellectual property or chooses to publish in a journal that allows deposit in an IR, the liaison has played an integral role in ensuring access to that research.

At this point, the subject liaison's familiarity with Beall's list (http://scholarlyoa.com/publishers) of potential predatory publishers can help scholars avoid any unsolicited or dubious publishing opportunities. Strong knowledge of authors' rights is vital, and with that knowledge liaisons can assist faculty who want to protect their copyrights and negotiate addenda with their publishers. For this purpose, familiarity with discipline publishers' CTAs and with the Sherpa/RoMEO tool (http://www.sherpa.ac.uk/romeo) is key to the subject liaison's duties.

Nuts and Bolts: Collection Development and Assisting Faculty with Deposits

Once the discipline scholar's manuscript is accepted for publication, the subject liaison's duties turn back to collection development. The inclusion of the faculty member's scholarship in the repository is known to be beneficial for the scholar. The open access exposure to search engine robots increases the discoverability of the work and its availability increases citation counts (Gargouri et al., 2010, p. 8). The institution hosting the work also benefits from the exposure through increased visibility and prestige. This support service involves the subject liaison depositing scholars' work on their behalf, a mediated-deposit model, which includes librarian-quality metadata. The mediated-deposit model creates a more sustainable repository depositing system, and reinforces the repository in the scholar's mind and habits as part of the research process.

By incorporating the duties of collection development to include collecting discipline scholars' work for deposit into the IR, the library will essentially "clone" the institutional repository librarian—in terms of content collection—by a factor of ten. Multiple librarians performing mediated deposit on behalf of faculty will lead to a more "sustainable system" for ingesting content into the repository, and create a "healthier" repository in the long term (Carr and Brody, 2007).

CONCLUSION

In order for the development of liaison librarians as scholarly communication support professionals to continue, it is essential that the library literature add reports of real-world experiences and data about those experiences. The addition of published strategies, successes, and failures from more institutions will contribute to the development of best practices. Additional surveys of discipline scholars' attitudes about their scholarly communication needs, similar to the University of California, Berkeley's Center for Studies in Higher Education's report *Assessing the Future Landscape of Scholarly Communication: An Exploration of Faculty Needs and Values in Seven Disciplines* (Harley et al., 2010), would be beneficial for institutions to accurately craft their programs to fit their faculty's needs.

Even as subject liaisons grow into their new roles as scholarly communication coaches in their disciplines or departments, scholarly communication methods and practices continue to evolve. Library digital publishing is a new trend in scholarly communication and could soon be considered a new core competency (Maria Bonn, 2014, p. 134). As the library profession moves from a faculty liaisonship that is primarily about building collections to a model that incorporates engagement with researchers in the research process, it must also adapt, shift, and grow along with the environment in which it operates. Open access is growing at a steady and strong pace. Unless and until the subscription model for journal publishing is made reasonable and fair, access to new knowledge will be limited to only those large and elite institutions that can afford it. For these reasons and many more, establishing sustainable repositories will be essential to maintain fair and equal access to research. This is also true for the larger institution. Prospective students have an opportunity to see their future professors' work. Boards of higher education, legislative bodies, and donors can see firsthand the intellectual artifacts of the faculty, and, perhaps more importantly (by virtue of download counts), how influential that work can be.

But that sustainable repository can only occur as a result of the service liaisons operating as scholarly communication coaches. As new knowledge proliferates in the digital age, scholars' needs for assistance with navigating the complexity of the scholarly communication world will establish librarians—who, Plutchak notes, are trained to "bring people together with the intellectual content of the past and present" (2012, p. 12)—at the heart of the research enterprise. Subject liaisons, transitioning to these new roles, will be at the forefront of this new librarianship.

The authors of this chapter are indebted to Megan Bresnahan and Andrew Johnson, Joy Kirchner, Kara Malenfant, and Andrea Wirth and Faye Chadwell, whose writing valuably informed the creation of this work.

APPENDIX

Scholarly Communication Coaching Toolkit

Tool	Source	Purpose	Just in Time Need(s)	
Directory of Open Access Journals	http://doaj.org/	Identify OA sources of scholarship	Literature research stage	
Digital Commons Network	http://network.bepress.com/	Identify OA papers and potential collaborators	Literature research stage	
OpenDOAR	http://www.opendoar.org/	Search OA repositories worldwide for resources	Literature research stage	
DMPTool	https://dmptool.org/	Develop a data management plan specific to scholar's home institution and granting agency	Grant proposal	Data management
Creative Commons	http://creativecommons.org/	Apply license to scholar's work	When scholar wants to assign rights privileges to their work	
Scholars Copyright Addendum Engine	http://scholars.sciencecommons.org/	Create an author's rights addendum	When scholar has been accepted for publication and wants to retain their copyright	
Beall's List	http://scholarlyoa.com/publishers/	Assist faculty with avoiding potentially predatory publishers	When scholar is solicited	When scholar is seeking publication avenues
Sherpa/ROMEO	http://www.sherpa.ac.uk/romeo/	Check publisher copyright policies	When faculty deposit past works and negotiate copyright transfer	When scholar is seeking publication avenues
Open Journal Systems or Digital Commons Network	OJS: https://pkp.sfu.ca/ojs/ Digital Commons: http://digitalcommons.bepress.com	Software platforms for launching OA journals	When faculty transition journals to OA or launch new OA journals	
Undergraduate Commons	http://undergraduatecommons.com/	Worldwide network of Digital Commons repositories' selected undergraduate scholarship	Promote faculty work with student scholars	Encourage potential students' interest in institution

REFERENCES

Adams, Tina M., and Kristen A. Bullard. (2014). "A Case Study of Librarian Outreach to Scientists: Collaborative Research and Scholarly Communication in Conservation Biology." *College and Undergraduate Libraries* 21: 377–395. doi:10.1080/10691316.2014.925415.

Allen, Barbara McFadden. (2008). "All Hype or Real Change: Has the Digital Revolution Changed Scholarly Communication?" *Journal of Library Administration* 48: 59–68.

Armstrong, Michelle. (2014). "Institutional Repository Management Models That Support Faculty Research Dissemination." *OCLC Systems and Services* 30(1): 43–51. doi:10.1108/OCLC-07-2013-0028.

Aston, Samantha, Steven McIndoe, and John Rylands. (2011). "Scholarly Communications for Post-Graduate Researchers." *ALISS Quarterly* 6(4): 30–32.

Bailey, Charles W. (2005). "The Role of Reference Librarians in Institutional Repositories." *Reference Services Review* 33(3): 259–267.

Bell, Suzanne, Nancy Fried Foster, and Susan Gibbons. (2005). "Reference Librarians and the Success of Institutional Repositories." *Reference Services Review* 33: 283–290.

Bonn, Maria. (2014). "Tooling Up: Scholarly Communication Education and Training." *College and Research Libraries News* 75(3): 132–135.

Bosch, Stephen, and Kittle Henderson. (2014). "Steps down the Evolutionary Road." *Library Journal* 139(7): 32–37.

Bresnahan, Megan M., and Andrew M. Johnson. (2013). "Assessing Scholarly Communication and Research Data Training Needs." *Reference Services Review* 41(3): 413–433. doi:10.1108/RSR-01-2013-0003.

Bruns, Todd A., and Harrison Inefuku. (2015). "Purposeful Metrics." In B. B. Callicott and David A. Scherer (eds.), *Making Institutional Repositories Work*. Chicago: ALA Editions, forthcoming.

Bruns, Todd A., et al. (2014). "It Takes a Library: Growing a Robust Institutional Repository in Two Years." *College and Undergraduate Libraries* 21(3–4): 244–262. doi:10.1080/10691316.2014.904207.

Budapest Open Access Initiative. (2012). "Ten Years On from the Budapest Open Access Initiative: Setting the Default to Open." http://www.soros.org/openaccess/boai-10-recommendations.

Bull, Jonathan, and Bradford Lee Eden. (2014). "Successful Scholarly Communication at a Small University: Integration of Education, Services, and an Institutional Repository at Valparaiso University." *College and Undergraduate Libraries* 21(3–4): 263–278. doi:10.1080/10691316.2014.932264.

Burns, C. Sean, Amy Lana, and John M. Budd. (2013). "Institutional Repositories: Exploration of Costs and Value." *D-Lib Magazine* 19(1–2): n.p. doi:10.1045/january2013-contents.

Carr, Leslie, and Tim Brody. (2007). "Size Isn't Everything: Sustainable Repositories as Evidenced by Sustainable Deposit Profiles." *D-Lib Magazine* 13(7–8): n.p. doi:10.1045/july2007-carr.

Creaser, Claire. (2010). "Open Access to Research Outputs—Institutional Policies and Researchers' Views: Results from Two Complementary Surveys." *New Review of Academic Librarianship* 16(4): 4–25.

Cullen, Rowena, and Brenda Chawner. (2010). "Institutional Repositories: Assessing Their Value to the Academic Community." *Performance Measurement and Metrics* 11(2): 131–147.

Davis, Philip M., and Matthew J. L. Connolly. (2007). "Institutional Repositories: Evaluating the Reasons for Non-use of Cornell University's Installation of DSpace." *D-Lib Magazine* 13(3/4): n.p. doi:10.1045/march2007-davis.

Dutta, Goutam, and Dibyendu Paul. (2014). "Awareness on Institutional Repositories-Related Issues by Faculty of University of Calcutta." *DESIDOC Journal of Library and Information Technology* 34: 293–297.

Gargouri, Yassine, et al. (2010). "Self-Selected or Mandated, Open Access Increases Citation Impact for Higher Quality Research." *PLoS ONE* 5(10): n.p.

Gordon, Gregory J. (2012). "Strategic Access." *Legal Information Management* 12(3): 198–202. doi:10.1017/S1472669612000461.

Hahn, Susan E., and Anna Wyatt. (2014). "Business Faculty's Attitudes: Open Access, Disciplinary Repositories, and Institutional Repositories." *Journal of Business and Finance Librarianship* 19(2): 93–113.

Harley, Diane, et al. (2010). *Assessing the Future Landscape of Scholarly Communication: An Exploration of Faculty Values and Needs in Seven Disciplines.* Berkeley: Center for Studies in Higher Education, University of California. http://escholarship.org/uc/cshe_fsc.

Harnad, Stevan. (2010). "Gold Open Access Publishing Must Not Be Allowed to Retard the Progress of Green Open Access Self-Archiving." *LOGOS: The Journal of the World Book Community* 21(3/4): 86–93. doi:10.1163/095796511X559972.

Inefuku, Harrison. (2013). *More than Seeing What Sticks: Aligning Repository Assessment with Institutional Priorities.* Poster presented at Open Repositories 2013, Charlottetown, Canada. http://lib.dr.iastate.edu/digirep_conf/3/.

Kelderman, Eric. (2014). "Higher Education Lobbyists Keep Expectations Low for Size of State Budgets." *Chronicle of Higher Education* 60(17): A6.

Kenney, Anne R. (2014). "Leveraging the Liaison Model: From Defining 21st Century Research Libraries to Implementing 21st Century Research Universities." *Ithaka S+R*: n.p. http://www.sr.ithaka.org/blog-individual/leveraging-liaison-model-defining-21st-century-research-libraries-implementing-21st.

Kim, Jihyun. (2011). "Motivations of Faculty Self-Archiving in Institutional Repositories." *Journal of Academic Librarianship* 37: 246–254.

Kirchner, Joy. (2009). "Scholarly Communications: Planning for the Integration of Liaison Librarian Roles." *Research Library Issues* 265: 22–28.

Konkiel, Stacy, and Dave Scherer. (2013). "New Opportunities for Repositories in the Age of Altmetrics." *Bulletin of the Association for Information Science and Technology* 39(4): 22–26.

Laughtin-Dunker, Kristin. (2014). "Assessing the Scholarly Communication Attitudes and Practices of Faculty: Lessons from a 'Failed' Survey." *Journal of Librarianship and Scholarly Communication* 2(3): eP1164.

Linlin, Zhao. (2014). "Riding the Wave of Open Access: Providing Library Research Support for Scholarly Publishing Literacy." *Australian Academic and Research Libraries* 45(1): 3–18. doi:10.1080/00048623.2014.882873.

Malenfant, K. J. (2010). "Leading Change in the System of Scholarly Communication: A Case Study of Engaging Liaison Librarians for Outreach to Faculty." *College and Research Libraries* 71(1): 63–76.

Mullen, Laura Bowering. (2011). "Open Access and the Practice of Academic Librarianship: Strategies and Considerations for 'Front Line' Librarians." *IATUL Annual Conference Proceedings* 21: 1–8.

Neugebauer, Tomasz, and Annie Murray. (2013). "The Critical Role of Institutional Services in Open Access Advocacy." *International Journal of Digital Curation* 8(1): 84–106.

Nicholas, David, et al. (2014). "Trust and Authority in Scholarly Communications in the Light of the Digital Transition: Setting the Scene for a Major Study." *Learned Publishing* 27(2): 121–134. doi:10.1087/20140206.

Park, Ji-Hong, and Jiyoung Shim. (2011). "Exploring How Library Publishing Services Facilitate Scholarly Communication." *Journal of Scholarly Publishing* 43(1): 76–89.

Plutchak, T. Scott. (2012). "Breaking the Barriers of Time and Space: The Dawning of the Great Age of Librarians." *Journal of the Medical Library Association* 100(1): 10–9. doi:10.3163/1536-5050.100.1.004.

Prottsman, Mary Fran. (2011). "Communication and Collaboration: Collection Development in Challenging Economic Times." *Journal of Electronic Resources in Medical Libraries* 8: 107–116. doi:10.1080/15424065.2011.576585.

Royster, Paul. (2014). *The Advice Not Taken: How One Repository Found Its Own Path.* Presented at Open Repositories 2014, Helsinki, Finland. http://digitalcommons.unl.edu/cgi/viewcontent.cgi?article=1101&context=library_talks.

Sterman, Leila. (2014). "Institutional Repositories: An Analysis of Trends and a Proposed Collaborative Future." *College and Undergraduate Libraries* 21(3/4): 360–376. doi:10.1080/10691316.2014.943919.

St. Jean, Beth, et al. (2011). "Unheard Voices: Institutional Repository End-Users." *College and Research Libraries* 72: 21–42.

Suber, Peter. (2012). *Open Access.* Cambridge, MA: MIT Press.

Taylor, Michael, Pandelis Perakakis, and Varvara Trachana. (2008). "The Siege of Science." *Ethics in Science and Environmental Politics* 8: 17–40.

Tewell, Eamon C. (2014). "Administrator Interest Is Perceived to Encourage Faculty and Librarian Involvement in Open Access Activities." *Evidence Based Library and Information Practice* 9(3): 80–82.

Thomas, Wm. Joseph. (2013). "The Structure of Scholarly Communications within Academic Libraries." *Serials Review* 39(3): 167–171.

Thorn, Sue, Sally Morris, and Ron Fraser. (2009). "Learned Societies and Open Access: Key Results from Surveys of Bioscience." *Serials* 22: 39–48.

Tolppanen, Bradley P., and Janice Derr. (2010). "Interlibrary Loan Patron Use Patterns: An Examination of Borrowing Requests at a Midsized Academic Library." *Journal of Interlibrary Loan, Document Delivery and Electronic Reserve* 20: 303–317.

Way, Doug. (2010). "The Open Access Availability of Library and Information Science Literature." *College and Research Libraries* 71(4): 302–310. http://works.bepress.com/doug_way/2.

Wiegand, S. (2013). "Beginning the Conversation: Discussing Scholarly Communication." *Serials Librarian* 65(3–4): 335–349. doi:10.1080/0361526X.2013.833883.

Wirth, Andrea A. (2011). "Incorporating Existing Library Partnerships into Open Access Week Events." *Collaborative Librarianship* 3(4): 197–204.

Wirth, Andrea A., and Faye A. Chadwell. (2010). "Rights Well: An Authors' Rights Workshop for Librarians." *portal: Libraries and the Academy* 10: 337–354.

Xia, Jingfeng. (2010). "A Longitudinal Study of Scholars' Attitudes and Behaviors toward Open-Access Journal Publishing." *Journal of the American Society for Information Science and Technology* 61: 615–624.

Xia, Jingfeng, and David B. Opperman. (2010). "Current Trends in Institutional Repositories for Institutions Offering Master's and Baccalaureate Degrees." *Serials Review* 36(1): 10–18.

Chapter Three

Driving Partnerships for Assessment and Engagement

Understanding Users and Outcomes

Katy Mathuews

In a higher education environment increasingly focused on student success, funding issues, and accreditation pressures, the need to analyze, understand, and communicate library data is greater than ever. The Clark Memorial Library at Shawnee State University initiated a collaborative assessment project in response to external institutional pressures. Blending library data with institutional data allowed the library to better understand the student population and the library's impact on student success. These measures informed internal strategic planning to align with institutional goals.

BACKGROUND

Shawnee State University is a regional open access institution located in the Appalachian region of southern Ohio with an approximate enrollment of four thousand students. With first-generation students comprising approximately three-quarters of the student population, many students are academically underprepared and require developmental coursework. Serving this unique population is challenging for the twenty-eight-year-old university, where graduation rates average 22%.

The challenge to serve this population of students was magnified in 2011 with the issuance of *The Chancellor's Plan for Shawnee State University to Improve Course Completion, Retention and Graduation Rates*. This directive initiated a plan to increase course completions and degrees awarded. This effort occurred simultaneously with a transition to a performance-based funding model in 2012, as outlined in the University System of Ohio publication *Recommendations of the Ohio Higher Education Funding Commission*. Along with a decreasing population of new high school graduates, these developments created internal budget concerns. These developments spurred the university to develop a culture of data-driven analysis to understand the student population and the impact of various measures on student success.

In response to these institutional pressures and inspired by the call for increased alignment of library assessment initiatives with institutional goals outlined in *The Value of Academic Libraries: A Comprehensive Research Review and Report* (Oakleaf, 2010, pp. 13–17), the library initiated a project to blend library data with institutional data to gain a better understanding of the library user and nonuser population and the library's impact on student success, as defined by GPA and graduation rates. Similar studies have analyzed the impact of library resource use on GPA (Jantti and Cox, 2013, p. 163; Wong and Webb, 2011, p. 361; Odeh, 2012, p. 222) and on retention and graduation rates (Emmons and Wilkinson, 2011, p. 128; Haddow and Jayanthi, 2010, p. 233; Haddow, 2013, p. 130; Stone and Ramsden, 2013, p. 546). This literature moves library assessment beyond traditional input-output methods to focus on student outcomes, which can speak more directly to library value and impact.

ALIGNING DATA

Since the library's data management program was in its early development, the most accessible data to help measure library use was patron circulation data. The library was able to extract data from its integrated library system to provide patron circulation data including total number of checkouts, total number of renewals, and patron type, among others. Circulation data included, but was not limited to, books, laptops, and media.

As the central data repository on campus, the Office of Institutional Effectiveness was able to provide access to a rich collection of student demographic and performance-based outcome information. Using the institution's relational database, an extract containing six years of student data was retrieved. The data ranged from summer 2007 to spring 2013 and included 11,150 students. The extract included student high school class rank, ACT score, declared major, sex, residency, age, cumulative GPA, courses enrolled with corresponding grades, and graduation status, among other demographic and success outcomes. Using student identification number as the common variable, the institutional data was blended with library circulation data using Microsoft Access, with the data further analyzed using Tableau analytic software. To address privacy concerns, all identifying information beyond the student identification was stripped from the data.

UNDERSTANDING USERS

After the data were combined, a thorough examination of the user and nonuser population was conducted to gain a better understanding of the potential needs of students. Library users were defined as having at least one checkout. The data was sorted by number of checkouts to create user and nonuser groups.

Many demographic characteristics of both groups were similar. It was found, however, that first-generation students made up approximately 81% of the library user population. This was a higher percentage than the general student population, of which first-generation students comprised approximately 73%. This indicated that library material usage may be an important component of the first-generation student's college experience. This was a valuable discovery that enabled the library to enhance programming and materials offerings to better meet the needs of first-generation college students.

Another helpful discovery was the distribution of checkouts by academic area. Figure 3.1 shows the number of students who checked out library materials by academic area. This information was compared to the total number of students within the academic areas to provide context. This information helped the library in strategic planning with subject liaison duties.

In addition to first-generation status, the library was able to examine the use behaviors of students who were college ready versus students who were not college ready. College readiness is of increasing concern as the university strives to improve the success of high school students transitioning to their first year of college. Using ACT subject benchmark scores for college readiness, it was determined that college-ready students use the library at higher percentages (49%) than those students who are not college ready (41%), as shown in figure 3.2.

UNDERSTANDING LIBRARY IMPACT

Though it was valuable to understand the makeup of the library user and nonuser population, exploring outcome measures allowed for a deeper understanding of the library's impact on student success. The library was able to observe a correlation between library checkouts and student GPA. As shown in figure 3.3, increased library checkouts correlated with increased student GPA. In fact, the correlation coefficient was .82, indicating a fairly strong correlation between the two variables.

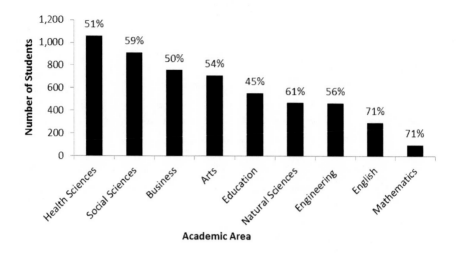

Figure 3.1.   Number of Students per Academic Area with Checkouts

It was also important for the library to contribute to the conversation surrounding the institution's commitment to improving graduation rates. Mimicking the Integrated Postsecondary Education Data System (IPEDS) graduation rate calculation, the library was able to compare the graduation rates of the user and nonuser populations. The IPEDS graduation rate calculation focuses on all first-time, full-time, bachelor's degree–seeking students who enter in the summer or fall term of a particular academic year. The rate is calculated as the percent of these students who have graduated at 150% of the time it would take to earn a bachelor's degree. Using the appropriate cohort from the data extract, it was determined that the graduation rate for those who checked out materials was 52%, while the rate for those who did not check out library materials was 22%. This information created opportunities for enriching discussions with campus administrators about the value of the library in supporting institutional goals.

INFORMING STRATEGIC PLANNING

Informed by this analysis, the library restructured staffing to better align library service with student needs and institutional goals. A position was repurposed to create an outreach librarian specifically tasked with supporting student research, success, and retention. The duties of the outreach librarian focus on supporting first-year students and developing collaborations with other campus units to magnify impact. Given the makeup of the student population and the positive correlation of student success with library use,

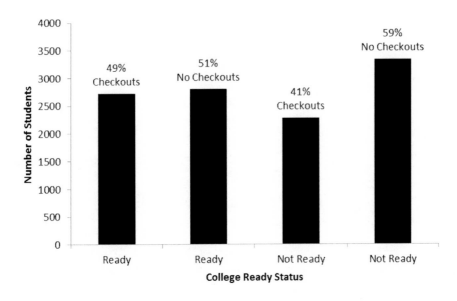

Figure 3.2.   **Student Circulation of Materials by College-Ready Status**

communicating the value of the library to students and parents became a priority of the outreach librarian. This aligned with the goals of other campus units such as University College and the Admissions Department, entities heavily involved with orientation and the first-year experience.

   With the support of these campus units, the outreach librarian helped the library gain greater visibility at fall orientation. The library was included in an informational table session, which gave the outreach librarian the opportunity to informally chat with students and parents, offering library information specific to major, interest, and need. Additionally, the library was allocated twenty minutes during the parent informational session. During this session, assessment data was used to communicate the impact of library use on student success. Students were also able to visit the library during a campus tour to chat with a library student employee to hear firsthand how the library supports student success. The outreach librarian achieved sustained contact with students throughout the year by visiting courses in academic development skills, developmental math, and developmental writing. This was an intentional effort as part of the Personal Librarian initiative, which included students in the Success Curriculum, a support program designed for academically underprepared students.

   Assessment efforts have also helped to build new partnerships on campus. The campus Writing Center recently relocated to the library, providing an enhanced service to students, who can now have research and writing support

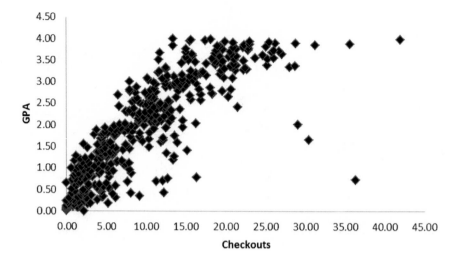

Figure 3.3.   Student Checkouts by GPA

needs met in one location. This also allows for easy collaboration for assessment purposes. Writing Center use can now be included in library assessments, offering an expanded view of student academic activity beyond the classroom. Writing Center representatives also often accompany the outreach librarian to orientation activities and classroom visits in addition to co-hosting events and workshops at the library.

CHALLENGES AND NEXT STEPS

Initiating a project like this did come with several challenges and considerations for the future. First was the concern to maintain privacy. The library participated in the university's institutional review board training process and submitted a proposal describing methodology, purpose, and the nature of the data included. Upon receiving approval, the library ensured that all identifiable information beyond student identification number was deleted from the data file. Additionally, the library committed to only report data in the aggregate.

There were also challenges in blending two distinct data sets created by separate campus entities. Institutional data is very specific to each academic term. One is able to see a student's performance in any given course in any given semester. Library data, on the other hand, is entirely cumulative. The library is not able to tell, for example, how many checkouts a particular patron had in any given semester. This constrained analysis in the short term, as the library was not able to get a granular perspective on the impact of library use on student success. To increase analysis options in future projects, the library initiated a data management plan in which snapshots of library data are taken at the conclusion of each semester to enhance the ability to examine semester-specific performance.

It is also necessary to expand the definition of library use in order to gain a more robust understanding of library impact. Circulation data is likely the most accessible data for libraries to initiate this type of study. In future iterations of this study, the library plans to continue to use existing data to expand the understanding of library use. For example, patron records include a field that indicates if a patron has signed a terms of use agreement to check out laptops and consortial materials. Converting this to a data field can provide insight into the types of materials used. Efforts were also initiated to capture the student identification numbers of students who are enrolled in courses that receive library instruction sessions and those who participate in library events and workshops.

Integrating electronic resource use measures is a particular challenge. The computer systems and network at SSU are administered through University Information Services, a department that serves and maintains information systems and policy for the entire campus. It is challenging to resolve data needs with privacy and network security concerns. For example, it would be very useful to obtain the student identification numbers of those students who log in to library computers, as many students come to the library solely to use computers for writing or researching, never checking out a physical resource. Obtaining this type of data, however, involves many complex conversations to ensure security and privacy remain intact.

One electronic resource measure the library has been able to obtain is off-campus authentications via EZproxy. Library vendor software allows the library to obtain the usernames of those who access electronic resources from off campus. Using this information, the library can match usernames to identification numbers as a means to blend this variable with existing data sets for library impact measurement. This can be useful in understanding the population of students accessing library resources in this manner. For example, the library is able to see which academic areas have the highest instance of off-campus authentications. This is valuable insight as approximately three-quarters of the student population are commuters and distance-learning courses are increasingly offered. These students have unique needs, as they are not able to be in the physical library as much as on-campus residents. In fact, as shown in figure 3.4, approximately 35% of the student population accessed library resources off campus during spring semester 2014.

A final challenge is establishing true correlation between library use and student success. While the measures described here and in similar studies are invaluable to help gain an understanding of library user and nonuser popula-

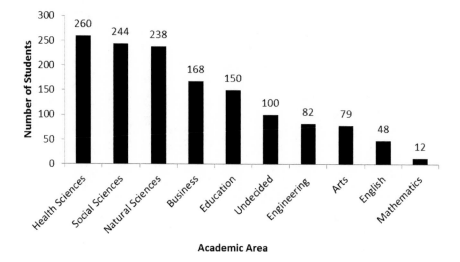

Figure 3.4.   EZproxy Authentications by Academic Area, Spring 2014

tions, true correlation is the gold standard of this type of assessment. Expanding the number of measurable variables will expand the definition of library use, and a more robust understanding of library use and impact can be gained.

CONCLUSION

The current higher education climate encourages increased collaboration to fully understand the components of student success. This study shows one way the library can prove to be a valuable partner in a university's strategic goals to address internal and external pressures. Blending data from various areas on campus can help the entire university understand the best practices to support student success. This approach also keeps the library at the forefront of such initiatives, providing the avenue for the type of collaborative support that will ensure the library remains a vital partner in student success.

Many thanks to Rebekah Kilzer, Kimberly Patton, and Vickie Crawford for their guidance, support, and assistance in this project.

REFERENCES

Emmons, M., and F. C. Wilkinson. (2011). "The Academic Library Impact on Student Persistence." *College and Research Libraries* 72(2): 128–149.

Haddow, Gaby. (2013). "Academic Library Use and Student Retention: A Quantitative Analysis." *Library and Information Science Research* 35: 127–136.

Haddow, Gaby, and Joseph Jayanthi. (2010). "Loans, Logins, and Lasting the Course: Academic Library Use and Student Retention." *Australian Academic and Research Libraries* 41(4): 233–244.

Jantti, Margie, and Brian Cox. (2013). "Measuring the Value of Library Resources and Student Academic Performance through Relational Datasets." *Evidence Based Library and Information Practice* 8(2): 163–171.

Oakleaf, Megan J. (2010). *The Value of Academic Libraries: A Comprehensive Research Review and Report*. Chicago: Association of College and Research Libraries, American Library Association.

Odeh, Atif Yousef. (2012). "Use of Information Resources by Undergraduate Students and Its Relationship with Academic Achievement." *Libri: International Journal of Libraries and Information Services* 62(3): 222–232.

Ohio Board of Regents. (2011). *The Chancellor's Plan for Shawnee State University to Improve Course Completion, Retention and Graduation Rates*. http://www.shawnee.edu/offices/president/media/shawnee-state-report.pdf.

Stone, G., and B. Ramsden. (2013). "Library Impact Data Project: Looking for the Link between Library Usage and Student Attainment." *College and Research Libraries* 74(6): 546–559.

University System of Ohio. (2012). *Recommendations of the Ohio Higher Education Funding Commission*. https://www.ohiohighered.org/sites/ohiohighered.org/files/uploads/financial/ssi/Ohio%20Higher%20Education%20Funding%20Commission%20-%20Report.pdf.

Wong, Shun Han Rebekah, and T. D. Webb. (2011). "Uncovering Meaningful Correlation between Student Academic Performance and Library Material Usage." *College and Research Libraries* 72(4): 361–370.

Chapter Four

Embedding Libraries in the University Commercialization Process

Jason Dewland and Cynthia M. Elliott

Universities are increasing efforts to assist faculty, students, and community partners to bring inventions to market. As state funding for higher education continues to shrink, universities are looking for new revenue streams to support teaching, research, and learning. Campus commercialization efforts are a strategy to promote economic development opportunities that benefit the community and society at large. Commercialization efforts on campus include technology transfer offices, incubator parks, and joint ventures between the university, investors, and corporate entities. Academic libraries have the opportunity to partner with campus technology transfer efforts and expand librarian roles and responsibilities to support commercialization, innovation, and entrepreneurship on campus.

LITERATURE REVIEW

Global changes in the economy and increasing competition of products and services drive innovation. Technologically advanced countries like the United States rely on sophisticated, novel inventions that develop into products with commercial value (Geiger and Sá, 2008, p. 1) to sustain a robust economy. Colleges and universities provide a strong base of science and technology researchers with the capacity to innovate. Commercial entities are partnering more with academic peers to gain access to advances in basic science (Geiger and Sá, 2008, pp. 31–32). Academic institutions have utilized an organizational model for technology transfer since the end of World War II (Miller and Acs, 2013, pp. 407–408). As the US economy slowed in the 1970s, concerns about inconsistent patent policies, lack of incentives to commercialize early-stage high-risk technologies, and growing competition from Europe and Asia led federal policy makers to make changes to spur economic growth and development (Schacht, 2012). After Public Law 96-517, Amendments to the Patent and Trademark Act (commonly called Bayh-Dole), was enacted, the utilization of inventions from federally funded research programs allowed for collaboration between commercial and nonprofit organizations and universities (Schacht, 2009). The Bayh-Dole Act allows universities and researchers to retain title to inventions made using federal research dollars, incentivizing universities to transfer technology to the private sector (Association of University Technology Managers, 2012).

In the last thirty years, many studies have discussed the success of the technology transfer model (Siegel et al., 2007; Grimaldi et al., 2011; Wright, 2014; Bozeman, 2000; O'Shea et al., 2005; O'Shea et al., 2008; Phan et al., 2005). Since Bayh-Dole, scientific discovery itself has advanced, providing more opportunities for scientists to become entrepreneurs (Geiger and Sá, 2008, p. 2), and university and industry relationships are now the norm. In a study of fifty large research universities, half of all academic life scientists had at least one form of direct industry relationship in the last three years, principally serving as consultants, paid speakers, and scientific advisory board members (Zinner et al., 2009, p. 5).

The authors found little in the literature review addressing specific library partnerships with technology transfer offices and commercialization efforts on campus. The role of librarians partnering specifically with technology transfer efforts (Pinelli, 1991; Steinke, 1990; Pensyl, 1991; Borovansky, 1987) was documented in the 1980s and 1990s, but little has been written about partnerships and outcomes with technology transfer offices and libraries today. Traditionally, the academy was not attuned to seeing librarians as providers of market information, or "economic change agents" who actively contribute to the growth of their communities (Pensyl, 1991, p. 30). Despite this perception, librarians were able to overcome this obstacle and partner with researchers by saving time and improving the quality of the information evaluated for the researcher, and librarians benefited by experimenting and improving searching and analysis abilities (Pensyl, 1991, pp. 35–36).

In recent years, academic libraries have added value to economic development efforts through entrepreneurial outreach, by building relationships with university technology transfer offices, and by collaborating with local economic development offices and public libraries. One recent survey of the academic business librarian community found that librarians collaborate with community groups and other libraries to assist local entrepreneurs with their information needs (Feldmann, 2014). In 2001, the University of Alabama developed the Alabama Entrepreneurial Research Network (AERN), which partners with the University of Alabama business librarians and local chamber of commerce offices in Alabama counties to provide research materials and reference support for entrepreneurs and small businesses (Pike et al., 2010). Libraries are piloting "economic gardening" projects, an approach to local economic development that involves academic business librarians and public librarians to provide research and reference support to entrepreneurs (Hamilton-Pennell, 2008; Leavitt et al., 2010). The Northwest Ohio Regional Growth Partnership received support from the University of Toledo business librarian to create the Launch business development library for new small business ventures (Martin, 2010). The University of Toronto Libraries and the MaRS Discovery District, a hub for entrepreneurial activity, collaborated to launch a market intelligence service aimed at science and technology entrepreneurs in the province of Ontario (Fitzgerald et al., 2010). The University of Arizona Libraries and the campus technology transfer unit Tech Launch Arizona teamed up to create a business intelligence unit to gather information that helps researchers and faculty members make smart, well-informed business decisions. Librarians have the expertise to develop, manage, and share access to resource collections focused on entrepreneurs, and to provide training on how to utilize collections and share links, but librarians do not always synthesize data to help the user digest the results (Feldmann, 2014, p. 120). The literature discusses a need for information consulting that provides high-value and impactful information for scholars leading to effective partnerships (Frank et al., 2001, p. 90).

CHALLENGES

Academic libraries can play a significant role in the commercialization efforts on campus, but in order to be a partner in these efforts, libraries must create a structure that allows them to react quickly and efficiently to the needs of the commercialization process. The initial partnership by the University of Arizona Libraries and the commercialization unit is exciting, but there is potential for increased cooperation in the form of resource sharing, research support, and other areas. The literature reflects that academic libraries have not been embedded in campus commercialization processes up to this point. One of the challenges that the authors recognize is that libraries are not structured in a way that recognizes the importance of coordinating librarian contributions to the commercialization process of bringing products and services to the marketplace. The traditional subject specialist librarian model in place at many academic libraries is one in which a librarian works directly with specific departments, but does not typically partner or coordinate efforts across disciplines with other librarians or units to serve researchers. When a librarian works with one small area, it is easy to miss the big picture and difficult to identify opportunities to work across disciplines to better serve researchers. The traditional subject liaison model creates opportunities for duplicative work, and does not easily allow for recognition of all of the people, work, and research steps that contribute to the commercialization process. For example, medical librarian A may work with a faculty researcher in an initial exploration of a research topic in a particular area as part of her disciplinary area of expertise. Business librarian B could be assisting an MBA entrepreneurial student team with market research for a project that happens to be from the same faculty researcher that medical librarian A was assisting. Meanwhile, this faculty researcher has enlisted the assistance of law librarian C to help with the patent search as well. The faculty researcher has engaged three separate librarians in the process of conducting research in the development of a technology intended for the marketplace.

In this scenario, the three librarians are not aware of each other's work and contributions on the same project, and hence the library is unaware of each of its contributions throughout the process. Each librarian has spent considerable time learning about the technology in order to provide the information services needed, resulting in the doubling of efforts. An argument can be made for developing a coordinated model in which the librarians communicate and assist each other throughout the research project. This model would increase the speed by which the research project is completed, save time and effort for both the researcher and the librarians, and recognize the contribution of librarians to the commercialization process.

Another challenge the authors have found is that many of the students and employees working with commercialization units on campus are accomplished researchers in their own studies and disciplines, often holding advanced degrees in the sciences and law, but are not good searchers outside of their own disciplines. Students hired to work with commercialization units must research novel technologies outside of their specialties and conduct in-depth market research, often for the first time, which requires the use of specialty business databases. Students do not always have a strong understanding of the importance of high-quality market research, because the colleagues managing the students do not emphasize quality research. For example, the authors conducted a database training and observed employees explaining to the new student trainees, "All the market analysis needed is available via Google on the Internet." In the past, this level of searching may have been viewed as adequate, but as universities compete to increase revenue and develop and spin off new technologies, the level of sophistication of analysis needed is increasing dramatically.

Another challenge to overcome is that librarians often undervalue their services, expertise, and contribution to the commercialization effort. One reason for this is the aforementioned challenge of coordinating efforts among librarians in the commercialization cycle. Academic librarians have not traditionally billed customers for access to information; the mission of the academic librarian is to provide services that support teaching and learning campus goals. Since commercialization groups are viewed as profit centers on most campuses, it may be time to reevaluate how libraries provide access, and demonstrate to units on campus how librarians are providing value and contributions to their research efforts.

RECOMMENDATIONS

Some libraries are experimenting with a pay-for-use or corporate library model and consulting services. For example, the Entrepreneurial Library Program of the John Hopkins University Sheridan Libraries creates customized library and information services for clients in the academic, corporate, allied health, nonprofit, and other sectors (Sheridan Libraries, 2014, para. 1). The pay-for-use model requires all departments to have a strong understanding of what information is available to them for a fee, outside of the resources they use as faculty for teaching and general research, and a fee for service may deter them from using additional library services. Entrepreneurial programs and commercialization initiatives on campus present an opportunity for science, medical, law, and business librarians to collaborate and embed in the entire research cycle. Librarians collaborate in the development of information literacy course components when multiple skills and disciplines are needed. For example, Mary Feeney and Jim Martin partnered to develop coursework to engage engineering majors in the development of plans to design and engineer products and address fundamental business considerations such as cost analyses and market research (2003).

The work of the commercialization process requires an interdisciplinary library approach to better serve this clientele. Research areas are very different from each other, and a wide breadth of knowledge is necessary to walk a research idea from concept to commercialization. A librarian with subject expertise in the health sciences may not be an expert in business or engineering resources, and thus it is not sufficient to assign one librarian to be the "commercialization subject librarian." Several librarians working together can fill in each other's gaps in a model called the commercialization library group (CLG). This model, as shown in figure 4.1, can help in facilitating this process and understanding when and to whom the research is passed to support the changing needs of the technology as it moves through the commercialization process.

The proposed organizational structure of the CLG is based on the experience the authors have had at the University of Arizona (Elliott and Dewland, 2013). Each library's CLG structure will vary based on the university's unique mixture of academic specialties and relative vibrancy of the program's commercialization effort. The proposed structure for the University of Arizona Libraries is based upon data collected locally, in which 65% of all

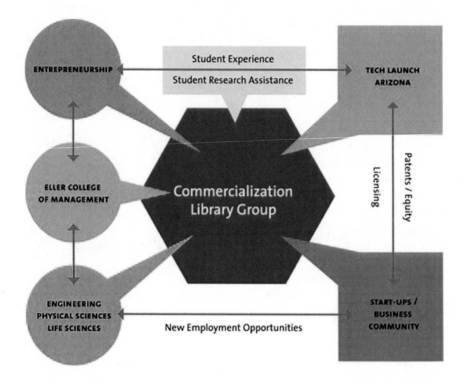

Figure 4.1. Commercialization Library Group Model

new technology commercialization efforts is health sciences related; therefore, a core group could consist of a small group of librarians who specialize in health sciences, business, engineering, and other sciences. The model will vary from group to group depending on the needs of the entrepreneurial community, but could consist of a business specialist, technical/patent specialist, law contact, and medical contact to provide coverage in the steps of technology transfer.

The workflow can be characterized as dynamic and iterative depending on the activity level at any given time. One key aspect to ensure a smooth process for each project is to assign a project manager to each item in the commercialization pipeline. In 65% of the projects at the University of Arizona, one subject specialist is the project manager along with one of the primary researchers for medical technologies; the business librarian manages the rest of the projects. As projects move through different stages of completion, different individuals will step in and contribute. One of the key dependencies in this system is the project manager's ability to communicate with the different librarian liaisons on the UA Libraries Research and Learning team about potential projects emanating from their schools. These may be projects that the project manager has become aware of through Tech Launch Arizona, or work that the library liaison is aware of through work with the faculty and graduate students in their assigned disciplines.

The project manager ensures that all of the liaison librarians are aware of the services that the CLG provides, and have a general understanding of what is needed to point researchers in the right direction for their information needs. Partnering with faculty early in the research process may lighten the load or set a better level of understanding of what is involved and expected throughout the commercialization process. Another important role for the assigned project manager librarian will be to engage with the embedded technology licensing managers that are located in each of the colleges devel-

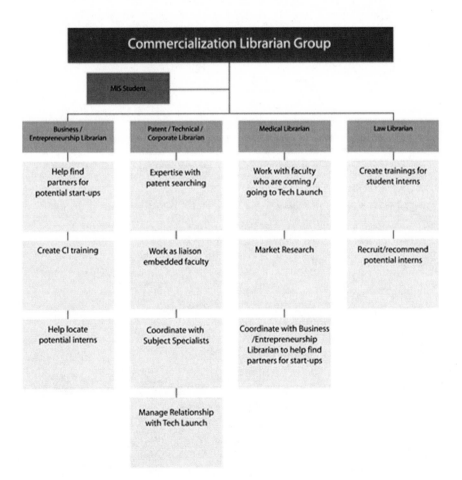

Figure 4.2. Commercialization Librarian Group Hierarchy

oping technologies for market. This provides another avenue to assist the CLG in becoming involved with the researcher early and developing an understanding of how the project will proceed in order to help the faculty locate the relevant research. If the patent/technical librarian is tied into the Office of Technology Transfer's embedded technology managers at the beginning of the process, the patent/technical librarian will be able to provide additional environmental knowledge of the research and information needs of the college back to the library. One concern noted for the project managing librarian is that, as the library becomes more involved with the commercialization process, workload may become an issue. In addition to the CLG model, the business/entrepreneurship librarian could work closely with the university entrepreneurship and business programs to partner with the embedded Tech Launch Arizona licensing managers to pair an MBA student with an inventor who is considering developing a technology for the marketplace. The authors expect that as groups of MBA students are paired with an inventor, these students will develop a business plan to assist the inventor in exploring how to move their ideas to market in the early stages.

FUTURE DIRECTIONS

Librarians are uniquely situated to reach across walls to see potential opportunities to partner with units on campus. The distinct borders between the academic institution and the private sector are eroding and libraries can embed within the commercialization process. In order to better serve researchers developing new technologies, librarians will want to increase their presence in the research process by embedding to a greater extent, both physically and virtually. It may be advantageous to embed physically at various locations to serve as a reminder that the library is present and available to help with research needs. Embedding within course management systems will serve as the major way for the library to be virtually present on campus, but there are other outside opportunities that the library can explore. Business librarians can partner with local public library business librarians and provide feedback on some of the resources they provide to the business community. Academic librarians can attend meetings held by organizations working toward local economic development, new business incubators, and start-ups, and network and partner with local organizations that work closely with entrepreneurs and small businesses. Another issue to explore is how to provide affordable access to the information resources themselves, along with identifying opportunities for partnering effectively with database and market research providers with regard to licensing agreements for entrepreneurs as well as campus units. Libraries should explore ways to provide ongoing research support for the fledgling companies once they form and move off campus to an incubator or small business development center. In this new stage of development, companies lose access to the resources provided by the library once they move from the academic sphere to the commercial sphere. Two of the librarians at the University of Arizona are currently reaching out to their existing information providers and exploring cost-effective solutions so that these newly formed companies still have access to high-quality information resources.

CONCLUSION

Libraries should consider new models for delivering services to all of their users, and increase efforts to assist faculty, students, and the community to bring inventions to market through technology transfer. The model that the authors propose, the academic commercialization librarian (ACL), was developed out of assessing the needs of users of library information resources and services. The authors propose that librarians engage and collaborate with faculty, researchers, and those on campus involved in commercialization efforts in this conversation, and try out this model to extend and expand library services to support entrepreneurial and technology transfer efforts on campus.

REFERENCES

Association of University Technology Managers. (2012). *The Bayh-Dole Act: Issues in Patent Policy and the Commercialization of Technology*. Accessed October 20, 2014. https://www.autm.net/Bayh_Dole_Act_Report.htm.

Borovansky, V. T. (1987). *Technology Transfer and Academic Libraries*. Proceedings of the IATUL conferences. Paper 13. Accessed June 28, 2013. http://docs.lib.purdue.edu/iatul/1987/papers/13/.

Bozeman, B. (2000). "Technology Transfer and Public Policy: A Review of Research and Theory." *Research Policy* 29(4), 627–655.

Elliott, C., and J. Dewland. (2013). *The Academic Commercialization Librarian: The Next Role for Academic Librarians*. Special Libraries Association Conference, June 9–11, San Diego, CA.

Feeney, M., and J. Martin. (2003). "The Business of Science: Cross-Disciplinary Information Literacy in the Applied Sciences and Business." *Issues in Science and Technology Librarianship* 37. Accessed June 30, 2013. http://istl.org/03-spring/article4.html.

Feldmann, L. M. (2014). "Academic Business Librarians' Assistance to Community Entrepreneurs." *Reference Services Review* 42(1): 108–128. doi:10.1108/RSR-04-2013-0021.

Fitzgerald, K., L. Anderson, and H. Kula. (2010). "Embedded Librarians Promote an Innovation Agenda: University of Toronto Libraries and the MaRS Discovery District." *Journal of Business and Finance Librarianship* 15(3–4): 188–196.

Frank, D. G., G. K. Raschke, J. Wood, and J. Z. Yang. (2001). "Information Consulting: The Key to Success in Academic Libraries." *The Journal of Academic Librarianship* 27(2): 90–96.

Geiger, R. L., and C. M. Sá. (2008). *Tapping the Riches of Science: Universities and the Promise of Economic Growth*. Cambridge, MA: Harvard University Press.

Grimaldi, R., M. Kenney, D. S. Siegel, and M. Wright. (2011). "Thirty Years after Bayh–Dole: Reassessing Academic Entrepreneurship." *Research Policy* 40(8): 1045–1057.

Hamilton-Pennell, C. (2008). "Public Libraries and Community Economic Development: Partnering for Success." *Illinois Institute for Rural Affairs* 10.

Leavitt, L. L., C. Hamilton-Pennell, and B. Fails. (2010). "An Economic Gardening Pilot Project in Michigan: Libraries and Economic Development Agencies Collaborating to Promote Entrepreneurship." *Journal of Business and Finance Librarianship* 15(3–4): 208–219. doi:10.1080/08963568.2010.487692.

Martin, J. A. (2010). "A Case Study of Academic Library and Economic Development Center Collaboration at the University of Toledo." *Journal of Business and Finance Librarianship* 15(3–4), 237–252.

Miller, D. J., and Z. J. Acs. (2013). "Technology Commercialization on Campus: Twentieth Century Frameworks and Twenty-First Century Blind Spots." *The Annals of Regional Science* 50(2): 407–423. http://dx.doi.org.ezproxy1.library.arizona.edu/10.1007/s00168-012-0511-7.

O'Shea, Rory P., et al. (2005). "Entrepreneurial Orientation, Technology Transfer and Spinoff Performance of US Universities." *Research Policy* 34(7): 994–1009.

O'Shea, Rory P., Harveen Chugh, and Thomas J. Allen. (2008). "Determinants and Consequences of University Spinoff Activity: A Conceptual Framework." *The Journal of Technology Transfer* 33(6): 653–666.

Pensyl, M. (1991). "Emerging Roles for Academic Librarians in the Technology Transfer Process." *Science and Technology Libraries* 11(2): 29–38. doi:10.1300/J122v11n02_03.

Phan, P. H., D. S. Siegel, and M. Wright. (2005). "Science Parks and Incubators: Observations, Synthesis and Future Research." *Journal of Business Venturing* 20(2): 165–182. http://dx.doi.org/10.1016/j.jbusvent.2003.12.001.

Pike, L., K. Chapman, P. Brothers, and T. Hines. (2010). "Library Outreach to the Alabama Black Belt: The Alabama Entrepreneurial Research Network." *Journal of Business and Finance Librarianship* 15(3–4): 197–207.

Pinelli, T. E. (1991). "The Information-Seeking Habits and Practices of Engineers." *Science and Technology Libraries* 11(3): 5–25.

Schacht, W. H. (2009). *The Bayh-Dole Act: Selected Issues in Patent Policy and the Commercialization of Technology*. Washington, DC: Library of Congress Congressional Research Service.

Schacht, W. H. (2012). *Technology Transfer: Use of Federally Funded Research and Development*. Washington, DC: Library of Congress Congressional Research Service.

Sheridan Libraries. (2014). *Entrepreneurial Librarian Program*. John Hopkins University. Accessed November 14, 2014. http://elp.library.jhu.edu/.

Siegel, D. S., M. Wright, and A. Lockett. (2007). "The Rise of Entrepreneurial Activity at Universities: Organizational and Societal Implications." *Industrial and Corporate Change* 16(4), 489–504.

Steinke, C. A. (ed.). (1990). *Technology Transfer: The Role of the Sci-tech Librarian*. Psychology Press.

Tumarkin, P. (2014). "Monday May 19, 2014, TLA, University Libraries Partner to Support Commercialization of UAInventions." *Tech Launch Arizona*. Accessed November 13, 2014. http://techlaunch.arizona.edu/article/tla-university-libraries-partner-support-commercialization-ua-inventions.

Wright, M. (2014). "Academic Entrepreneurship, Technology Transfer and Society: Where Next?" *The Journal of Technology Transfer* 39(3): 322–334.

Zinner, D. E., D. Bolcic-Jankovic, B. Clarridge, D. Blumenthal, and E. G. Campbell. (2009). "Participation of Academic Scientists in Relationships with Industry." *Health Affairs* 28(6): 1814–1825.

Chapter Five

Embedded Support of Adult Students in the Online Environment

Jessica Alverson and Susan Shultz

Librarians are accustomed to adapting their professional roles in an environment of rapidly evolving technology. Additional shifts in higher education, including changing student demographics and new instructional modes, are impacting the work of academic librarians. Instead of transplanting current models of information literacy instruction and reference service into this emerging environment, 21st-century librarians have the opportunity to reimagine their roles. Academic librarians can be at the forefront of this change, collaborating with campus partners to create new instructional models tailored to adult learners in e-learning environments. Key to adequately supporting adult e-learners are gaining a better understanding of this population and identifying relevant educational theories with applications for academic librarians.

In this chapter, the authors describe adult and online learners; present selected e-learning and adult learning theories; discuss appropriate assessment models; and outline best practices for working with adult e-learners. The authors also incorporate relevant literature with their own experiences and include insights from three faculty members with whom they collaborate in the online environment.

MOTIVATION FOR THIS CHAPTER

Jessica Alverson and Susan Shultz began their research as an endeavor to inform their work with adult learners in the online environment. However, as they investigated the relevant literature, gaps were identified. Librarians have published articles that discuss instruction and support for adult students (Caravello, 2000; Cooke, 2010; Gold, 2005; Harrison, 2000; Logan and McCaffrey, 2001). The library e-learning literature tends to focus on support services and access to library resources (Cannady et al., 2013; Johnson et al., 2008; Leeder and Lonn, 2014); creating online tutorials or information literacy courses (Barnhart and Stanfield, 2011; Clapp et al., 2013; Cuthbertson and Falcone, 2014; Hahn, 2012); or choosing and teaching with technology (Hess, 2013; Li, 2014). Literature on embedded librarianship does address models of support for e-learners (Carlson and Kneale, 2011; Meredith and Mussell, 2014; Shumaker, 2012). Some authors acknowledge that many online learners are adults with unique needs (Figa et al., 2009; Stielow, 2014); however, the literature does not deeply explore library instructional support at the intersection of adult learning and e-learning. This chapter aims to address this gap.

HIGHER EDUCATION IN THE 21ST CENTURY

Higher education, and by extension academic libraries, is facing tremendous challenges due to demographic, technological, and economic factors. Part and parcel of these changes is a shift in the age of students enrolling in higher education. For the years 2000–2011, the National Center for Education Statistics (NCES) reported that the increase in postsecondary enrollment for students twenty-five and older surpassed the eighteen to twenty-four age group by a 30% difference. While the NCES projects a slowdown in the enrollment of adult students in the future, it continues to forecast a healthy 14% increase during this decade (National Center for Education Statistics, 2013).

As these demographics shift, the meaning of the term "nontraditional student" is also morphing. Where better to gain an understanding of this turnabout in terminology than in the *Chronicle of Higher Education*: "What we used to call 'nontraditional' students . . . are fast becoming the new traditional" (Jenkins, 2012, para. 4). This chapter uses the terms "adult learners" and "adult students" to refer to this population.

An equally disruptive change in higher education is the move to online course delivery. While online education is not a new phenomenon, the compound annual growth rate of students taking at least one online course in the decade 2002–2012 was 16.1%; the enrollment growth in higher education for the same decade was 2.5% (Allen and Seaman, 2014).

In this chapter, the following definition of e-learning is applied: "the use of the Internet to access learning materials; to interact with the content, instructor, and other learners; and to obtain support during the learning process, in order to acquire knowledge, to construct personal meaning, and to grow from the learning experience" (Ally, 2008, p. 5). Alverson and Shultz focus on courses completely delivered online asynchronously.

LIBRARIAN ROLES IN E-LEARNING ENVIRONMENTS

Librarians have developed various approaches for supporting e-learners; however, embedded librarianship appears to hold the most promise. The term "embedded librarian" is well established in the professional lexicon. Although librarians have long provided this type of service, publications about embedded librarianship did not appear until the early 2000s. The term "embedded journalist" was first used during the Iraq War; librarians quickly adopted the term to represent their own integrated work partnerships (Schulte, 2012).

What does it mean to be an embedded librarian? Many different models have been developed, reflecting the myriad roles librarians perform. Presented below is a snapshot of the evolution of embedded librarianship.

While the term "embedded librarian" is relatively new, the work and relationships it represents are not. Beginning with a reflection on the library as place, libraries were often discipline-specific and the relevant collection was physically located in the academic department (Dewey, 2004, p. 6). Today, librarians may be physically embedded in an academic department, holding office hours or even having a dedicated office space. This model is often embraced in medical and business colleges.

One area of academic librarianship that generates many models of and participation in embeddedness is instruction, for both face-to-face and online classes. While one-shot instruction sessions are still common, more extensive collaborations with faculty that integrate the expertise of librarians into the course have also become part of the landscape. These collaborations vary and may include assignment creation, co-teaching, grading, consulting, and even curriculum development (Shumaker, 2012).

Librarians have adapted the embedded model to support online courses. John Shank and Nancy Dewald (2003) provide a useful lens for viewing the myriad ways that librarians are involved in online courses, distinguishing between macro and micro levels of involvement. Macro levels of involvement integrate general library resources and learning objects into a learning management system (LMS). For example, using links or widgets, librarians provide access to chat reference, course reserves, interlibrary loan, or databases. Micro-level involvement occurs at the course level in collaboration with the instructor and creates value-added interaction with students. Examples of micro-level involvement include monitoring and responding to discussion boards, co-teaching, creating customized learning objects, designing assignments, and posting introductions or announcements (Bezet, 2013;

Schulte, 2012). The model described in this chapter is a micro-level embeddedness.

SCHOOL FOR NEW LEARNING (ADULT PROGRAM): DEPAUL LIBRARY COLLABORATIONS

Motivated by reports from the Carnegie Commission on Higher Education that addressed nontraditional students, as well as internal discussions about the effectiveness of the university's evening college, DePaul University founded the School for New Learning (SNL) in 1972 (Strain, 1998). From the outset, this competence-based program was designed around the belief that life experiences of adults are fundamental to their learning process. SNL is an interdisciplinary, liberal arts program for adult students, granting bachelor's and master's degrees to students twenty-four years of age and older. All undergraduate students must complete the Research Seminar course in order to meet their formal inquiry competency and receive their bachelor's degrees.

DePaul librarians have a long history of collaborating with SNL faculty to support their students, and in fact the early partnerships were forms of embedding. These collaborations began in 1978 with a library research workbook that included exercises students were required to complete (Logan and McCaffrey, 2001). Over the past thirty-six years, this collaboration has evolved so that the librarians now provide face-to-face instruction for all on-the-ground sections of two required courses: Foundations of Adult Learning and Research Seminar. Additionally, all Foundations of Adult Learning students complete an online research tutorial that is graded by the librarian providing instruction for that class.

In 2002, SNL began offering Research Seminar online. Librarians have continued to provide support for these online students through different models of embeddedness. In Research Seminar, students must complete an annotated bibliography, a literature review, and a research proposal addressing an original research question. In 2008, librarians began embedding in the online sections of Research Seminar through the LMS. Librarians were assigned a "librarian" role in the LMS, providing them with full access to the course. The librarian's involvement consisted of grading two library-related assignments that students submitted via the LMS, and responding to students' postings on the "Ask a Librarian" discussion board. In summer 2013, Alverson and Shultz decided to revisit their model, taking a more holistic approach to supporting DePaul's adult e-learners. In the following sections, they share a summary of the research that has informed their process.

CHARACTERISTICS AND CHALLENGES OF ADULT STUDENTS

Who are these adult students? Malcolm Knowles, commonly referred to as the father of adult education, brings this population into focus with the following four working definitions of "adult." Adulthood arrives when individuals are able to biologically reproduce; are afforded legal privileges such as voting; take on responsible roles such as full-time employee; or "arrive at a self-concept of being responsible for [their] own lives, of being self-directing" (Knowles et al., 2005, p. 64). Knowles considers this last definition to be the most crucial to learning.

The constellation of circumstances that adults bring to their education significantly influences their ability to learn. While there is considerable diversity in the population of adult students, several characteristics are consistently mentioned in the literature as hallmarks of these students (Cooke, 2010; Jenkins, 2012):

- Family: Adult students are often responsible for family members including partners, children, or aging parents. Single parent and extended, multigenerational family responsibilities are not uncommon.
- Work: Many of these students are employed full-time or are working multiple part-time positions in order to make a living.
- Academic Preparation: Many adult students have been away from an educational environment for extended periods of time. Consequently, their academic skills may have eroded, or they never previously developed the skills of writing, close reading, studying, and time management.
- Technology: Closely aligned with the skills mentioned above, adult students may not be knowledgeable of or comfortable with current technologies that are essential for academic work.
- Finances: Not only can the stress of financial problems impede adult students' ability to learn, but budget constraints make it difficult to purchase textbooks, course materials, technology, and even transportation to campus.
- Self-Efficacy: The critical learning component of self-efficacy is often missing for adults returning to the classroom. Self-efficacy is an individual's belief that he or she possesses the ability to manage the processes involved to influence events in his or her life. For adults who have decided to participate in higher education, self-efficacy plays an important role in their academic performance (Bandura, 1997).
- Cognitive Function: Research on the plasticity of the brain has helped to dispel long-standing myths about age, cognitive decline, and the inability to learn beyond a certain age; however, the brain does change with age, and one cognitive function that may affect adult students is slower reaction time. This translates into the potential for additional time require-

ments for reading, synthesizing, and ultimately learning for the older adult student (Merriam et al., 2007; Wlodkowski, 2008).

- Self-Directedness: This characteristic is often attributed to adult students in the education literature, and while many adults exhibit this type of independence and persistence in their learning, equally important to consider are the many adults who need thoughtful and consistent direction to achieve learning (Cercone, 2008).

CHARACTERISTICS AND CHALLENGES OF E-LEARNERS

Alverson's and Shultz's work with adult students on the ground through instruction sessions, research consultations, and reference interactions provides them with a deeper understanding of this population. But the online students they support as embedded librarians are more enigmatic. Therefore, the literature about online students has been helpful in their quest to more fully know and support these students.

As with the adult population, students who participate in online classes comprise an increasingly diverse group of learners. Consequently, neatly identifying specific characteristics is problematic. Instead, the relevant literature often discusses measures such as students' perceptions or dissatisfaction/satisfaction with online courses and how this influences their ability to learn (Smart and Cappel, 2006). Based on the literature reviewed, the following portrait of the e-learner emerged:

- Demographics: Adult students account for the majority of students in online courses; this is not surprising given the complexity of their lives and the flexibility online learning provides. The increasing diversity in terms of race and gender of e-learners is also reflected in the literature (Ashong and Commander, 2012).
- Perceptions: From an analysis of twenty research studies that addressed students' perceptions in online courses, Karen L. Milheim (2012) found that e-learners experienced dissatisfaction with the following aspects of the online environment: limited or no interaction with the instructor; lack of collaboration or support available in the course; inappropriate design and delivery of content; limited skills and comfort with technology on the part of the student; and lack of student motivation.

The undergraduate enrollment in the School for New Learning reflects the demographic diversity of adult students (DePaul University, 2014). Gender distribution of SNL fall enrollment 2013/2014 was 61% female and 39% male. See table 5.1 for the racial distribution.

As these two populations came into focus for the authors, it was apparent that they needed to gain an understanding of the relevant theories addressing these two groups of students in order to anchor their model.

OVERVIEW OF SELECTED ADULT AND E-LEARNING THEORIES AND FRAMEWORKS

As practitioners, librarians are often mired in day-to-day activities. Busy schedules make it difficult to find time to reflect on teaching and examine it from a theoretical perspective. In librarians' roles as educators, however, understanding how they teach and connect to the bigger picture helps to enrich their practice. Terry Anderson (2008) states, "This broader perspective helps us to make connections with the work of others, facilitates coherent frameworks and deeper understanding of our actions, and perhaps most importantly allows us to transfer the experience gained in one context to new experiences and contexts" (p. 45). To that end, the authors outline key adult learning and e-learning theories and frameworks. They do not aim to provide a comprehensive overview—many others have already done this work—but to familiarize the reader with a selection of theories and frameworks that guide their work. In addition, a summary of theories used by the SNL faculty they interviewed is included.

Adult Learning Theories

While many different frameworks for and theories about adult learning exist, all operate on the tenet that adult learners differ from the traditional-age college student in motivation, how they learn, expectations, and goals for

Table 5.1. Racial Distribution by Percentage SNL Fall Enrollment 2013/2014

Race Category	Percentage SNL Fall Enrollment
African American	21
American Indian/Alaska Native	0.2
Asian	2
Hispanic	14
Multiracial	3.0
Native HI/Pacific Islander	0.2
Nonresident Alien	0.2
Unknown	11
White	48

learning. The theories/frameworks selected for inclusion in this chapter address both the adult learner and the educator of the adult learner.

Andragogy

Although others preceded him, Malcolm Knowles is most often associated with andragogy. In his seminal work *The Adult Learner: A Neglected Species*, Knowles defines andragogy as "the art and science of helping adults learn" (1990, p. 54). The andragogical model views the relationship between educator and the adult student as bidirectional. Andragogy acknowledges that adult learners come to the classroom with their own set of experiences, and therefore the educator and adult student contribute to each other's learning. The andragogical model is offered in contrast to the pedagogical model, which is viewed as unidirectional, with educator as the authority on content that he or she then conveys to the student. While the andragogical model is bidirectional, it is not necessarily an equitable relationship. The educator often carries more authority in his or her role as the facilitator of learning, depending on where the adult student is in the process of managing his or her individual learning.

Andragogy is based on six core principles (Knowles, 1990):

1. Learner's Need to Know: Adult learners need to have a reason for or understanding of why they need to know something.
2. Self-Concept of the Learner: Adult learners already have an independent identity. Learning environments in which the educator assumes an authoritative position can be threatening to adult learners.
3. Prior Experience of the Learner: Adult learners bring life experience to the classroom. Cumulatively, these life experiences can make for a diverse learning environment; however, life experiences can also result in students being opinionated and having certain biases that must be managed and challenged in the classroom.
4. Readiness to Learn: Adult learners are often driven to complete a degree by real-life needs or circumstances.
5. Orientation to Learning: Adult learners are focused on learning as "life-centered" as opposed to other learners who are "subject-centered." Education is valuable to the adult learner when it helps him or her in real-life situations.
6. Motivation to Learn: Adult learners are more intrinsically motivated. Adult learners may not be motivated by grades or other rewards.

Mezirow's Transformative Learning

Transformative learning theory acknowledges that adult learners come to learning with a preexisting frame of reference consisting of habits of mind and points of view. The goal of adult learning is to have the adult learner move away from authority-directed learning (the pedagogical model) and toward "autonomous" or self-directed learning. Jack Mezirow (1997) defines autonomy as "the understanding, skills, and disposition necessary to become critically reflective of one's own assumptions and to engage effectively in discourse to validate one's beliefs through the experiences of others who share universal values" (p. 9). In this metacognitive model, it is the goal of the adult learner to learn how to learn.

Educators help adult learners move toward autonomous learning by creating what Mezirow terms a communicative learning environment. In this model, both the adult students and the educator play a role in moving individuals toward autonomous learning. The educator may expose students to content and challenge their thinking, but the diversity of the adult students within a single classroom will also present learners with new experiences and challenges to their individual points of view. The educator functions as a "facilitator and provocateur" (p. 11) rather than as an authority on subject matter and ultimately becomes a co-learner. Like Knowles, Mezirow operates from the perspective that both the educator and the adult learner have something to learn from each other.

Pratt's Five Perspectives on Teaching Adults

With Daniel Pratt (1998), the focus shifts from the adult learner to the educator of the adult learner. Pratt's work emphasizes reflective teaching and challenges educators to first identify the perspective from which they are teaching. Pratt defines a perspective as "an interrelated set of beliefs and intentions which give meaning and justification for our actions" (p. 33). Perspectives are first formed by personal experiences as a learner, but they may evolve over time through teaching and life experiences.

Pratt identifies the following five perspectives:

1. Transmission: From the transmission perspective, the educator views his or her primary role as effectively teaching content to the adult learner. In this teacher-centered model, educators are viewed as experts in their content areas. For certain subject areas, teaching from the transmission perspective is very effective—especially those areas where the body of knowledge is well defined.
2. Apprenticeship: Educators teaching from the apprenticeship perspective view teaching as "the process of enculturating learners into a specific community." The educator may not be an expert in content, but is an experienced professional within the community. Within the apprenticeship model, Pratt notes, "learning is directed as much at

learning to be someone, as learning to do or know something" (pp. 44–45).

3. Developmental: This model is learner-centered and views learning as an experience in which students are challenged to incorporate new ideas and adjust their existing frames of reference. The educator must first identify the frames of reference or habits that the adult learners bring into the classroom and then challenge students to create new mental models. Pratt summarizes this perspective as follows: "Learning is a change in the quality of one's thinking rather than a change in the quantity of one's knowledge" (p. 47).

4. Nurturing: The nurturing perspective is also learner-centered, but focuses more on the learner's self-concept as a learner. Adult learners bring prior learning experiences, both positive and negative, into the classroom. The educator's goal is to be empathic and help students to become "confident and self-sufficient learners" (p. 49).

5. Social Reform: When teaching from the social reform perspective, educators have the ultimate goal of creating an improved society through education. The ideals take the most important role in teaching, overshadowing the learners, the teacher, and the content.

It is important to note that Pratt does not advocate for any one perspective as being preferable to another. In fact, if adult learning is viewed as Mezirow's continuum moving from dependence toward autonomy, this illustrates how it is beneficial for a student to have someone teaching from the transmission perspective (i.e., delivering content, laying the foundation) at the beginning of his or her education. In addition, Pratt distinguishes between the perspectives from which one teaches and the techniques that are used to teach. One may teach from a transmission perspective, but still create an engaging classroom environment.

E-learning Theories and Frameworks

Designing effective e-learning entails more than merely transporting content from the face-to-face environment to a learning management system. The goal of the educator in e-learning is to 1) design a learning experience that effectively translates the basic fundamentals of good learning into the online environment, and 2) effectively use the unique affordances of the online environment to enrich the learner's experience.

T. Brinthaupt et al. state:

> Thinking of online teaching as a shortcut—that is, approaching online teaching and learning as easier, or taking less time, or as something that can be put on "autopilot"—leads to much less effective teaching and learning. A more productive and transformational approach to online teaching is to recognize that it

allows teachers to transfer time from content delivery to time that can be devoted to fostering student engagement, stimulating intellectual development, and building rapport with students. (2011, p. 6)

Anderson's Theory of Online Learning

In his chapter "Towards a Theory of Online Learning," Terry Anderson (2008) argues that effective e-learning environments are learner-centered, knowledge-centered, assessment-centered, and community-centered and offer one form of interaction (student-student, student-teacher, student-content) at a high level. While Anderson's theory is seemingly simplistic, it provides a foundation for understanding how the fundamental characteristics of effective learning environments translate into the online environment.

Anderson draws from the work of John D. Bransford et al. (2000), who first articulated the four characteristics of effective learning environments: learner-centered, knowledge-centered, assessment-centered, and community-centered. Learner-centered instruction entails understanding what knowledge, skills, and attitudes students bring into the classroom and how these both impact and can be leveraged to improve learning. Knowledge-centered learning environments focus on the content that is taught, why it is taught, and what it means to have mastered the content. Assessment-centered classrooms incorporate formative assessment and include assessments that are "learner-friendly." Community-centered environments acknowledge that context is important to learning and seek to create collaborative learning environments with a set of defined and shared class norms and expectations.

Anderson also argues that successful learning relies on quality interactions between the teacher, students, and content. He explains (as cited in Anderson, 2008):

> Sufficient levels of deep and meaningful learning can be developed, as long as one of the three forms of interaction (student-teacher; student-student; student-content) is at very high levels. The other two may be offered at minimal levels or even eliminated without degrading the educational experience. (Anderson, 2002, p. 54)

Connectivism

George Siemens (2004) argues that technology has profoundly changed the way individuals live, work, communicate, and learn, and that older learning theories—constructivism, behaviorism, and cognitivism—do not reflect this new social environment. Connectivism provides a theory of learning that is flexible, responsive to this new and changing social environment, and learner-centered. Metacognition, not content, becomes the focus of learning. Knowing where to find information; making connections among different information types; and understanding when there is a new information need and when to discard old information become the goals of learning. It is easy to draw strong parallels between the aims of connectivism and information literacy.

Technology has rewired the brain, and the technology itself impacts learning. Siemens states, "The pipe is more important than the content within the pipe" (para. 31). Many of the traditional processes used to learn, including memorization, recall, and calculation, can now be offloaded to or supported by technology, leaving space for more meaningful learning. In other words, any learning theory must acknowledge the role technology plays.

Technological Pedagogical Content Knowledge Model (TPCK)

In their TPCK model, Punya Mishra and Matthew J. Koehler (2006) examine what knowledge and skills teachers should have in order to successfully integrate and use technology in the classroom. While this model looks at the use of *any* technology in the classroom, it provides a nice foundation for examining e-learning from the educator's perspective.

Drawing on Shulman's PCK (pedagogical, content, knowledge) model, Mishra and Koehler argue that three overlapping knowledge domains play into creating effective learning environments that integrate technology: content knowledge, pedagogical knowledge, and technological knowledge. Content knowledge is knowledge about the content being taught, and the required depth of that knowledge varies according to the level of the students being taught. Pedagogical knowledge is knowledge about teaching practices and theories, as well as an understanding of learning. Educators who create effective learning environments operate within the overlap of pedagogical and content knowledge, using teaching techniques appropriate to the type of content being taught. Mishra and Koehler add a third knowledge area to Shulman's model: technology knowledge. Technology knowledge is knowledge about how to operate and use various technologies.

Mishra and Koehler argue that these areas cannot be examined as separate domains, but must be combined to create the technological pedagogical content knowledge framework:

> TPCK is the basis of good teaching with technology and requires an understanding of the representation of concepts using technologies, pedagogical techniques that use technologies in constructive ways to teach content; knowledge of what makes concepts difficult or easy to learn and how technology can help redress some of the problems that students face; knowledge of students' prior knowledge and theories of epistemology; and knowledge of how technologies can be used to build on existing knowledge and to develop new epistemologies or strengthen old ones. (p. 1029)

An Educator's Perspective

SNL faculty members mentioned several theorists that inspired their work with adult learners. While Knowles was among them, Piaget and Dewey were also mentioned. Transformation and acknowledgment of prior experience were a common thread among the theories that guide their work. In addition, faculty noted that they apply the same adult learning theories to learners both on the ground and online. Faculty members emphasized that adult learning was a reciprocal exchange between the learner and the teacher. And at least one professor viewed the adult learning process through a spiritual lens: "In general, I understand that education should be holistic, meaning that everything we learn in class should be connected with every aspect of human and cosmic life, and also meaning that what we learn in class should inform the mind, inspire the heart and nourish the body of instructors and learners alike" (SNL professor, September 22, 2014).

ASSESSING THE ADULT LEARNER IN E-LEARNING

Librarian presence in the e-learning environment is still in its nascent stages, and developing appropriate assessment tools will be critical to achieving success. Assessment not only allows librarians to understand if their students are achieving learning outcomes, but also provides feedback that can be used to improve teaching. Perhaps most importantly, librarians can use assessment results to demonstrate the need to allocate proper resources to support this growing educational model.

Within the field of librarianship, assessment has mostly revolved around demonstrating student learning. This type of assessment can either be formative (low-stakes assessment to assess how the student is learning along the way) or summative (a final evaluation—usually evidenced in a grade—of the student's cumulative learning at the end of a course). In addition, librarians need to develop appropriate methods to analyze the ease and effectiveness of delivery of content via e-learning technologies.

Assessment in Adult Learning

Adult learners may resist traditional assessment tools (e.g., tests, quizzes) because they may interfere with the adult learner's concept of self as an autonomous individual. Previous negative experiences with these traditional assessment methods may resurface for the adult learner. Raymond Wlodkowski (2008) explains:

> In training and more formal learning experiences, assessment exerts a powerful motivational influence on adults because it is the socially sanctioned edu-

cational procedure to communicate about their competence. Historically, more than any other action, assessment by the instructor has validated learners' competence. Our comments, scores, grades, and reports affect learners in the present and future. Assessment often leaves a legacy for adults, directly or indirectly, by having an impact on their careers, vocational opportunities, professional advancement and acceptance into various schools and programs. (p. 312)

Librarians need to be sensitive to adult learners' prior learning experiences and self-concept when designing assessment tools.

Since many learning theories focus on developing adult students into self-directed, lifelong learners, self-assessment and self-monitoring tools need to be used when working with adult learners. Adult learners may only superficially learn content and focus on the evaluation tools themselves if assessment is only centered on tests (Pratt, 2008). Assessment tools that support self-directed learning include checklists, portfolios, self-reflective questions, note-taking pairs, post-writes, and worksheets (Costa and Kallick, 2004; Pratt, 2008).

Authentic assessment techniques align well with the andragogical model. Authentic assessment measures the acquisition of knowledge by focusing on applications of that knowledge through real-world scenarios or problem solving. Authentically designed assessments may also be a motivating tool for the adult learner (Wlodkowski, 2008).

Assessment tools should incorporate constructive feedback that is given in a timely manner. Feedback should address whether or not the learner achieved the intended outcomes of the assignment and explain any gaps or misunderstandings. Frequent feedback throughout the course provides the learner with opportunities to develop and correct any misunderstandings as their learning progresses (Wlodkowski, 2008).

In summary, effective assessment techniques for the adult learner demonstrate growth in learning; are scheduled; communicate expectations for successful completion in advance; provide penalty-free ways for students to improve learning; include feedback from both peers and the instructor; and are flexible enough to allow individual learners to demonstrate their strengths (Wlodkowski, 2008).

Assessment in E-learning

E-learning environments require new forms of assessment. Ellen Mandinach states, "E-learning is more than a new and emerging technology-based instructional delivery mechanism. It is a new form of teaching and learning that requires educators to rethink how the evaluation of process and outcomes should be conducted" (2005, p. 1815). Formative assessment opportunities are especially important in the e-learning environment, since instructors do not have consistent face-to-face interactions with students to inform their understanding of the students' progress (Rocco, 2007).

The e-learning environment should incorporate the fundamentals of assessment used in the face-to-face environment. Stevie Rocco (2007) outlines two approaches to assessment in the online environment: learner-centered methods and content-acquisition methods. Learner-centered methods measure how the learner perceives his or her own learning progress. Learner-centered methods may function as self-monitoring tools, making them especially appropriate for adult learners. Content-acquisition methods focus on whether students are meeting learning goals as determined by the instructor.

E-learning environments offer new affordances for assessment not available in the face-to-face classroom. Learning management systems provide educators with an ongoing record of student performance and participation. For example, discussion boards may demonstrate a student's evolving understanding. Learning management systems also provide metrics, such as amount of time spent on a page, to help educators assess student engagement with the material. Quizzes or other checks for understanding can easily be built into learning modules. Librarians can work with instructors to leverage these built-in assessment tools for their specific purposes.

In addition, it is important to assess whether the technologies being used to deliver e-learning are effectively supporting student learning. When implementing new technologies to deliver instruction, educators may use simple techniques such as an affordance analysis to evaluate the tool under consideration. Using an instructional design process such as ADDIE (Analysis, Design, Development, Implementation, Evaluation) can help to ensure a quality product. Librarians may consider using Char Booth's USER method (Understand, Structure, Engage, Reflect), which is an adaption of ADDIE (2011). Fee-based programs such as Quality Matters (www.qualitymatters. org) provide peer review of online courses to ensure ongoing quality.

It is also important to be aware of how the use of technology for assessment impacts the learner. Rocco (2007) notes, "Online instructors should recognize that there is a technical component to assessment in the online environment. . . . It is vital that these tools are easy for both students and teachers to use" (p. 77). Librarians must evaluate technology-based assessment tools for their effectiveness or possible hindrance in the assessment process. Technology is another critical consideration when designing assessment tools for adult learners.

PUTTING THEORY AND KNOWLEDGE INTO PRACTICE: APPLICATIONS

Consistently, the DePaul librarians experienced several issues that proved problematic for students trying to complete Research Seminar. Many of these issues occurred for both the face-to-face and online Research Seminar students. At the outset, students are confronted with challenging their mental models for research. For most of these students, "research" means gathering information. This makes it difficult for students to identify an original research question that is manageable. Low self-efficacy in adult learners also factors into their ability to embrace the research process. Since many students have returned to school after a period of absence, they often encounter a much different library and also have to deal with the technostress of learning how to manipulate and use new research tools. These issues are compounded and become even more evident in the online Research Seminar sections.

Informed by their research, in summer 2013, Alverson and Shultz decided to take action and revisit their model of support for Research Seminar online; reenvisioning their involvement was influenced by Pratt's nurturing perspective. Teaching from this perspective allowed them to focus their model on the librarian-student interaction and less on the content-student interaction, as articulated by Anderson's theory of online learning.

Their new model retains the original embedded roles: each online section is assigned a librarian who has full access to the course through the learning management system. The new model, however, moves toward a deeper level of embedding by incorporating multiple support structures. In order to achieve sustained presence, librarians communicate with all students via email or news items within the LMS at least once a week. A portfolio of canned messages was developed to introduce appropriate library services and resources. The messages explaining the application of the resource/service were designed to correspond with the student's stage in the research process. Students also receive an introductory, welcoming email from the librarian in the first week explaining her role in the course.

Students now complete only one library assignment. This guided assignment walks students through the process of identifying and searching appropriate article databases through a scaffolded approach that includes short videos. Students are required to submit two citations for articles as part of the assignment. Designed to minimize technostress, the assignment is a downloadable Word document of questions for students to complete and upload to the LMS assignment drop box. The library assignment was repositioned in the course and is now timed to correspond with the course assignment that requires students to submit five annotated sources. With this repositioning, students can now immediately apply what they learn from the library assignment, as well as use the two articles toward that week's course assignment.

To increase personalization and provide more responsive support, librarians meet with each student for a fifteen-minute research consultation, either via instant messaging (chat) or phone. The consultations are timed to correspond to the most research-intensive modules of the course. Students are required to complete the consultation as part of their coursework and can easily sign up for appointments using an online scheduling system. For both the librarians and the students, the research consultation works as a bidirectional exchange. The librarian learns more about the student and his or her motivations for research, providing richer information for tailored guidance. In addition, consultations allow the librarians to easily address any challenges the students may be facing. The significance of the personal connection created through the interaction cannot be overstated. For many students, librarians are also able to provide emotional support and reassurance. Students are more likely to reach out for additional help after having their research consultation; this demonstrates the importance of personal contact in creating a sustained relationship.

The "Ask a Librarian" discussion board was retained with the goal of creating a peer learning space; students are encouraged to post any research-related questions to that board. Students can read librarian responses, as well as provide their own suggestions.

BEST PRACTICES FOR WORKING WITH ADULT E-LEARNERS

Librarians need to examine what and how they teach when working with adult e-learners: embedding is key. While it is technically possible to translate the one-shot library instruction session into the e-learning environment, it is not the most effective teaching method—especially for adult learners. In this section, a list of best practices for librarians working with adult e-learners is provided.

The DePaul librarians operate under the following principles:

1. Create a nurturing environment for students. Librarian involvement should be sustained and personalized.
2. Allow for flexibility. Understand that adult students may have other, competing real-life commitments.
3. Acknowledge and consider the adult learners' prior experiences. Prior learning experiences may negatively impact their views of the research process if not addressed.

4. Use the affordances of the technology, but only if they make sense. Understand that students come to the online classroom with various experiences with technology, both good and bad.
5. Librarians are facilitators of learning. Teaching from an andragogical perspective, above all, requires that the librarian view himself or herself as a partner in constructing knowledge with the students.

Before the course:

1. Establish relationships with the course instructor, program administrator, and instructional designer. Having a personal rapport with the instructor helps librarians to clearly define their roles and also solidifies the collaborative roles important to supporting students. Program administrators can provide information on the student population, as well as keep librarians informed of ongoing issues such as retention or planned developments for online programs. In many cases, instructors will also be working with an instructional designer. Depending on the role and privileges a librarian is given in the LMS, the instructional designer may be a key partner for incorporating content and assignments in a course, as well as making any corrections to outdated content or broken links.
2. Review the course content. E-learning affords librarians an opportunity not available in the face-to-face environment—the ability to see all of the course content. Reviewing all of the course content will allow librarians to better identify where to include library instructional objects or assignments so that they are appropriately timed.
3. Become familiar with the e-learning delivery platform and its affordances and understand the capabilities of the learning management system or platform. It is important for librarians to be knowledgeable of the various communication channels (e.g., discussion boards, email functionality, news items). Understanding what content can be embedded directly into the LMS is also essential; third-party or library platforms for hosting certain types of content may be necessary.

ESTABLISHING RAPPORT WITH STUDENTS AND CREATING A SUPPORTIVE ENVIRONMENT

1. Librarians should introduce themselves to students in a personalized message the first week of class. In this message they should explain who they are, what their role will be in the course, and include the best method of communicating (e.g., email, phone, chat). Students will more easily connect if the librarian includes a picture or a brief, infor-

mal video of introduction. These introductions will be most effective if the communication channels available via the LMS are used.

2. Create a friendly, helping environment. Embed a widget to the institution's chat and email reference services in the LMS. Alternatively, include a personal chat widget that allows students to contact librarians when they are online. Provide students with options for getting assistance after hours, since many students may be doing their work at night.
3. Communicate with students weekly. This allows librarians to create a sustained presence in the course, as well as giving them the opportunity to pass along other timely information to students.
4. Go offline. Contact students via phone, or even arrange an in-person meeting—many online students may actually be local. Because students often feel isolated in the online environment, providing them with a human connection gives them a lifeline. Adult students are especially appreciative of this type of contact. It has become apparent that the best mode of communication for these research consultations is the phone. A personal discussion on the phone allows for a richer and more nuanced exchange of information and questions, and the ability to build rapport with the student. In addition to developing this bond, dialogue is an important component of the learning process for students (Jacobs, 2013).

CONTENT

1. Before each semester, content (e.g., tutorials, documents, assignments) should be checked for accuracy and to ensure that all links work. If students are not able to accomplish basic tasks, such as getting to the course content, they may lose motivation early in the course (Milheim, 2012).
2. Work with the instructor and instructional designer to ensure that library-related links are correct. In addition, librarians might also recommend third-party links or tutorials for the instructor to include—especially if they are aware of a stronger example.
3. Library instructional content and/or assignments should be appropriately timed within the context of the class. Librarians should work closely with the instructor to ensure that the library content load is balanced with course content from week to week in order to avoid overwhelming students.
4. Library content should be tied to the larger framework of the course, and if possible beyond the course. Adult students need to understand

the bigger picture and how content and assignments are going to help them toward accomplishing their individual goals.

5. Keep recommended resources to a minimum. When providing students with options for getting additional help beyond what is required for the course, be very selective. Provide a link to the best APA citation style tutorial, not three different ones.

6. Identify exactly what the students need to be able to do, and work from there when including content or assignments. Content should be focused on the course learning outcomes.

7. Offload process-oriented and short tasks to videos. These videos may be included as a required part of the instructional content or may be optional, for those who need the help.

8. Carefully consider the technology used for any assignments or delivery of content. The technology should work seamlessly for the student, with no learning curve involved. If the technology is not user-friendly, students may see it as an undue burden (Tabak and Nguyen, 2013). Do not introduce new technologies into the course for purposes of library content.

ASSESSMENT AND FEEDBACK

1. Design informal check-ins throughout the course to measure where students are in the research process. Create a feedback loop with the course instructor, allowing ease of communication for students who may need additional assistance.

2. Incorporate self-monitoring assessment methods so that adult learners are able to measure where they are in the learning process. Examples include providing a checklist for completing research or including self-graded quizzes related to library content, allowing students to test their understanding without fear of receiving a bad grade.

3. Include a librarian-graded assignment in the course. An introductory email should be sent that explains the purpose of the assessment, as well as outlined expectations for completing the assignment. Although research reveals that many adult learners are intrinsically motivated without accountability, reviewing library-related content may be viewed as an optional activity. Unfortunately for the student, his or her research skill deficits may only come to light in a final project, when it is too late.

4. Feedback should be personalized, substantive, and timely. "Good job!" does not provide the student with much to reflect on. The feedback should acknowledge what the student achieved, as well as address any gaps or areas for improvement. If the student needs to cor-

rect something, clear instructions about what should be corrected (and why it is important) should be included. Finally, feedback should provide students with additional suggestions. It is important to make the feedback meaningful; otherwise, students may not devote time to reading it.

5. Incorporate assessment techniques that allow librarians to measure and reflect on their own teaching and delivery methods. Review students' end products and apply a rubric to assess whether students met the learning outcomes as outlined for their research. Provide students with a survey asking about their experiences with librarian involvement in the course.

PUTTING THEORY AND KNOWLEDGE INTO PRACTICE: CHALLENGES

Despite careful planning, preparation, and renewed energy, unanticipated problems may surface at any point in the course. The DePaul librarians developed several of the best practices discussed above in response to issues that were consistently experienced in the early phases of their embedded program. As is often the case, problems in a dynamic environment such as an online course may take time to crystallize. The following are challenges that librarians identified in working with fourteen Research Seminar courses after their revision of the program. They begin with several tangible issues to keep in mind when working with students, and then talk about considerations for sustaining, and perhaps growing, an embedded program for the long run.

1. Research Consultations:

    a. Each quarter there are students who are no-shows for their scheduled appointments. This has implications for librarian schedules; the specific weeks in which these research consultations take place are the busiest weeks in the quarter for librarians in terms of instruction and reference workloads.

    b. The librarians observe the busy lives of these adult students firsthand when trying to match their availability to the schedules of the students. Many times students have requested an appointment in the evening or on a weekend. To provide adequate support for these students, it is important for librarians to be sensitive to their schedules, but cautiously flexible with their own time.

2. Role Confusion: The boundaries between the instructor's and librarian's roles can sometimes be confusing for students. Occasionally, librarians field questions that are clearly more appropriate for the instructor to answer (e.g., questions about the literature reviews and research proposals, which are graded by the instructor). Knowing when to gently refer the student to the instructor for answers to a question is informed by a thorough understanding of the course content, assignments, and instructor's expectations of the students.

3. Mind-Set: The academic abilities of adult students range widely on a long continuum. It is important, and can at times be challenging, for librarians to keep the uniqueness of each student in mind as they support them in their learning. It can be useful to visualize helping students move in a positive direction along the continuum of learning, instead of striving to move them to the most successful end point (SNL professor, 2012).

4. Workload: The DePaul librarians' holistic model of embedded support requires a sizable and continuous time commitment that extends throughout the quarter/semester. Based on this, they recommend two fundamental considerations when designing an embedded program: a) do not overcommit; begin with one librarian integrated into one course at a time; and b) capture all relevant statistics that are generated from embedding in an online course, including time spent, research consultations, email transactions with students and faculty, and postings to the discussion boards. The literature on embedded librarianship reflects a similar concern with time commitment (Bezet, 2013; Schulte, 2012).

5. Administrative Support: Related to the issue of workload is the importance of communicating with library administration and gaining their support for an embedded program and the requisite commitment of time. To dedicate the time necessary to adequately support and engage with students in a holistic-embedded model, library administration will need to provide parallel support to a librarian in this role. Administrative support is also recommended in the distance education literature as an essential program structure for online course development and teaching (Fish and Wickersham, 2009).

In addition to the inherent challenges of teaching in online courses discussed in the literature, the School for New Learning faculty members who were interviewed also shared complexities they encounter. Awareness of the many dynamics experienced by all participants in the online course (students and faculty) helps to inform the support librarians provide.

CHALLENGES FOR SNL PROFESSORS IN THE ONLINE RESEARCH SEMINAR COURSE

1. Ambiguity: Students sometimes misinterpret or do not understand the written documents in an online course (e.g., assignments, explanatory text, discussion board postings). While this can also happen in a face-to-face classroom, students in an online course struggle with this in isolation (SNL professor, October 2, 2014).
2. Lack of the Five Senses: The richness of interactions in a face-to-face classroom is not possible to achieve online. The online classroom is a "very bounded environment" (SNL professor, October 2, 2014), and this can negatively impact the learning experience. In a face-to-face classroom, "instructor and students interact in a profoundly human way, in their discussions, in their use of body language, in the human-touch moments and experiences not possible in the online experience" (SNL professor, September 22, 2014).
3. Online Distractions: Students struggle with comprehension, and this can be compounded by the many distractions that are available when they are working online in the LMS. Students may approach their online learning as just one more activity in their online behavior; they may not devote the quiet time and space necessary for learning (SNL professor, October 2, 2014).
4. Student Engagement: Students who fall behind in the work for an online course can be more challenging to motivate and keep on task (SNL professor, October 2, 2014).

CONCLUSION

Reflecting on the process of researching and writing this chapter, a clear and consistent theme surfaced, both in the literature and in the authors' thoughts. Many layers of assistance are provided to these adult students in the online Research Seminar course—all are important to adequately support these students in their academic success. But the vital element that permeates this model is the sustained relationship the DePaul librarians offer these students through the ten weeks of the course.

This chapter has presented theories and ideas from several of the most influential experts in this field, and the authors introduce one more in their concluding thoughts: Laurent Daloz. He developed his keen understanding of adult learners through an active career of teaching, mentoring, and administration in adult education. It is not surprising that a more meaningful analogy for embedded librarianship was discovered in his book *Mentor: Guiding the Journey of Adult Learners*. Drawing from work by Robert Kegan, Daloz highlights the importance of holding environments or "cultures of embeddedness" in the many different phases of an individual's development and relates these to mentoring adult students (1999, p. 185). As with the mentoring relationship, the DePaul librarians provide a similar type of holding environment that allows students to experience the three essential environmental components for development: confirmation (acknowledge where they are in the research process); contradiction (model research skills, but allow them to develop the skills for themselves); and continuity (remain available to them throughout the course as they continue to develop these skills) (pp. 187–188).

Working with adult students, both face-to-face and online, is a richly rewarding experience. The authors learn many things from these students, but perhaps most importantly, they learn about the perseverance of the human spirit.

Jessica Alverson and Susan Shultz would like to thank Dr. Corinne Benedetto, Dr. Kenya Grooms, and Dr. Raymond Mosha for their valuable insights on adult students.

REFERENCES

Allen, I. E, and J. Seaman. (2014). *Grade Change: Tracking Online Education in the United States*. http://www.onlinelearningsurvey.com/reports/gradechange.pdf.

Ally, M. (2008). "Foundations of Educational Theory for Online Learning." In T. Anderson (ed.), *Theory and Practice of Online Learning*, 2nd ed., pp. 3–31. Edmonton, AB: Athabasca University Press. Available online.

Anderson, T. (2008). "Towards a Theory of Online Learning." In T. Anderson (ed.), *Theory and Practice of Online Learning*, 2nd ed., pp. 33–60. Edmonton, AB: Athabasca University Press. Available online.

Ashong, C. Y., and N. E. Commander. (2012). "Ethnicity, Gender, and Perceptions of Online Learning in Higher Education." *MERLOT Journal of Online Learning and Teaching* 8(2): 98–110.

Bandura, A. (1997). *Self-Efficacy: The Exercise of Control*. New York: W. H. Freeman.

Barnhart, A., and A. Stanfield. (2011). "When Coming to Campus Is Not an Option: Using Web Conferencing to Deliver Library Instruction." *Reference Services Review* 39(1): 58–65. doi:10.1108/00907321111108114.

Bezet, A. (2013). "Free Prize Inside! Embedded Librarianship and Faculty Collaboration at a Small-Sized Private University." *The Reference Librarian* 54(3): 181–219.

Booth, C. (2011). *Reflective Teaching, Effective Learning: Instructional Literacy for Library Educators*. Chicago: American Library Association.

Bransford, J., A. Brown, and R. Cocking. (2000). *How People Learn: Brain, Mind Experience and School*. Expanded ed. Accessed October 2, 2014. http://www.nap.edu/openbook.php?record_id=9853.

Brinthaupt, T., L. Fisher, J. Gardner, M. Raffo, and J. Woodard. (2011). "What the Best Online Teachers Should Do." *MERLOT Journal of Online Learning and Teaching* 7(4).

Cannady, R., B. Fagerheim, B. Williams, and H. Steiner. (2013). "Diving into Distance Learning Librarianship." *College and Research Libraries News* 74(5): 254–261.

Caravello, P. S. (2000). "Library Instruction and Information Literacy for the Adult Learner: A Course and Its Lessons for Reference Work." *The Reference Librarian* 33(69–70): 259–269.

Carlson, J., and R. Kneale. (2011). "Embedded Librarianship in the Research Context: Navigating New Waters." *College and Research Libraries News* 72(3): 167–170.

Cercone, K. (2008). "Characteristics of Adult Learners with Implications for Online Learning Design." *AACE Journal* 16(2): 137–159.

Clapp, M., M. Johnson, D. Schwieder, and C. Craig. (2013). "Innovation in the Academy: Creating an Online Information Literacy Course." *Journal of Library and Information Services in Distance Learning* 7(3): 247–263. doi:10.1080/1533290X.2013.805663.

Cooke, N. A. (2010). "Becoming an Andragogical Librarian: Using Library Instruction as a Tool to Combat Library Anxiety and Empower Adult Learners." *New Review of Academic Librarianship* 16(2): 208–227. doi:10.1080/13614533.2010.507388.

Costa, A., and B. Kallick. (2004). *Assessment Strategies for Self-Directed Learning.* Thousand Oaks, CA: Corwin Press.

Cuthbertson, W., and A. Falcone. (2014). "Elevating Engagement and Community in Online Courses." *Journal of Library and Information Services in Distance Learning* 8(3/4): 216–224. doi:10.1080/1533290X.2014.945839.

Daloz, L. A. (1999). *Mentor: Guiding the Journey of Adult Learners.* 2nd ed. San Francisco: Jossey-Bass.

DePaul University. (2014). *DePaul Fact File: 2010/11–2013/14.* http://oipr.depaul.edu/market_analytics/FFPlus.asp?cont=FFP.

Dewey, B. I. (2004). "The Embedded Librarian: Strategic Campus Collaborations." *Resource Sharing and Information Networks* 17(1–2): 5–17.

Figa, E., T. Bone, and J. R. Macpherson. (2009). "Faculty-Librarian Collaboration for Library Services in the Online Classroom: Student Evaluation Results and Recommended Practices for Implementation." *Journal of Library and Information Services in Distance Learning* 3(2): 67–102. doi:10.1080/15332900902979119.

Fish, W. W., and L. E. Wickersham. (2009). "Best Practices for Online Instructors: Reminders." *The Quarterly Review of Distance Education* 10(3): 279–284.

Gold, H. E. (2005). "Engaging the Adult Learner: Creating Effective Library Instruction." *portal: Libraries and the Academy* 5(4): 467–481. doi:10.1353/pla.2005.005.1.

Hahn, E. (2012). "Video Lectures Help Enhance Online Information Literacy Course." *Reference Services Review* 40(1): 49–60. doi:10.1108/00907321211203621.

Harrison, N. (2000). "Breaking the Mold: Using Educational Pedagogy in Designing Library Instruction of Adult Learners." *The Reference Librarian* 33(69–70): 287–298. doi:10.1300/J120v33n69_26.

Hess, A. (2013). "The MAGIC of Web Tutorials: How One Library (Re)focused Its Delivery of Online Learning Objects on Users." *Journal of Library and Information Services in Distance Learning* 7(4): 331–348. doi:10.1080/1533290X.2013.839978.

Jacobs, P. (2013). "The Challenges of Online Courses for the Instructor." *Research in Higher Education Journal* 21: 1–18.

Jenkins, R. (2012). "The New 'Traditional Student.'" *Chronicle of Higher Education* 59(8): A31–A32.

Johnson, K., H. Trabelsi, and E. Fabbro. (2008). "Library Support for E-learners: E-resources, E-services, and the Human Factors." In T. Anderson (ed.), *Theory and Practice of Online Learning*, 2nd ed., pp. 397–418. Edmonton, AB: Athabasca University Press. Available online.

Knowles, M. (1990). *The Adult Learner: A Neglected Species.* 4th ed. Houston: Gulf Publishing.

Knowles, M. S., E. F. Holton, and R. A. Swanson. (2005). *The Adult Learner: The Definitive Classic in Adult Education and Human Resource Development.* Amsterdam: Elsevier.

Leeder, C., and S. Lonn. (2014). "Faculty Usage of Library Tools in a Learning Management System." *College and Research Libraries* 75(5): 650–663. doi:10.5860/crl.75.5.641.

Li, J. (2014). "Greeting You Online: Selecting Web-Based Conferencing Tools for Instruction in E-learning Mode." *Journal of Library and Information Services in Distance Learning* 8(1/2): 56–66. doi:10.1080/1533290X.2014.916246.

Logan, F., and E. McCaffrey. (2001). "New Partnerships for New Learning." *Journal of Library Administration* 32(1–2): 309–318.

Mandinach, E. B. (2005). "The Development of Effective Evaluation Methods for E-learning: A Concept Paper and Action Plan." *Teachers College Record* 107(8): 1814–1835.

Meredith, W., and J. Mussell. (2014). "Amazed, Appreciative, or Ambivalent? Student and Faculty Perceptions of Librarians Embedded in Online Courses." *Internet Reference Services Quarterly* 19(2): 89–112. doi:10.1080/10875301.2014.917.

Merriam, S. B., R. S. Caffarella, and L. M. Baumgartner. (2007). *Learning in Adulthood: A Comprehensive Guide*. San Francisco: Jossey-Bass.

Mezirow, J. (1997). "Transformative Learning: Theory to Practice." *New Directions for Adult and Continuing Education* 74: 5–12.

Milheim, K. L. (2012). "Toward a Better Experience: Examining Student Needs in the Online Classroom through Maslow's Hierarchy of Needs Model." *MERLOT Journal of Online Learning and Teaching* 8(2): 159–171.

Mishra, P., and M. J. Koehler. (2006). "Technological Pedagogical Content Knowledge: A Framework for Teacher Knowledge." *Teachers College Record* 108(6): 1017–1054.

National Center for Education Statistics. (2013). *Fast Facts: Enrollment*. http://nces.ed.gov/fastfacts/display.asp?id=98.

Pratt, D. D. (1998). *Five Perspectives on Teaching in Adult and Higher Education*: Malabar, FL: Krieger Publishing.

Rocco, S. (2007). "Online Assessment and Evaluation." *New Directions for Adult and Continuing Education* 113: 75–86.

Schulte, S. J. (2012). "Embedded Academic Librarianship: A Review of the Literature." *Evidence Based Library and Information Practice* 7(4): 122–138.

Shank, J. D., and N. H. Dewald. (2003). "Establishing Our Presence in Courseware: Adding Library Services to the Virtual Classroom." *Information Technology and Libraries* 22(1): 38–43.

Shumaker, D. (2012). *The Embedded Librarian: Innovative Strategies for Taking Knowledge Where It's Needed*. Medford, NJ: Information Today.

Siemens, G. (2004). "Connectivism: A Learning Theory for the Digital Age." *Elearnspace*. http://www.elearnspace.org/Articles/connectivism.htm.

Smart, K. L., and J. J. Cappel. (2006). "Students' Perceptions of Online Learning: A Comparative Study." *Journal of Information Education* 5: 201–219.

Stielow, F. (2014). *Reinventing the Library for Online Education*. Chicago: ALA Editions.

Strain, C. R. (1998). "We Ourselves Are Plural: Curricular Change at DePaul, 1960–1997." In J. L. Rury and C. S. Suchar (eds.), *DePaul University: Centennial Essays and Images*, pp. 291–342. Chicago: DePaul University.

Tabak, F., and N. Nguyen. (2013). "Technology Acceptance and Performance in Online Learning Environments: Impact of Self-Regulation." *MERLOT Journal of Online Learning and Teaching* 9(1): 116–130.

Wlodkowski, R. J. (2008). *Enhancing Adult Motivation to Learn: A Comprehensive Guide for Teaching All Adults*. 3rd ed. San Francisco: Jossey-Bass.

Chapter Six

Creativity, Collaboration, and Connectedness

Going Radical with a Librarian-Faculty Partnership to Transform Learning in the 21st Century

Troy Davis and Ann Marie Stock

Academic libraries are purportedly committed to student learning and faculty engagement. That commitment, however, is often unrealized. Despite impediments, libraries are poised to become renaissance places, environments that invite the librarian and the professor to learn together with students and continue "becoming" so as to contribute to the transformation of their institutions.

This chapter reflects upon the origins, evolution, and continuing trajectory of a deliberative experiment in collaboration. A librarian and a professor actively sought to explore the nature of student learning and their capacities to influence, shape, and produce it, all the while realizing that this required a preoccupation with *their own learning* and an imaginative remix of roles.

In the end, this endeavor necessitated an examination of the institutional, professional, and intellectual limitations inherent in the undertheorized roles of the "librarian" and the "professor."

This chapter does not provide appendices of lesson plans or rubrics for innovative assignments. Nor does it embrace a language of "information literacy" or its standards, or even its recent reinvention in the registers of "metaliteracy" (Mackey and Jacobson, 2014). (The authors are, however, heartened by an emerging conversation in the library world that seeks to critique purpose and pedagogy, most notably via social media platforms like Twitter via the #critlib community). Instead, it communicates a journey, a protracted experiment and experience in collaboration. The conclusions suggest that academic libraries must, if they are to remain relevant, mobilize resources to examine, reinvent, and ultimately transform their missions, practices, organizational structures, and philosophies of "instruction." Like Robert Barr and John Tagg (1995), the authors believe that the "mission is not instruction but rather that of producing *learning* with every student by *whatever* means work best" (p. 13). To this end, librarians and faculty must develop partnerships that are at once generative and authentic, and devoted to learning as well as teaching. This is increasingly necessary for empowering learners in the 21st century. While seeking to outline the contours of an ongoing experience of collaboration, the authors also strive to foreground the collaborative nature of this writing experience. In doing so, they envision a reading audience composed of curious librarians and professors who seek to understand and ultimately strive to eliminate the barriers to meaningful collaboration. They are aware that this reimagining could leave them at the periphery in both worlds, yet believe the risk is worth taking. Using the word "radical" in the title might seem a bit ambitious. It is employed purposefully, however, in adherence to Paulo Freire's notion of "critical pedagogy." Like this theorist, the authors resist the "banking" concept of education in which teachers deposit money (knowledge) into the accounts (brains) of students, agreeing that it "transforms students into receiving objects" rather than active agents equipped to take charge of their learning." Moreover, "it attempts to control thinking and action, leads men and women to adjust to the world, and inhibits their creative power" (Freire, 1970, p. 77). In casting teachers as active and students as passive, the power imbalance is reinforced, the agency of learners is limited, and creativity is curtailed. What is "radical," then, in Freire's formulation and in the employment of the term here, is the potential for new self-knowledge and the reshaping of one's identity through education. In Freire's words, "education makes sense because women and men learn that through learning they can make and remake themselves, because women and men are able to take responsibility for themselves as beings capable of knowing—of knowing that they know and knowing that they don't" (Freire, 2004, p. 15). Education can and must transform individuals and institutions. To realize this potential, or even attempt to do so, is to "go radical."

LITERATURE REVIEW

Recent interventions in theories of information literacy echo this emphasis on "going radical." Andrew Whitworth (2014), for example, argues for a "radical information literacy"; this occurs, he observes, "whenever the assumptions around which we base our learning and practice are called into question and scrutinized in democratic, participatory ways" (p. 168). Whitworth goes on to assert that radical information literacy "is also a theory that suggests why change is difficult. Institutionalization, authority in texts, and the presence of unscrutinized assumptions and values in many landscapes help explain why collaboration, whether between librarians and faculty or between communities and formalized educational institutions, has proven so elusive" (p. 168). Of interest in undertaking the collaboration examined herein was figuring out precisely how to identify these assumptions and call them into question.

In terms of librarian-faculty partnerships, there are perhaps more questions than answers: What are the institutional and intellectual conditions necessary for fruitful collaboration? What are the theories that inform practice and what limitations do they impose? Under what conditions can something radical emerge? Even a cursory survey of the literature on librarian-faculty collaboration shows an active and intellectual turbulence (Bausman et al., 2014; Kotter, 1999; Brown and Duke, 2005; Keil, 2014; Kenedy and Monty, 2011; Meulemans and Carr, 2013; Mounce, 2010; Raspa and Ward, 2000). Why is it so difficult to collaborate? And what, in the end, constitutes a productive collaborative experience?

The safest answer suggests that partnerships make sense only in the context of producing student learning. This chapter proposes a different answer: A partnership is radical when it activates the learning process of the collaborators. It is in the messy, redemptive, multifaceted, intellectual, and at times banal process modeled for students. What is radical, then, is not the results of collaboration (although some outcomes and ongoing initiatives will be shared), but rather the reframing of the questions asked about partnerships formed around a devotion to student learning. If collaboration does not generate something *transformative*, then it is not radical. And if it is not radical it remains limited at best. What is necessary for higher education in the 21st century is nothing less than significant transformation: of roles, of relationships, and of institutions.

Academic libraries, now more than ever before, are poised to become places committed to student learning and faculty engagement as well as persistent and sustainable learning environments that invite librarians, professors, students, *and the institution* to learn together, to change, and to contribute to ongoing transformation.

SNAPSHOT OF THE INSTITUTION AND THE PARTICIPANTS

The College of William and Mary in Virginia is a public liberal arts institution that enrolls some five thousand undergraduates and two thousand graduate students across five schools, the largest of which is Arts and Sciences. The institutional culture values both teaching and research as critical for "encourag[ing] creativity, independent thought, and intellectual depth, breadth and curiosity" (http://www.wm.edu/offices/fye/about/mission/index. php). Members of this academic community—students, faculty, librarians, administrators, alumni, and others—often cite the integration of teaching and research as a hallmark of a William and Mary education. And in fact, this feature provided the framework within which a librarian and a professor teamed up to enhance student learning, transform their respective profession- al roles, and contribute to their institution in new ways.

One of the authors (Troy Davis) is an academic librarian with a special- ization in media production; he was hired to establish and lead a media services division in the college's Earl Gregg Swem Library. As a result of this collaboration, he has designed and taught courses in the interdisciplinary Film and Media Studies Program. The other author (Ann Marie Stock) is a professor of Hispanic studies in the Modern Languages and Literatures De- partment and also a member of the Film and Media Studies faculty. She teaches courses in Spanish related to Cuban and Latin American cinema and in English on film and media theory and practice. When they began the collaboration outlined in these pages, Davis had been at the college seven years and Stock fifteen years; during their respective careers, both embraced interdisciplinary inquiry, both valued the blending of teaching and research, and both were committed to experimentation.

The impetus for their collaboration was an arts and sciences initiative promoting undergraduate research for the university's accreditation process for the Southern Association of Colleges and Schools. The opportunity drew Stock's attention because she was completing a book manuscript and wanted to integrate this scholarly endeavor with her teaching. (Stock has authored and edited books on the subject, among them *On Location in Cuba: Street Filmmaking during Times of Transition* and *World Film Locations: Havana*, as well as numerous articles.) She had this vision: engage students in her ongoing exploration of the work of emerging Cuban filmmakers, specifically by translating dialogues and creating subtitles for documentaries and by film- ing interviews for the Cuban Cinema Classics DVD series she had created (www.cubancinemaclassics.org). But she lacked some basic infrastructure to pull this off, e.g., access to professional media creation tools. Even more significantly, she lacked the know-how for these hands-on projects. So in order to expand her knowledge, and engage others in the process, she set out to find someone with the necessary expertise. After several queries, in vari- ous units across the institution, she located her hoped-for partner. What was to have been a brief meeting with the director of media services in the university library extended into a lengthy and impassioned conversation: about film and media, cultural studies theories, pedagogical principles, and the institutional mission. It was clear from the outset that Davis shared Stock's commitment to enhancing student learning and willingness to engage in an ongoing critique of institutional structures and professional parameters in order to do so. They were, in short, willing to challenge the status quo and take risks. (Also evident was their shared passion for film; years later they still recall their lively exchange about the Soviet-Cuba coproduction *Yo soy Cuba/I Am Cuba*.) Flash forward: they drafted a grant proposal, garnered funding, and listed their New Media Workshop among the college's course offerings the following year.

NEW MEDIA WORKSHOP: DESIGN AND IMPLEMENTATION

In order to design this workshop, Davis and Stock met regularly for an entire semester. While familiarizing themselves with the texts and textures of their respective fields, they struggled with some entrenched perceptions and practices—"modes of being" and "ways of doing"—in the institution as well as in their respective specializations. The professor comes to this from a culture that values autonomy and influences institutional governance and curriculum development; and the librarian from a culture all about support and service, a culture with increasing anxieties over relevance. In grappling with learning and teaching, their conversations became particularly animated, for they realized that despite their diverse institutional identities, they shared an increasing restlessness and a growing frustration with a series of binaries that seemed all too prevalent:

- teaching/learning
- theory/practice
- librarian/professor
- library/classroom
- thinking/doing
- producing/consuming
- expert/amateur
- local/global
- university/world

Such dualities were at odds with their interdisciplinary frameworks, professional practices, and world views; these oppositions seemed unproductive (counterproductive, in fact) to the learning experiences they sought to create, and to their vision of engendering creativity, fostering collaboration, and forging connections. Having discovered their shared commitment to moving from an "either-or" to a "both-and" mind-set, they set out purposefully to explore the in-between spaces.

Their common aim: to collapse a series of distinctions, including those between *teaching* and *learning*, *librarian* and *professor*, *research* and *crea-*

tive practice, and *library* and *classroom.* In order to do so, they examined the convergence—and collision—of paradigms emanating from theories of critical pedagogy, critical information literacy, and postcolonial studies. They returned to Paulo Freire and found renewed inspiration in his view of pedagogy as political, and in his insistence on the need for learners to develop a critical consciousness.

Another source of inspiration emanated from the field of cultural studies, in general, and the work of postcolonial critics in particular. Stock and Davis were informed by the productive coming together of multiple languages and cultural forms, the transnational and transmodal features of creativity and cultural expression, and the intersection of disciplinary paradigms with interdisciplinary modes. Whether termed a "borderland" (Anzaldua, 1987), "contact zone" (Pratt, 1991), or "third space" (Bhabha, 2004), these sites permit individuals, institutions, and communities to connect in new ways. Such "in-between" spaces and mind-sets foster this generative process. Building on these concepts, then, and remaining intent on resisting dualities, Davis and Stock began to articulate objectives, create assignments, and determine preliminary criteria for evaluation and assessment. Engaged with these paradigms, and in dialogue with one another, they created the New Media Workshop.

The New Media Workshop, now an integral part of the curriculum for undergraduates at the College of William and Mary, requires students to take responsibility for making discoveries, developing their creativity, collaborating with their peers, and connecting with individuals in local and distant communities. They do this through some traditional modes—extensive reading, intensive discussion, thoughtful writing—and also by working together on projects they help design and assess, ones that cast them as "cultural agents" (Sommer, 2005) interacting with filmmakers, photographers, writers, and others. Course content and activities vary from one semester to the next, but there are some constants in the design and structure:

- The workshop enrolls sixteen students with complementary areas of knowledge and skills. Each participant brings experience in at least one of these areas: familiarity with Hispanic culture; fluency or advanced proficiency in Spanish; knowledge of world cinema and film analysis; background in filming, editing, graphic design, information architecture, or music composition. In this way, all workshop participants contribute knowledge and skills at the same time that all (instructors included) must rely on others for help in some areas. As a result, notions of "expert" and "amateur" are called into question.
- All workshop participants share in the design of the syllabus and contribute to the evaluation of the collective experience. During the first session, the instructors present a "prospectus," a preliminary program of possible

activities and a schedule with some tentative dates (the authors acknowl-edge the inspiration of their colleague, Gene Roche, for this idea). Work-ing in small groups, participants then brainstorm ideas and begin to articu-late interests and priorities. These ideas are developed further during a class discussion. Through this process the syllabus emerges. The metrics for assessing progress and evaluating products are also generated in this way. So, unlike traditional courses "owned" by the instructor, in this one students share responsibility for the creation and implementation. The instructors guide the process and are ultimately accountable to the institu-tion, but students participate in setting the agenda. The space separating "teacher" from "student" shrinks, and at times disappears.

- The workshop is held in the library, an ambient learning space that facili-tates access to media equipment, expertise, and collections; proffers multi-ple options for film screenings; and permits the creation of conditions necessary for media making and other creative practice. Situated at the center of campus, this locale is a crossroads of sorts. Of even greater importance is the symbolic significance. Students see the library as an active agent in their learning. Not associated with a particular program or discipline, the library is a neutral space where all students (regardless of major) can feel "at home." This space permits reconfiguration: the roles of "librarian" and "professor" are remixed and the boundaries between li-brary and classroom are blurred.

- The workshop presupposes a willingness to take creative risks. Even be-fore the initial session, students are aware of the "hands-on" nature of the course. All must be willing to explore and expand their creativity and that of their classmates. Whether writing a poem to read during a session or sharing some project created outside of class (a video, scrapbook, draw-ing, website), students are exposed to multiple modes of "making." By enhancing their own creativity, and reflecting on the process, the acts of "making" and "doing" come together with that of "thinking." No longer is creativity relegated to specific courses nor is it owned by particular depart-ments. Instead, it becomes open to all.

- In this workshop, research, discovery, and scholarship are redefined to include dissemination. The emphasis on creativity and collaboration ne-cessitates curating, performing, and communicating. Participants' collec-tive work done as part of the workshop is circulated outside the class-room—whether during an end-of-semester showcase open to the campus and community, throughout the semester in a series of conference or film festival presentations, through electronic or print publications, in a perfor-mance or exhibit, or more likely in some combination of these. Even as the workshops are under way, students and instructors identify ways to share products and works in progress (in past installments, students pre-sented at an undergraduate humanities conference at Longwood University in Farmville, Virginia; instructors contributed reflections in a session at the Middle Atlantic Council of Latin American Studies Conference in Baltimore; and a New Media Workshop documentary was included at the Havana Film Festival in New York). The preparation for these events— identifying opportunities, drafting an abstract, preparing a presentation— as well as the reflections on audience reception are then integrated into subsequent class discussions. This dissemination component serves to underscore the relevance of the work, establishes a connection between production and consumption, and generates enthusiasm. Invariably, workshop participants arrive to sessions eager to hear how the projects went and report on what people had to say about them. In communicating their ideas and sharing their creativity with an audience beyond the workshop, students hone their curatorial and communication skills, confront a range of scholarly issues, and gain important feedback. Research as a private undertaking confined to the classroom becomes instead a public mode for engaging others beyond the university.

• At least one artist visit is scheduled during each workshop installment. Guests have included photographers and filmmakers, producers and editors, writers and critics, and a special effects artist. The workshops have been enriched by the presence of Carlos Rodríguez, Aram Vidal, Oneida González, Esteban Insausti, Angélica Salvador, Alfredo Ureta, Susel Ochoa, Laimir Fano, Gilberto Martínez, Miguel Coyula, and others. Still others—including Samuel Riera, Alina Rodríguez, Juan Carlos Cremata Malberti, and Karel Ducasse—have participated via the Internet. Students take part in planning and organizing activities related to the visits. They film interviews with these artists, and then edit their material along with other footage (some filmed by the instructors during recent research trips to Cuba) in order to create original projects. These products—videos, websites, multimedia presentations, and exhibits—are curated and then introduced, often along with the guest, to a broader audience. Through these artists' visits, students connect with individuals from previously unfamiliar cultural contexts. They have the opportunity to engage face-to-face with creators. At the same time, the invited guests benefit from participating in conversations about their work, and others on campus and in the community are privy to a cross-cultural dialogue. Activities like these serve to reposition the local classroom within an expanded global framework, one attuned to practices and perspectives emanating from outside the United States.

The constants outlined above could be overlaid onto any cultural context. In other words, artists from any country, or indeed from within diverse communities in the US, could be invited to participate. In the installments thus far, however, Davis and Stock focused on hosting Cuban artists. One reason, as already explained, is that Stock's recent research examines Cuban film and media, so she has a long list of contacts. Another is that the Cuban context is relatively unfamiliar to US students. Generally, their experience with Hispanic cultures centers on Spain and Mexico, the sites most frequently offered for study abroad. The inclusion of artists from Cuba provides students with a unique opportunity to engage with this island's people and culture. The converse is also true: Cubans have very few opportunities to experience the United States despite the proximity of the two nations and their shared history and traditions. So the sustained engagement with *Cuban* artists, while not essential for an initiative like this one, has enriched the experience for all involved.

NEW MEDIA WORKSHOP: OUTCOMES, NEXT STEPS, BEST PRACTICES

These high-tech (and high-touch) student-faculty research endeavors have yielded concrete outcomes: workshop participants have subtitled Cuban documentaries and distributed them on DVD in the US; created original documentaries, one of which was screened at the Havana Film Festival in New York and another of which was shown at the Festival de Cine Pobre (Festival of Low-Budget Cinema) in Gibara, Cuba; presented their findings at regional and international conferences; curated exhibits of Cuban photographs and films; and begun work creating an archive called *Fabrica/Factory: Cuban Film and New Media Project*. These student-faculty research endeavors have also resulted in publications, community events, web resources, and various digital media. A filmed overview of the initiative, *Subtitling Cuban Culture*, can be accessed at http://www.wm.edu/news/stories/2009/cuban-film-stock-davis-1112.php. Footage filmed and edited by the instructors, titled "On Location in Cuba: Montage," can be accessed at https://www.youtube.com/watch?v=5qO0tMteRhE. Other projects include a documentary about the Cuban filmmaker Miguel Coyula, a *video-carta* (video letter) capturing student responses to a documentary by Esteban Insausti; English-language subtitles for several animated shorts by Ernesto Piña, numerous documentaries by Sara Gómez and Nicolás Guillén Landrián, and the documentary *Zona de silencio* (*Zone of Silence*) by Karel Ducasse; a website for the creator and curator of "outsider art," Samuel Riera; and an exhibit installed in the library gallery devoted to the photographs of Gustavo Pérez; as well as many others. In addition, a filmed interview with each of the visitors contributes to an ever-expanding archive of Cuban culture.

The number of high-quality projects suggests that meaningful learning is taking place. But success can also be measured in the students' approach to their own learning, noting that they tend to become more independent. One example illustrates this: During a New Media Workshop session halfway through the semester, students were grouped at stations around the classroom. The discussion of one team at work editing a filmed interview developed into a heated debate; opinions differed as to whether a particular filmed sequence was best included or left out. Without seeking any instructor mediation or intervention, students made their arguments, negotiated their positions, and eventually came to an agreement about how to proceed with the editing. By this time, the students were not dependent on the instructors to provide "right" answers or trying to figure out "what the professors wanted"; instead, they were empowered to rely on their own developing knowledge, and on one another, in determining how to best proceed.

An investigation of the impact of evolving technologies brings together creators and consumers in new ways. Located at the center of that process, students consistently "get it." When reflecting on the impact of these learning experiences, they remark on the value of the research experience and its relevance, all the while underscoring their new knowledge about Cuban culture. Frequently, students note that they "forget" about the grade; their motivation emanates from enthusiasm for the projects, a desire to "come through" for their classmates, and a belief in the significance of their work. They also credit this experience as instrumental in propelling them into careers in television, journalism, media production, education, and a variety of other fields.

There have been other outcomes, as welcome as they are unexpected. One is that the artists and filmmakers insist that these efforts have been transformative for them; oftentimes the investment in their work enables them to connect with audiences at international venues and across the globe through cyberspace. They express gratitude in emails, on Facebook, and even in the credits of their films. And many stop over on their way to and from festivals and exhibitions of their work elsewhere in the US, thereby positioning the institution as a crossroads of sorts for Cuban artists and filmmakers. Another outcome is that the library has allocated funds to support a media artist in residence, making it possible to host a guest for several weeks rather than just a few days. In doing so, the dean of university libraries and others have affirmed the efficacy of this learning model, demonstrated the library's commitment to faculty-librarian partnerships, and underscored the institutional commitment to fostering creativity and connections. Yet another outcome is that colleagues have begun developing initiatives that incorporate features of these workshops: subtitling films into English, assigning projects that integrate new media technologies, and emphasizing the coordinates of creativity, collaboration, and connectedness.

The authors acknowledge that this collaborative relationship has changed them. Davis has ventured further into the faculty arena, while Stock has moved further into the library world. And as a result, both have developed a more comprehensive perspective of the institution, in particular, and of higher education in general. In contributing in new ways, this partnership has enabled them to add value to their work at the college. Is it finished? Not yet, and likely not anytime in the near future. Some seven years after the initial conversation that sparked this collaborative experience, the authors remain energized by the possibilities for enhancing student learning, exploring new modes of creativity and intellectual development, and contributing to the institution and their professions in meaningful ways. Davis has just had published several photographs and an essay in a volume edited by Stock, and Stock has teamed up to coauthor this chapter. Davis is committed to further improving his Spanish language skills, and Stock continues to refine her abilities to film, record sound, and edit as well as to find information and keep it found. Even as this chapter was taking shape, the authors were traveling to Miami together to help a Cuban filmmaker, one of the artists hosted in a workshop, with the filming of interviews for her next documentary. The authors envision tackling many more projects in tandem: more installments of the New Media Workshop; the design of a theory-practice course probing creativity for the college's new curriculum; a research trip to Cuba to share the results of the workshop and to do more filming; the creation of a digital archive to better organize and improve public access to materials gathered and created with students; a documentary about the work of emerging Cuban filmmakers; and, of course, the preparation of grant proposals to support these and other initiatives. In addition, they are eager to involve more colleagues. As the authors plan and prepare, they take time out to share their experiences with engaged colleagues, and with others seeking to discern and develop best practices. To sum up: Did learning take place in ways considered effective and successful? Undoubtedly. Will the authors continue to team-teach workshop-style courses? Absolutely. Was this process easy? No, definitely not. For those considering an undertaking like this, these factors are important to consider:

- Your status at your institution and the context in which you work. Does your college or university embrace border-crossing and permit disruptive practices? If not, think about whether it would be wise to move forward, especially if you are untenured and/or newly hired. If you decide to proceed, do so with caution and make sure to have "buy-in" from your supervisor. It will certainly help if your colleagues are also affirming of your pedagogical innovation, but be prepared for some resistance, perhaps voiced in a reference to your "boutique" course. As a librarian, particularly in an institution that privileges and frames its contribution to learning and (uncritically) seeks to "achieve the educational missions of their institutions by teaching the core competencies of information literacy" (ACRL guidelines for instructional programs in libraries, 2003), be prepared to narrate the significance of these alternative interventions.

- The time available to contribute to this endeavor. If your hours are limited—whether from serving on multiple committees, teaching an overload, working on multiple research projects, mentoring a range of independent studies and theses, engaging in community service, or some other activity—consider waiting for a more opportune moment. As paradoxical as it may seem, to team up in creating learning opportunities like the one examined herein requires many more hours than going it alone.
- The availability of institutional resources. Do you have access to necessary space, equipment, and expertise? Are funds available for corollary activities such as group travel to a regional conference? If any of these answers are "no," think about whether you're prepared to invest your own resources and/or willing to add a grant proposal to your "to do" list (one semester, when the authors were anticipating offering the workshop, the library classroom became unavailable to them. Deeming the "right" space to be essential to this offering, they decided to defer and wait for that time when they could again make use of a particular library classroom).
- Perhaps most importantly, do you have an effective partner: someone willing to venture out of safe zones and take risks; someone who will share knowledge and also voice vulnerability; someone who speaks thoughtfully and listens respectfully, defending some positions while ceding others; someone whose commitment to the undertaking parallels your own; someone you find engaging and generative, affirming and energizing? While every relationship has its imperfections, great care should be taken in choosing a would-be partner for an endeavor of this nature. The selection of the person with whom you work will be, without a doubt, the most decisive factor in making or breaking the collaboration.

What follows is a short dialogue on the partnership between the two authors.

A LIBRARIAN-PROFESSOR DIALOGUE

Davis: For academic librarians, building deep relationships with teaching faculty, while encouraged *generally*, may not be something encouraged *systematically* at most institutions. The professional literature on the subject suggests that it is either impossible *and/or* inevitable. While an institution speaks a language of faculty engagement, it often lacks a coherent strategy to purposefully enact, consciously evaluate, and systematically overcome the barriers to activate that engagement. Librarians and teaching faculty are certainly motivated by their institutional goals, but they also come from different worlds. Authentic collaboration, in the end, is radical, not because it can provide examples for the newsletter or annual report; rather it is radical because it requires an uncomfortable critique of purpose. Even when librarians generally assent to the aims of "information literacy," they confront fundamental blind spots when trying to blend critical theory and creative practice in a sustained learning experiment with faculty.

Stock: Many professors have been conditioned to see librarians as "helpers." They can assist in filling in some blanks, but aren't often sought out as partners in crafting the larger narrative, be it for a course or a presentation or an article. Even when professors invite librarians to visit classes and meet with students, the results can be lackluster, and in fact, these "one-off" sessions may perpetuate this perception of librarians as supporters rather than collaborators. The presentations on searching (rather than finding) leave students (and professors) uninspired. While it might be easy to attribute this to inflated professorial egos or entrenched faculty-staff hierarchies, it likely has more to do with (contested) information literacy standards. Before meeting Davis and embarking on this shared journey, Stock had not envisioned working with a librarian in an ongoing and mutually beneficial way, in a way that would enhance the learning of her students as well as her own.

Davis: As a library liaison to Film and Media Studies, Davis had already established significant relationships with faculty members in the program. He attended faculty meetings to report news related to the library, and used his expertise in media production and graphic design to assist with program outreach, alumni relations, and curricular questions related to creative media practice. He had dutifully created a film and media research guide on which, to varying extents, program faculty relied for their teaching and scholarship. He had also contributed (reluctantly) the usual "one-off" library instructional session for undergraduates and performed various collection development duties. Even so, he began to see this type of liaison work as increasingly incomplete as a strategy for deep and sustained faculty engagement. He concluded that just as the library's instructional efforts might need to be rebooted, the liaison model of librarianship was equally in need of some rebooting. Davis saw that in order for this collaboration to be "authentic," he needed to completely reimagine and restate the liaison role. As Allan Parsons (2010) suggests, "these explicit functional roles mask a further implicit interpersonal, communicational or phatic role, harnessing a capability that, in the near future, may be of greater importance, relationship building" (para. 3). In many ways, his ideas became informed from adopting and advancing what Janice Jaguszewski and Karen Williams (2013) describe as a "hybrid model" combining "elements of the role of the liaisons and functional specialist" (p. 7). It became clear that the traditional role of the library liaison must be reexamined in the context of changing priorities in the teaching and learning community.

Stock: During her first decade as a faculty member, Stock did much of her work alone. There was the occasional exchanging of drafts of syllabi or articles or book chapters, and the sharing of a reference here and a review there, but for the most part she carried out her intellectual activity independently. And so did her colleagues as well as most academics in the profession. As cross-disciplinary inquiry increased, she experimented with "team teaching." In a multisection Introduction to Hispanic Cultural Studies, for example, she and her colleagues found that by combining their knowledge they could introduce a broader range of material. Their exploration of representation and identity construction in the Hispanic world has, in various iterations, included Latino *barrio* narratives, Basque film and poetry, Central American testimonial literature, Spanish Civil War representation, Cuba's revolutionary visual culture, and so on. The involvement of more faculty permitted more "coverage" and thereby expanded the course "content." And yet, despite the insertion of new topics and texts, this team teaching experience was (and continues to be) unsatisfactory for Stock. Why? Because it does not require or even invite a rethinking of roles and relationships—with one another, with students, with the institution, with the academy, or with Hispanic culture. Summing up, it changes the "what" but never elicits engagement with the "how" or the "so what." In the end, the actual teaching of the course remains a solitary endeavor for the most part; once the syllabus is designed and the work divided up, each professor returns to his or her office. And they remain unchanged. Stock was eager to team up with an intellectual partner in a way that was more generative and sustainable, in a way that would *move* her—intellectually, pedagogically, and personally.

Davis: Early on in this collaboration, Davis felt compelled to present concepts of information literacy (IL) as his unique "intellectual" contribution to the collaboration. He shared with Stock the ACRL standards and, after some impassioned conversation, it was clear that they were, ultimately, incomplete. While the standards obviously seek to advance a super-structured instructional program in libraries, they remain separated from "disciplinary knowledge" and, as Stanley Wilder (2005) observed, this separation "encourages librarians to teach ways to deal with the complexity of information retrieval, rather than to try to reduce that complexity" (para. 6). Since IL did not prove useful in theoretically framing the larger transdisciplinary aims of collaboration, Davis quickly abandoned it for a conversation about broadening notions of literacy, learning, and the limits of IL. It wasn't until he presented to Stock a *critique*, and shared his concerns that academic libraries had become beleaguered in their attempts to progressively impact larger institutional missions, that the collaborators' imaginations were activated. And, as the discussions of student learning objectives evolved, he discovered that his own understanding of information literacy represented a completely undertheorized approach to learning; as a result, his commitment to it became strained. At the time of this writing, the Information Literacy Competency Standards for Higher Education are being recast as a "framework" and, while they are not without controversy, he is encouraged by the claim that the revisions emerge "out of a belief that information literacy as an educational reform movement will realize its potential only through a richer, more complex set of core ideas" (Gibson and Jacobson, 2014). This is big-picture language—a language of impact.

Stock: Among the learning experiences students deem most productive, and most pleasurable, are those that yield new connections. Professors, too, find these to be most meaningful. So it is not surprising that these are the kinds of experiences they seek to create and develop. As a champion of what the American Council of Colleges and Universities deems "high impact" educational practices (https://www.aacu.org/leap/hips), Stock has worked to design and facilitate study abroad opportunities, internships, and student-faculty research initiatives, among others. These endeavors share certain features: all encourage students to link ideas being explored in class with their lived experiences beyond the campus; all introduce students to individuals with expertise and world views very different from their own; and all require that students occupy and explore a new space—whether that of another country, a different community, or a new theoretical landscape. Invariably, students note their initial discomfort with being on unfamiliar terrain; they also express, in diverse ways and at different junctures, the empowering nature of the process. Although she has created these opportunities for students in other sites, an ongoing challenge is effectively integrating these features into *on-campus* course offerings. Exploring ways to meet this challenge motivates Stock and shapes much of her pedagogical practice.

Davis: These conversations allowed Davis to evaluate faculty perceptions about the work of librarians. It was clear that Stock's perception of the library, one grounded in her experiences over time, was as a place of friendly and uncontroversial "transactions." Davis discovered a perception of library work as a preoccupation with undertheorized problems associated with the cultivation of skills. Lars Christiansen et al. (2004) put it another way: "The perception among faculty is that librarians' work is service oriented" and "faculty see their own work as focusing on the production and dissemination of knowledge" (p. 119), and these issues are "deep and important" and enact "superordinate-subordinate relations that are legitimized by assumptions of superiority and inferiority" (p. 120). It is very important that librarians collectively explore these perceptions, catalog them, and seek ways of deconstructing and reframing them.

What risks are taken when librarians seek to alter these perceptions? For one, librarians must ask a wide range of uncomfortably existential questions. Do librarians truly *believe* that librarian-faculty collaboration yields a more fruitful activation of institutional goals? Do they work within organizational structures that value collaboration at all? Do librarians really make a difference? Do institutions have the right leadership in place to move authentic collaboration from the margins to the center? No one is going to dismiss altogether an academic library; however, the next strategy in this century is not to unite around prescriptive standards of "literacy," but rather to create mechanisms to "blow up" the institutional roles of the "librarian" and the "professor" so that one cannot exist without the other. This is what the authors have tried to do in this collaboration. They still do.

Davis and Stock: Finally, this conversation must end with some existentially motivated questions. The 21st-century academic library must rally allies in the institution so as to become an increasingly disruptive voice in the academy's conversation and exploration of the contours of teaching and learning; this is possible if, and only if, it can present itself as an authentic and ideologically motivated partner in this conversation. A 21st-century model of collaboration among librarians and faculty can only exist in an academic library that seeks to do more than perpetuate what already exists. It must value and actively cultivate a culture of experimentation and risk-taking in research, teaching, and learning; resist efforts to minimize the uncertainties, miscellaneousness, and unfinishedness inherent in these processes; and refuse to evoke monolithic standards of learning and contrived programs of assessment. This collaboration has revealed new roles for librarians working in the academy. The good news is that opening up these questions of purpose with faculty and with students promotes the library as an active site of serious and relevant inquiry. It is not enough for the academic library of the 21st century to be prepared to answer questions; it must also be prepared to ask them, and do so publicly, thereby engaging in a broader, and sometimes contentious, dialogue.

CONCLUSION

As this partnership continues and subsequent research agendas evolve, many unknowns persist: What new questions can librarians and faculty ask *together* to overcome traditional institutional/professional boundaries? Can faculty and librarians, *together*, dream up domains of new research, new scholarship, new roles? Where are the formal and informal platforms of dissemination that can help them share questions of critical practice? How can this scholarship support institutions as they invent a language of both *local* and *global* purpose, a language that values, in fact depends on, the fruits of partnerships that are generative, creative, and intellectually productive relationships between librarians and faculty? The authors contend that empowering learners in the 21st century requires nothing less.

It is important to note that these inventive relationships tend to exist not at the center but rather in the periphery. This is not surprising, for they certainly pose less risk there. As Lawrence Dowler (1997) observes, "Our creativity is found not so much within our institutions but on their borders"; he goes on to acknowledge "the creative tension" that exists between librarians as the "custodian[s] of our nation's intellectual heritage and the library as a place for studying it," on the one hand, and "the emerging role of the librarian as teacher and the library as a classroom" (p. 217) on the other. The authors share his sense that this "tension" is productive, that it can serve as a "gateway" for moving libraries away from "the comfort of familiar forms toward different organizational structures and new modes of learning" (Dowler, 1997, p. 217). And these relationships, while situated at the margins, must ultimately become revalued at the center. David Lewis (2007) echoes Dowler, warning that to effect significant change, "incremental adjustments at the margins will not suffice." The authors agree that what is needed is nothing short of "alterations in fundamental practice" (p. 423). Perhaps it is time, again, to question and reimagine the ways in which academic institutions craft invitations to librarians and faculty to *experience* the library. For most academic libraries there is a significant historical and philosophical (and financial) investment in the preservation of instructional programs (and their evolved standards) as the privileged site of library-faculty engagement. There are even laudable attempts to explore more sustained modes of engagement in the metaphor of "embedded" librarians (Kvenild and Calkins, 2011). But beyond that, in academic libraries there is the lingering tradition of maintaining difference, of nurturing an ideology of "otherness" that characterizes faculty as the "problem" (McCarthy, 1985). One important question is what are the institutional risks involved when librarians invite faculty to "deconstruct" the roles, relevance, place, and purpose of librarians within the academy?

Through this ongoing endeavor, the librarian has become more of a professor, and the professor more of a librarian. More importantly, they have begun to activate a critique of the philosophical and institutional barriers to collaborative experiences that can enact *real* transformation. The academic library is poised to serve as a catalyst for this transformation, not through contrived standards, nor through monolithic instructional programs, but rather from assuming a critical position from which it is poised and prepared to ask questions, questions about whether these programs reinscribe institutional divisions, perpetuate binary oppositions, and construct otherness.

The authors' experiments in collaboration may, on the surface, seem to be the result of a uniquely institutional set of conditions. But they advocate institution-wide discussions, thoughtful and ongoing, to determine in what ways and to what ends faculty and librarians are working together. And the authors believe, as Wade Kotter (1999) articulates, that one strategy (and a potentially painful one) is figuring out how "to evaluate the quality of librarian-faculty relationships" (p. 295). To take this step is to enter a domain of critique, one that is resisted but necessary. Another key issue has to do with where and how collaboration can occur. Do these types of collaborative experiences happen only at the margins? If so, why is that? And while faculty generally "like" libraries, they do not necessarily see the library or the librarian as a partner in realizing institutional goals. Why is that? To be unwilling to ask these questions is to continue to operate uncritically and, most likely, on the margins. Unable to take on the "big questions," librarians and faculty will not be poised to participate in the transformation of their institutions. A reluctance to engage these questions often reveals an institution that operates uncritically, a culture that undervalues risk, a context that discourages innovation, and, most unfortunate of all, an institution that is itself incapable of *learning.* While this discussion may raise more questions than answers, it cannot emphasize enough that a deep and abiding relationship between librarians and faculty is a necessary condition for the transformation of academic institutions. For the authors, this relationship will invariably produce new conversations in the scholarly literature of both faculty and librarians. This book chapter signals their commitment to continuing to risk this conversation.

The authors dedicate this chapter to the memory of Joe Kennedy.

REFERENCES

Anzaldua, G. (1987). *Borderlands/La Frontera: The New Mestiza.* Aunt Lute Books.
Barr, R., and J. Tagg. (1995). "From Teaching to Learning—A New Paradigm for Undergraduate Education." *Change: The Magazine of Higher Learning* 27(6): 12–26.

Bausman, M., S. L. Ward, and J. Pell. (2014). "Beyond Satisfaction: Understanding and Promoting the Instructor-Librarian Relationship." *New Review of Academic Librarianship* 20(2): 117–136.

Bhabha, H. (2004). *The Location of Culture.* Abingdon: Routledge.

Brown, J. D., and T. S. Duke. (2005). "Librarian and Faculty Collaborative Instruction: A Phenomenological Self-Study." *Research Strategies* 20(3): 171–190. http://dx.doi.org.proxy.wm.edu/10.1016/j.resstr.2006.05.001.

Christiansen, L., M. Stombler, and L. Thaxton. (2004). "A Report on Librarian-Faculty Relations from a Sociological Perspective." *The Journal of Academic Librarianship* 30(2): 116–121. http://dx.doi.org.proxy.wm.edu/10.1016/j.acalib.2004.01.003.

Dowler, L. (1997). *Gateways to Knowledge: The Role of Academic Libraries in Teaching, Learning, and Research.* Cambridge, MA: MIT Press.

Freire, P. (1970). *Pedagogy of the Oppressed.* New York: Continuum.

Freire, P. (2004). *Pedagogy of Indignation.* Boulder, CO: Paradigm.

Gibson, G., and T. Jacobson. (2014). "Framework for Information Literacy for Higher Education." Draft 3. Association of College and Research Libraries. http://acrl.ala.org/ilstandards/wp-content/uploads/2014/11/Framework-for-IL-for-HE-draft-3.pdf.

Jaguszewski, J., and K. Williams. "New Roles for New Times: Transforming Liaison Roles in Research Libraries." Association of College and Research Libraries. http://www.arl.org/component/content/article/6/2893.

Keil, D. (2014). "Research Data Needs from Academic Libraries: The Perspective of a Faculty Researcher." *Journal of Library Administration* 54(3): 233–240. doi:10.1080/01930826.2014.915168.

Kenedy, R., and V. Monty. (2011). "Faculty-Librarian Collaboration and the Development of Critical Skills through Dynamic Purposeful Learning." *Libri: International Journal of Libraries and Information Services* 61(2): 116–124. doi:10.1515/libr.2011.010.

Kotter, W. R. (1999). "Bridging the Great Divide: Improving Relations between Librarians and Classroom Faculty." *The Journal of Academic Librarianship* 25(4): 294–303. http://dx.doi.org.proxy.wm.edu/10.1016/S0099-1333(99)80030-5.

Kvenild, C., and K. Calkins. (2011). *Embedded Librarians: Moving beyond One-Shot Instruction.* Chicago: Association of College and Research Libraries.

Lewis, D. W. (2007). "A Strategy for Academic Libraries in the First Quarter of the 21st Century." *College and Research Libraries* 68(5): 418–434. doi:10.5860/crl.68.5.418.

Mackey, T., and T. Jacobson. (2014). *Metaliteracy: Reinventing Information Literacy to Empower Learners.* ALA Neal-Schuman.

McCarthy, C. (1985). "The Faculty Problem." *Journal of Academic Librarianship* 11(3): 142.

Meulemans, Y., and A. Carr. (2013). "Not at Your Service: Building Genuine Faculty-Librarian Partnerships." *Reference Services Review* 41(1): 80–90. doi:10.1108/00907321311300893.

Mounce, M. (2010). "Working Together: Academic Librarians and Faculty Collaborating to Improve Students' Information Literacy Skills: A Literature Review, 2000–2009." *Reference Librarian* 51(4): 300–320. doi:10.1080/02763877.2010.501420. http://learning.writing101.net/wp-content/readings/pratt_arts_of_the_contact_zone.pdf.

Parsons, A. (2010). "Academic Liaison Librarianship: Curatorial Pedagogy or Pedagogical Curation?" *Ariadne* 65. http://www.ariadne.ac.uk/issue65/parsons/.

Pratt, M. (1991). "Arts of the Contact Zone." *Profession* 91: 33–40. Online.

Raspa, R., and D. Ward. (2000). *The Collaborative Imperative: Librarians and Faculty Working Together in the Information Universe.* Chicago: Association of College and Research Libraries.

Sommer, D. (2005). *Cultural Agency in the Americas.* Durham, NC: Duke University Press.

Stock, Ann Marie. (2009). *On Location in Cuba: Street Filmmaking during Times of Transition.* Chapel Hill: University of North Carolina Press.

Stock, Ann Marie. (2014). *World Film Locations: Havana.* Bristol, UK: Intellect.

Whitworth, A. (2014). *Radical Information Literacy: Reclaiming the Political Heart of the IL Movement.* Amsterdam: Chandos Publishing.

Wilder, S. (2005). "Information Literacy Makes All the Wrong Assumptions." *Chronicle of Higher Education* 51(18): B13. http://www.studystream.org/upload/data/6/Information%20Literacy%20Makes%20All%20the%20Wrong%20Assumptions.pdf.

Chapter Seven

Looking Both Ways

Seeing the Changing Roles of Librarians

John Weed, Eric Willman, Dana Whitmire, Katherine A. Prentice, and Kelley Minars

Academic health science libraries, like all libraries, are experiencing extensive changes. Librarians are part of these changes and at the University of Texas Health Science Center at San Antonio (UTHSCSA), librarians are developing partnerships and exploring new roles. In the context of change, many opportunities for growth and partnership have emerged. Since UTHSCSA was founded in 1959 as a school of medicine it has grown into five schools, including the School of Nursing, School of Dentistry, School of Health Professions, and Graduate School of Biomedical Sciences.

The Briscoe Library, the central library for the UTHSCSA, has always been part of the research and education tradition, but in recent years roles for the library as a physical place and for librarians have changed. The current library space opened in 1983 (University of Texas Health Science Center San Antonio, 2014), primarily as a print collection with expert librarians available to assist students and faculty with the research process. It goes without saying that much has changed in libraries since 1983, and the Briscoe Library has grown and changed during that time. The Briscoe Library building encompasses over seventy thousand square feet of usable space divided among four floors. At opening, the lowest floor was a teaching learning center, with a closed stack audiovisual collection, study rooms, and a few computers for a neurosciences project. Over time the space was converted into a computer lab and study space. Because of evolving campus and library needs, the most recent changes to this floor resulted in converting the former computer lab and study space to university classrooms with 24/7 access for student study.

Following this extensive renovation, the library retained a twenty-five-seat computer classroom, which is the location for hands-on computer-based classes for a dozen departments outside of the library as well as for library-sponsored classes. The third (also the main entrance) floor hosts the main service point for the library. Originally, it held the card catalog and later the catalog computers, the current journal collection, a large reference collection, and the print index collection. As the need for print indexes and reference materials declined, the third floor was adapted to become an information commons with study space, computers, a single service point circulation desk, a small reference collection, and a closed stack reserve collection. From the beginning, the fourth and fifth floors were designed to hold the library's extensive print collections. The fourth floor housed journals and a large photocopy room; the fifth floor was home to the library's book collection including the rare books and archives. Because of the need for additional student study space that could accommodate group and individual study as well as the need for a consolidated location for the university's Office of Undergraduate Medical Education, the book and journal collections were reduced in size and consolidated onto the fourth floor. Throughout these physical changes, the library space became home to the Center for Medical Humanities and Ethics, Office of Undergraduate Medical Education, and Pharmacotherapy Information Service.

Along with physical changes to the Briscoe Library building, the library staff has also changed over the years. The trend has been toward a smaller complement of staff with an emphasis on retaining professional staff, as the need for maintenance of a print collection has decreased. Figure 7.1 illustrates the change in the size of the staff from 1999 to 2014. With fewer librarians and staff overall, the Briscoe Library has moved with the changing nature of libraries from a physically centered library to a service-focused and electronically focused collection.

Looking at the past and to the future, the work outside of library walls has a greater role than ever before, with librarians engaging in campus partnerships and reporting outside traditional lines.

CURRICULAR INTEGRATION

Academic librarians are often found in classrooms across university campuses. The librarians of the Briscoe Library have worked diligently to integrate their expertise into curricular courses and to offer classes that students and faculty want and need. One of the library's longest-running partnerships was with the School of Medicine's third-year pediatrics clerkship. During each rotation, students attended a library instruction session and then completed a literature search assignment that was reviewed by a librarian, who

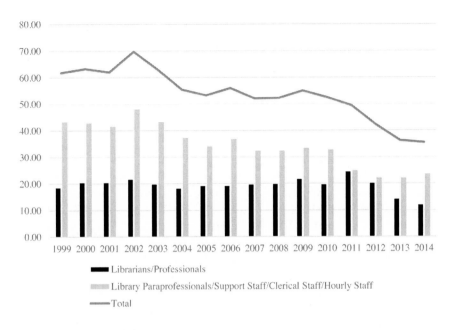

Librarians/Professionals

Library Paraprofessionals/Support Staff/Clerical Staff/Hourly Staff

Total

Figure 7.1. Library Personnel

provided feedback to the student. While this was a time-intensive activity, it was positive for the students and faculty as well as librarians. Over the years, this activity touched every medical student with a personal interaction, and some would comment years later during residency on the skills learned. This learning activity ended due to curricular revisions, but there are ongoing discussions on how to ensure every medical student has the skills necessary to find important information when needed in the clinical setting.

As the medical curriculum shifted, librarians worked with faculty in the School of Medicine over several years to try different methods of instruction. The first attempt was a large, whole-class (220 students) instructional session in a large lecture hall with interactive slides and clicker integration. Instruction was divided into two class sessions covering evidence-based medicine and basic search skills, and included hands-on exercises and discussion with the students. The challenges posed by the large space and the stadium-style seating led to changes in the content the following year, with more emphasis on whole-class interactions and less on small group discussion. This partnership is still changing with the constant curricular and faculty changes in the School of Medicine; however, the team of librarians continues to advocate for some form of the evidence-based medicine instruction to continue within the School of Medicine.

Librarian integration into the School of Health Professions (formerly the School of Allied Health) is quite different from that offered to the School of Medicine. Librarians have played important roles in physical therapy (PT), occupational therapy (OT), and respiratory therapy (RT). These programs' faculty have invited librarians to lecture and, in the case of RT, even assist with the grading of student research presentations. In the School of Health Professions, librarians have worked closely to develop curricular support so that as librarians return to classes, instruction can be planned progressively to build on prior sessions.

Instructional partnerships in the School of Nursing are very similar to those in the School of Health Professions. Nursing faculty have valued the time and attention librarians provide to their students. In addition to the traditional two-year bachelor of science in nursing, the School of Nursing offers an accelerated bachelor of science in nursing for students already holding a bachelor of science in another field. Master's, post-master's, and doctoral-level studies are also available to students. Librarians are embedded in the curriculum to provide instruction in evidence-based practice, finding and using literature, creating and presenting posters, locating resources for toxicology, and more. One semester, a team of librarians partnered with a nursing faculty to pilot a quality improvement project that examined how students report their utilization of library and other information resources. Interestingly, new classes were requested through serendipity when nursing faculty encountered librarians in so-called unusual places. For example, the toxicology resources class was developed after the campus 2014 Earth Day event. Librarians hosted a table to share resources on identifying toxic materials in and around the home, and a nursing faculty member came by to say hello and was thrilled to know the materials were available and librarians were prepared to share them with students.

The instruction provided by librarians for new students in the School of Dentistry has been organized somewhat differently from instruction in other schools. Traditional library orientation comprises a brief overview of library services in a large lecture hall with a variety of students. Dental students participate in this general orientation but also visit the library for an introductory session on finding articles in PubMed. It may seem "early" in their semester to offer such a class, but a curricular shift led to the development of this orientation session in the current format. Since there is an assignment that every student must complete, it is very clear what needs to be taught in the library session. Rather than teaching a traditional class on how to use PubMed, the National Library of Medicine's biomedical literature search system, librarians developed a set of exercises that require using different parts of the library home page and also PubMed to find answers to specific questions. This interactive and very hands-on orientation to library resources and services allows students to immediately use library materials during the session and gives them the opportunity to ask questions right away. The orientation also introduces students to the librarians and the idea of getting help from them later when the research questions become more in-depth. This type of instructional session has been popular with students and faculty because it is specific and focused on the students' task at hand.

OUTSIDE THE CLASSROOM

In addition to the standard curricular teaching, librarians have consistently worked to provide educational opportunities to the university community at large. One of the most popular set of classes is the Emerging Technologies Brown Bag (ETBB) series. The idea to offer these classes came about through discussions about information gaps on campus. Librarians realized there were negative associations and a general lack of understanding about social media, and decided to offer a series of classes to develop awareness and understanding of trending technology. One of the first classes offered was "Saving Face on Facebook," and it focused on privacy settings and staying safe. The class was popular, and over the next year that class was requested again and again by faculty and staff. Other classes included "Why Twitter"; "Knowledge Pursuit: Finding Online Learning"; a Halloween special, "When Zombies Attack: Protecting Your Information Online"; and an annual holiday special called "Tech the Halls." Attendance ranged from a handful of participants to a packed room—which for voluntary, lunchtime (no food provided) instruction was gratifying. These classes really pushed librarians into the limelight and helped administrators and other faculty value the knowledge and services provided by the library. For the librarian team, these classes were the chance to explore topics outside normal library activity and attract attention to the instruction available by librarians. Designed to be completed in fifty minutes or less, each ETBB class started with a short presentation and a handout with detailed instructions or sources of instruction, and whenever possible the sessions featured hands-on technology and equipment. The intent was not to provide every bit of information about a topic; instead, it was to provide an overview and then a venue for question-and-answer. As the ETBB sessions grew and developed, librarians presented all or part of the sessions at faculty meetings, other staff events, and department trainings. The road show of technology topics was fun for the librarian team to produce and conduct. Some topics were more challenging than others, but the point was to create relevant and interesting presentations. As the technology topics became less emerging and more mainstream, the classes were needed less, so the librarians chose to schedule them only by request rather than offer them on a regular basis.

Librarians have been involved in a variety of campus partnerships over the years and worked to embed themselves in multiple partnerships/consultation opportunities. Currently, the technology librarians work with the Academic Technology Services Council, Blackboard Partners, and the Information Security Council. Each of these partners provides the library with the expertise of staff embedded in jobs throughout the campus. Partnering with the various campus initiatives has allowed the library to stay in stride with other departments on campus and provide expertise/integration of library resources into new projects. Working with Blackboard Partners has allowed librarians to anticipate the upgrade/update cycle of Blackboard and become liaisons to students if any difficulty arises after traditional support hours. Working with the Information Security Council has allowed librarians to be the voice of persons who use library and other campus technology, helping to counterbalance security issues with real-world usability. This has allowed librarians to work with Information Security personnel on a variety of policies for the university that reinforce the security provided by the Family Educational Rights and Privacy Act, the Health Insurance Portability and Accountability Act, etc., while not impeding patrons' research opportunities.

THE LIBRARY AND TECHNOLOGY

UTHSCSA underwent a realignment of information technology resources beginning in the fall of 2012. Under the new direction of the chief information officer and vice president for Academic Faculty Student Affairs (AFSA), the library technology group transitioned from directly reporting to the executive director of the libraries to reporting to Academic Technology Services within the campus information technology infrastructure. This transition came to be as the university looked at the sustainability of multiple department-level IT solutions that had been created in the past. Administration found that many departments were functioning as fiefdoms, causing deployment of similar but separate solutions within their "walled gardens" and, as a result, not using resources effectively.

In this change, the director of Library Technology and Special Collections transitioned to become the director of Web Initiatives, a newly formed division in Information Management and Services, made up of library staff and other web professionals from across the university responsible for the revitalization of the university's web presence. The former director of Library Technology had been leading multiple online initiatives prior to the creation of Web Initiatives, including a social media interest group that met to discuss, create, and expand on the university's social media policies. Prior to this position, the university did not have formalized direction for the university's web presence. The library was looked upon as a model for web innovation that could be replicated on a larger scale throughout the university as a whole.

The systems librarian, in charge of the back-end infrastructure and the library systems department, then took over as the head of Library Technology. Library Technology continues to report to the director of Web Initiatives/ campus IT, allowing the synergy to continue across campus. Additionally, this realignment shifted the eight other departments that reported to the vice president for AFSA to receive IT support from Library Technology, followed by a revamp of the AFSA web presence to align with the university's mission.

The web services librarian works with the library as well as being involved with campus web initiatives, providing insight on a variety of subjects. The librarians' skills in being able to pick up technologies and processes as needed have helped bring a varied expertise that allows for movement among teams in Web Initiatives, including consulting on web analytics, search engine optimization, and user experience. In the library, the web services librarian focuses on development for the front end of the website, coding, user testing, and graphic design.

THE LIBRARY AND TECHNOLOGY EXPERTISE

In a world designed, written, and illustrated by librarians, the goal is to provide sound web design and infrastructure. Even though being "moved" out of the library reporting structure, while not physically removed from the library, would tend to be considered less than positive, librarian skills and versatility benefited the university as a whole by bringing a rounded insight into partnerships/committees on campus, print and copy, and the various websites that Web Initiatives/Library Technology support throughout campus. Integrating librarians into various departments outside typical organizational structures has allowed librarians to work in nontraditional settings. These nontraditional settings have allowed librarians to embed into the various technology departments and work on projects that have not been typically associated with libraries.

One example of such nontraditional roles is the Web Initiatives "Web Life" project. Web Initiatives was conceived to bring together skilled persons from departments across campus to provide web services and consultation free of charge. Due to the library Web Team's knowledge in this area, Library Technology was tapped to help form and lead this new group. The group has grown since inception, adding new members who are divided into teams where each best fits. These teams cover user experience, change management, development, content, analytics, and more. Web Initiatives' first big project was the redesign of the university's website. An outside vendor was brought in to help with this and the project was called Web Life. A choice was made to tackle different areas of the university separately to better address the needs of each. Over the course of a year, Web Initiatives worked with the vendor to learn its process for researching and creating large-scale websites, with the intent to take over when the contract with the vendor ended. Librarian input is very strong under the direction of the director of Web Initiatives, while the head of Library Technology and the web services librarian routinely consult and provide research and support to the project as needed.

The director of Web Initiatives leads the group as a whole, managing the teams and working with university departments to decide where to focus efforts. The head of Library Technology provides insight to the development team and supports the blog, which is used to disseminate information about the project as it progresses. The web services librarian provides guidance in analytics, creating reports and optimizing data and user experience to codify user research data. In the beginning, the librarians were able to bring traditional skills such as the reference interview and discovery of user needs into this new environment. Knowing how to interact with many different groups has been helpful when working with various departments and stakeholders in the project, many of whom have differing ideas. Reference skills have helped in the discovery process to define the needs of a department when it comes to web presence. Likewise, involvement with Web Life has allowed the librarians to bring learned skills back to the library to be implemented on a smaller scale. Most notably, the head of Library Technology has begun to introduce a culture of project management, which has had a positive impact on both large and small projects in the library, offering a formalized structure that did not exist before. In addition, new techniques for usability and analytics have been brought in and modified for the library's use.

The library is the "print and photocopy" resource center for the entire student population at UTHSCSA. In the past, the library dedicated rooms of copiers for faculty, staff, and students to be able to copy print resources that were stored in the library. Once computers became more prominent in the library, technology staff began migrating to a system that would allow patrons to print for a fee. The library has continued to play an intricate role in the print/copy service for all students here at the Health Science Center.

In recent years, the library has looked at partnering with the print/copy services department to reduce duplication of service around campus. The primary purpose and billing philosophy, however, have not allowed the two departments to merge various products into one cohesive service. Instead, the library has continued to be a leader in the entire process of print/copy for students. The library has attempted to upgrade the system that controls print/copy payment and billing whenever possible to enhance the user experience. Adding laptop/wireless printing, integrating Active Directory into print authentication, and upgrading the system allows users to print via their mobile devices.

Additionally, the library has quickly integrated with the schools in providing print services outside the library's traditional buildings. First, working with the School of Nursing, the library quickly began integrating into copy services and soon expanded into allowing printing in the building. The library migrated its print/copy services to the School of Health Professions and most recently the School of Dentistry. The library will be placing printers at the forthcoming Academic Learning and Teaching Center being built on campus, and will continue to look for ways to integrate services into other campus initiatives.

In 2010, the library Web Team made the decision to redesign the library's website based on data from a series of usability tests over the course of several months. Interviewing university students, faculty, and staff revealed that the library's website was not effectively meeting their needs and that change was needed. Prior to the new library website, the infrastructure was based on a ColdFusion and MSSQL back end. As team members familiar with these systems left the library, it became increasingly difficult to rely on this complex, expensive, and homegrown content management system. The Web Team began working with WordPress, which up until that point had been used for a few years for the various blogs written and maintained by the library. Part of the process for the Web Team was learning to use WordPress as a full site rather than just a blogging platform. Utilizing WordPress' open source model allowed the library to free up financial obligations, leverage predeveloped code, and employ a rapid development model. WordPress' user-friendly interface empowered library staff to become content owners, providing them with a platform to create their online voice.

Prior to the library's practice of web usability testing, there had been no history of user testing of websites at the university. The library Web Team kept themselves knowledgeable about best practices and trends in web development, including the need for user testing, which enabled the team to adapt those methods to a library environment. Given the library's small size, librarians on the Web Team chose to follow the model set forth by Steve Krug in his book *Rocket Surgery Made Easy: The Do-It-Yourself Guide to Finding and Fixing Usability Problems* (Berkeley: New Riders, 2010). Krug's method involves testing small groups of people (no more than three each session) while a group of observers takes notes. Afterward, the group identifies the issues each tester had in common. Instead of making large sweeping changes all at once, this method encourages tackling "low hanging fruit" and making small incremental changes based on those observations. This method helped library staff who are not part of the Web Team understand "why" some changes were made to the website while other requests by staff were not fulfilled.

After learning of the benefits of testing and familiarizing themselves with the model, library staff decided to move forward and received support from library administration to perform the tests, including approval of staff time and funds to purchase incentives for participants. Testing included a variety of participants in the university community. These included students from first year to graduate, university staff members, faculty, and local area health professionals. Despite their often different needs and backgrounds, the testing provided valuable feedback and their observations helped to raise a number of issues during each test. These included difficulty finding resources linked to the library's website, obtuse naming, buried content, and other problems. In the end, it was discovered that the library website had been designed more for library staff than for the users. In certain places it was more like a digital filing cabinet than a living site meant to serve user needs.

The aggregated usability data was presented to library leadership and staff to engage their help in a site-wide redesign. A library web committee was formed of library staff members representing all divisions, and under the guidance of the Web Team it restructured the website architecture and taxonomic structure in preparation for the move to WordPress. The redesign process allowed the Web Team to reiterate to library staff that they should begin thinking like a "fish," not a "fisherman," viewing the site the way faculty, students, and staff view and use the site. This process extended over six months, until the launch of the newly redesigned library website. The site was completely overhauled with a back end running on WordPress, an updated visual design, and new site architecture and navigation. Usability testing after redesign showed greatly improved ease of use.

WORKFLOW, PLANNING, AND CHANGE MANAGEMENT

Though the formal meetings of the library web committee have ended, the culture and engagement it created continue on. The members of that group came away with a deeper understanding of how websites work and the importance of user experience in the process of design, and took that knowledge back to their own functional areas. This fostered a greater sense of ownership of the website and stronger partnerships between other library staff and the Web Team in the creation of web content. In the past, the library suffered badly from a bottleneck in web content publishing, but with WordPress, content flows freely with only top-level supervision from the library Web Team.

Developing and growing this newly realized culture has allowed the library Web Team to focus their energies on other web development projects, rolling out new creative tools that allow library patrons to take advantage of a larger breadth of resources. Moreover, moving to university IT has brought a greater understanding in project management, project charter creation, and lessons learned after product launch. This allowed library technology person- nel to correctly define the scope of projects prior to launch and keep scope creep to a minimum, something that librarians had struggled with prior to the transition.

These efforts did not go unnoticed and soon the library was partnered in working with AFSA to redesign the websites of several departments outside the library, including Financial Aid, Registrar, Student Life, and others. Due to the extensive work done on the library website, the Web Team was able to utilize the model followed to re-create the process for these other depart- ments, from discovery to research to eventual rollout. Given WordPress' ease of use and ready adoption by library staff, the decision was made to also use WordPress for these sites. The Web Team had to expand their knowledge again, however, as the AFSA sites were to be implemented as a larger Word- Press multisite, a new process that had not been done before. Under this model, each site in the larger group would be connected under an umbrella network. This would allow the Web Team to administer and update the network on a super level while also allowing each site its own users and individuality. While WordPress fully supports multisite functionality, re- search and testing had to be done to assure a proper setup, and the Web Team learned through the process how to implement and administer the multisite.

Once the multisite had been successfully created, the department staff users were brought in and set up in their own individual sites. Departmental training was done in person by the Web Team to familiarize the users with WordPress, since staff were to be the primary content managers and creators. Once the training was done staff could start to move, create, and adapt content from the old site to the new. Though these sites are now all self- sufficient and the department members are in charge of the content, the library Web Team still consults, trains, and oversees updates to the multisite and installed plug-ins. The Web Team continues to work with AFSA depart- ments to ensure their websites meet their needs.

PHYSICAL COLLECTIONS AND THE JOINT LIBRARY FACILITY

Libraries across the country are experiencing changes in their collections and spaces. Physical collections are shrinking while electronic collections contin- ue to increase. Space demands on the library building are transitioning from storage and maintenance of physical collections to individual and group study, classrooms, coffee bars, and other interactive spaces. With these changes in mind, an opportunity arose in Texas in which librarians saw the potential to reduce local collection footprints while adding to a statewide shared collection.

The University of Texas (UT) System and Texas A&M University (TAMU) System first began a dialogue in 2008 focused on a joint storage facility to address collection concerns on a wide scale. Endorsed in 2009, the Joint Library Facility (JLF) completed construction in spring 2013 and officially opened May 24, 2013. The eighteen-thousand-square-foot facility will house approximately one million volumes and will be available for use through interlibrary lending by other academic and medical institutions across the country. Due to the evolving mind-set of repurposing library space on campus, UTHSCSA chose to join the joint storage initiative.

TAMU commissioned a task force to implement technology features for the JLF and another to develop policies and procedures. Both task forces consisted of librarians across the TAMU and UT Systems. The technology task force evaluated integrated library systems (ILS) and selected Generation Fifth Applications. A librarian from UTHSCSA participated on the policies and procedures task force, which developed documentation for various guidelines, recommendations, and policies for JLF. The final versions of these documents and more information can be found on the Joint Library Facility website, http://library.tamu.edu/joint-library-facility.

The guiding principle of the Joint Library Facility is the concept of the resource-in-common (RIC) model for materials. Applicable to both general academic and medical campuses from both systems, this model allows libraries to withdraw their print copy after one library deposits its copy in JLF. Items submitted to JLF are permanent; requests may be made through interlibrary loan but will not return to an individual library's collection. For holdings count purposes, any library that had a copy and either submitted to JLF or withdrew the copy could still maintain those volumes in their overall holdings count as volumes housed off campus. If a library never had a print copy of an item it cannot claim that particular volume as an RIC.

TAMU submitted the first collection spreadsheets in February 2013 detailing items to be offered for the JLF collection. Only a single copy of any item will be held at JLF, so these spreadsheets were made available to all participating libraries to view. Libraries then compared their potential collection spreadsheets to the initial A&M list to remove any duplication. Once a library finalizes its collection spreadsheet it is sent to JLF for approval. As more spreadsheets were added to the JLF site, libraries could see the potential collection growing.

Shipments are scheduled on a quarterly basis and libraries must schedule a shipment time in order to send their materials. Originating libraries are responsible for sending the materials to JLF in an organized fashion. Prior to shipment, all bibliographic and item records are uploaded by the originating library to an FTP (file transfer protocol) site where JLF staff can import them into their ILS. This process allows for records to already be in the JLF ILS when the materials are received. JLF staff began accepting and processing materials from the first collection lists in June 2013. Once received on site, JLF staff process the materials and edit the records previously loaded in the ILS for all libraries to view.

Librarians across the UT and TAMU systems are able to make the items at the Joint Library Facility available through a variety of means. Items claimed as a resource-in-common are still findable through individual library OPACs (online public access catalogs). The UTHSCSA Library, for example, notes a new location and status for these volumes along with a link in the OPAC to request the item through interlibrary loan. All items going into JLF or claimed as an RIC must have their DOCLINE symbol (TXUOGR for medical libraries) and OCLC symbol updated to reflect the JLF Library symbol (TXJLF). It is the responsibility of the individual libraries to reflect the proper holdings. Once DOCLINE and OCLC symbols are updated and the volumes are fully processed at JLF, these items are then eligible for interlibrary loan to all patrons.

The UTHSCSA Libraries did not have the opportunity of a remote storage location prior to JLF, so this truly was a new way of thinking for librarians and the institution. Internally, collection resources librarians had to rethink the collection as a whole. Mentally, librarians had already shifted their thinking to the electronic version as the copy of record for journals, so that was not a difficult task; however, workflows, shelving, and space all required a shift in thinking.

Over the course of several months, titles were selected from the print collection for potential transfer into JLF. Librarians established transfer criteria early in the process, thus documenting the decisions that would need to be made regarding storage and deaccessioning of titles, as shown in the textbox below.

Criteria for Transfer Consideration
Journals

Titles beginning with volume 1
Titles shelved with at least 20 years of volumes

Books

Older than 2000
Little or no usage
Not authored by UTHSCSA faculty or staff

Book and journal titles with electronic access were given first preference for storage or deaccessioning. While some titles did meet the criteria for offsite storage, not all are planned for removal from the collection. Those that are considered "core" or heavily used will remain in the library unless per-petual online access has been obtained.

Constituents on campus from which librarians first wanted to get buy-in for off-site storage included the Library Committee and Student Government Association, which consists of faculty and students across all disciplines. Both groups were comfortable with the concept of off-site storage at JLF as long as interlibrary loan was quick, reliable, and cost-effective. Librarians also met with the Faculty Senate, who were more attached to the older print copies, especially of journals. Faculty felt more comfortable knowing the print copies are housed on location in the library, even though most admitted-ly preferred to use electronic journals whenever possible. Executive leader-ship on campus was extremely interested in space within the library and creating more group and individual study areas, so librarians had to delicate-ly balance these competing interests. Once the UTHSCSA Libraries decided to move forward with the Joint Library Facility initiative, interlibrary loan staff had to be apprised of the concept of a resource-in-common, how OPAC records would change, and how off-site storage would affect interlibrary loan both lending and borrowing.

CURRENT FIGURES AND LESSONS LEARNED

As of August 2014, the Briscoe Library has removed 5,667 volumes (182 titles) from its collection and plans to ship 1,799 titles to the JLF in 2015. A benefit of sharing resources across the consortia was that many of the UT health science libraries have an overlap of titles in their collection. As one of the last libraries to ship items, the Briscoe Library was able to weed out the majority of selected titles without having to pay shipping costs to the Joint Library Facility. Shared resources were then marked for removal but would not be weeded until the item was transferred and processed into the JLF.

During the weeding process, library staff discovered a long-standing issue with the catalog. In the late 1990s, the decision was made to share print and electronic records. The shared records allowed users to easily access both print and electronic information on one record. After updating the first item records to reflect the Joint Library Facility as the current location, librarians realized that the shared records would cause a problem because of multiple ISSNs. Before moving physical volumes to the facility, all combined records had to be separated to ensure a smooth migration process. Input into union lists was another issue related to the combined print and electronic records. Holdings entered into OCLC were inconsistent, showing both print and elec-tronic formats on one record. At the same time, all of the Briscoe Library OCLC serial records were encoded as level 3, a level provided by vendors

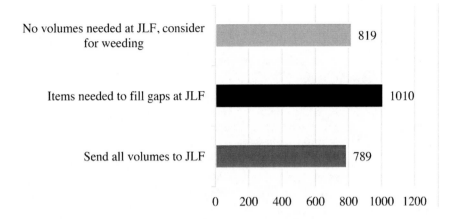

Figure 7.2.   Journal Titles to Be Removed from Collection

and publishers. Each encoding level had to be updated to the highest level of hierarchy and then transferred to the JLF location.

Since 2011, the Briscoe Library has gone through a number of weeding projects. October 2011–May 2012 marked a large weeding process in which 18.11% of the collection was removed (21,635 bound journals and 16,928 books). That being said, the process of transferring or removing items for JLF inclusion was a more complicated process than simply removing a title from the collection, resulting in a more time-consuming process. In the event that a title was offered by another contributing library, UTHSCSA library staff then removed that same item from the shelves. Only exact matches were removed, so if the original contributing library had a missing volume or issue, Briscoe Library would keep that copy in order to fill the gaps once the local materials were shipped. After the item had been removed from the stacks, changes would be made to the item record. For each item removed, the barcode, item location, and borrowing rules were updated. An 856 line was added to the bibliographic record to easily access ILLiad, the interlibrary loan system used by the Briscoe Library. Global editing was not an option for this process due to differing bindery decisions across multiple campuses. To match the records listed in the JLF OPAC, each local item record had to be updated by hand. The time-consuming process was not ideal but allowed for the ability to update and clean up records that had been overlooked for numerous years.

CONCLUSION

Over the last several years, change has been the constant theme at the Briscoe Library. The librarians worked very hard to create new roles and redefine traditional ones by embracing communication. One form of communication during this time of disruption was a librarian discussion group called Why We Exist. Why We Exist used a journal club and open-format style to engage staff on challenging issues. This led to interesting and open conversations about external forces and the current services and trends at the library. One metaphor that was consistently explored was the image of a rowboat and having everyone row in the same direction.

An important lesson learned is that library programs and activities, such as the pediatrics clerkship program or the ETBB classes, did not continue forever. Each served a purpose for a time and both internal and external decisions led to these activities coming and going. By approaching many new activities as pilots, librarians had the opportunity to try new services and still recognize the possibility of an ending. Challenges in library services and the collection remain, but the decision to enable communication and open discussion allowed projects and programs to grow on the campus overall. As a result of the overall growth, librarians are seen as leaders across campus.

Looking ahead, the authors are aware of the history and accomplishments of the librarians who came before while looking for a future that may not resemble the library of today. Every part of the library, from the mission to every service, should be considered according to the present needs of students, faculty, and staff. It is expected that budgetary challenges will be ongoing, the staff will remain small yet mighty, and the roles for librarians outside the library walls will continue to grow.

REFERENCES

Krug, Steve. *Rocket Surgery Made Easy: The Do-It-Yourself Guide to Finding and Fixing Usability Problems.* Berkeley: New Riders, 2010.
University of Texas Health Science Center San Antonio. (2014). "A Brief History of UTHSC-SA." http://uthscsa.edu/hr/briefhistory.asp.

Chapter Eight

The "Commons" Manager

Coordinator and Collaborator of New Learning Spaces in Academic Libraries

Joseph Fennewald

The way in which one accesses and provides information through technology has changed not only the way in which academic libraries operate but also the way they look. In new buildings—and renovated areas—less emphasis is given to collections storage and greater emphasis to comfortable spaces. The library is no longer a place with food and drink restrictions or imposed silence, but rather a place where students rearrange furniture, bring food and drink, and regulate their own noise level with headphones and ear plugs. Librarians no longer sit at reference desks but instead advise students and faculty on their research online, in the privacy of their offices or in their liaison departments. Library staff are likely to work alongside, or be replaced by, information technology consultants and multimedia specialists. Writing tutors, academic advisors, and financial counselors can now be found in many of the public spaces once dedicated to traditional library operations.

To reflect these changes, libraries have even renamed themselves as information, learning, or knowledge commons. Although the rationale for these names has already been much discussed (Beagle, 1999; Beagle, 2010; Bonnand and Donahue, 2010; Cowgill et al., 2001; Halbert, 2010; Leeder, 2009; Malenfant, 2006; Ren et al., 2009), it is often difficult in practice to distinguish one type of commons from another. The features found in any given *knowledge* commons, for example, may resemble those in an *information* or *learning* commons as much as they do those in another known knowledge commons. Consequently, the unmodified term "commons" will be used to refer to these new spaces that have been appearing in so many libraries over the past two decades.

While the choice of the adjective modifying "commons" often seems quite arbitrary, the noun itself is not. The *Oxford English Dictionary* traces the usage back to the 1300s, defining it as "provisions provided to a community or company in common" (*OED online*, retrieved December 7, 2014). These provisions, originally monetary or commodities, were made for the benefit of all members of a given group. Library commons are, after all, physical spaces where all students have ready and equal access to a range of information, learning and knowledge resources and services in an inviting and welcoming environment. Although these spaces sometimes seem radically different from those of the traditional library, they foster, using contemporary technologies, the library's mission to provide students, faculty, and researchers with the resources needed to succeed in educational endeavors. The commons staff not only direct users to the physical and online collections they require, but also help them create new works and intellectual products. The commons may have changed the way libraries look, but its services—access to information and information specialists in a central location—remain true to the traditions of librarianship.

When designing commons, library administrators and planners face many decisions. Among them is deciding who will oversee these new spaces. Pennsylvania State University's library administrators debated whether this management should be assigned to an individual or a department. If an individual, should it be a librarian or another specialist, and should this person report to a department head or directly to one of the associate deans? In the end, they conducted a national search for a librarian who would report directly to the associate dean for learning, undergraduate services, and commonwealth campuses. In doing so, they linked this position to an existing unit (Library Learning Services), identified the targeted audience (undergraduates), and projected expanding the commons to its twenty-four campuses across the commonwealth. They decided that the person's primary responsibilities would be to provide oversight of the knowledge commons, engage in continuous assessment, manage relationships with the various departments providing services in the space, and work closely with other library units.

The author, as head of the Tombros McWhirter Knowledge Commons, has faced many challenges since it opened in January 2012. As with other newly created positions, the job duties and responsibilities provide only a general overview. Many of the specifics of the job, from identifying how to provide technical support to clarifying who reports to whom, were developed within the first six months. Some aspects of the job continue to be defined. Other features were established inadvertently, or so it seems. The planners' decision to place his office in the center of the newly created space and to wall it with glass, for example, proved advantageous. The author sees how people use the space. He is highly visible to visitors who want to learn more about it. And he is accessible to the partners from Information Technology Services, the Media Commons, and the Learning Center. This exposure has been rewarding and balances the frustrations that inevitably come with new positions.

As the author felt his way into this new position, he wondered how and whether his professional education and past experience had prepared him for responsibilities beyond imagining when he was in library school. He has questioned (and has asked) whether a librarian should even be in this position. As in many newly created positions, he has wondered how what he is experiencing compares with the experiences of others in similar positions. How are commons being managed elsewhere? What expectations have been emerging within the field of those who have been entrusted with the management of these innovative, expensive, and still uncertain undertakings seemingly so important to the future of academic libraries?

To satisfy his curiosity and reassure himself, the author decided to review some data readily at hand—the job descriptions of positions like his own posted over the past decade or so. Virtually all of these have appeared in the *InfoCommons and Beyond* blog and are archived there. This resource describes itself as a "directory to library websites (234 as of 4/10/14) where one can find models of the innovation that started as the information commons and has evolved into the learning commons, knowledge commons, and many variations" (retrieved from *InfoCommons and Beyond* blog archives: http://listserv.binghamton.edu/scripts/wa.exe?A0=INFOCOMMONS-L). It makes available more commons postings than either the *ALA JobLIST*, which only lists the past two months online, or *College and Research Libraries News*, which has posted fewer examples. In the end, twenty-five vacancy postings were identified in the *InfoCommons and Beyond* blog between 2004 and 2014. Although they provide insight into the qualifications and responsibilities of these new positions, it is understood that these twenty-five positions represent but a small proportion of the 200 or so new "commons" academic libraries claim to have created in the past two decades. It is likely, however, that management of many of these facilities was assigned to an existing library position or filled internally, thus precluding the need for a search and vacancy posting.

The postings reviewed contained information typical of academic job announcements. This includes job title, position description, institution, institutional description, responsibilities, qualifications (required and/or preferred), and salary and benefits. The order in which they appeared varied slightly. The announcements also varied in length. The average was 515 words; the shortest was just under 200 words, and the longest closer to 1,200.

Shorter postings often included websites where additional information about the position and/or institution could be found.

This chapter focuses on the responsibilities and qualifications of the positions posted. It does not explore the institutions nor the salaries and benefits they offered. A future study will explore how responsibilities and salaries may have varied with an institution's geographic location and Carnegie classification.

JOB TITLE

It was interesting to find that position titles varied greatly (see table 8.1). North Carolina State University and Southern Maine Community College sought *directors* of their commons. Penn State and Brigham Young University sought a *head*, and Old Dominion an *operations manager*.

The University of Kansas advertised for a learning studio *coordinator*. The University of Illinois at Urbana-Champaign and the University of Louisville simply titled the position *commons librarian*.

Several institutions clearly linked responsibilities for their commons to other units. "Student services" was specified in the postings by the University of Massachusetts, the University of Maryland, and the University of Texas at San Antonio. Traditional library services (i.e., public services, reference services, or library instruction) appeared in the job titles for positions at Seattle University, James Madison University, University of Georgia, and Queen's University.

As much as titles varied, there was also variation in reporting lines. When the title alone did not provide a clear connection, where the position fit within the organization often did. One found the commons manager reporting to the head of public services, to the head of reference and information literacy, or to research and information services. And there were positions seemingly independent of traditional library units that reported directly to an associate university librarian, associate dean, or library director.

RESPONSIBILITIES

Regardless of the title or reporting line, the announcements for all of the positions examined indicated that management of the library's commons was the primary responsibility.

How these responsibilities were described varied. The person might "manage all operations," "supervise daily operations," or "coordinate the delivery of services." With the newer commons—those recently completed or still under development—importance was given to promoting the "implementation of the Commons," or to "develop Commons services," or to "par-

Table 8.1. Job Announcements, *InfoCommons and Beyond* Blog, 2004–2014

Item #	Date Posted	Position Title	Institution
0003	2004-5-19	Information Commons Section Head	Brigham Young University
0189	2005-4-28	Head, Learning and Research Services	Queen's University
0391	2006-3-15	Coordinator, Learning Commons and Undergraduate Library Services	University of Massachusetts Amherst
0897	2007-8-2	Coordinator, Learning Commons	University of Louisville
1114	2007-11-13	Head of Integrated Public Services	SUNY Brockport
1163	2008-01-25	Librarian for Information Commons	University of North Carolina at Charlotte
1241	2008-3-4	Learning Commons Librarian	University of Illinois at Urbana-Champaign
1518	2008-12-4	Assistant Director of Public Services	James Madison University
1896	2009-12-14	Head, First-Year Services	University of Texas at San Antonio
1911	2010-1-7	Head of Research and Education Librarian	Providence College
2112	2010-6-3	Director, Learning Commons Services	North Carolina State University, Raleigh
2335	2011-2-9	User Experience Librarian	University of Texas at San Antonio
2356	2011-3-21	Learning Commons Operations Manager	Old Dominion University
2386	2011-3-17	Head of Terrapin Learning Commons and Student Support Services	University of Maryland
2387	2011-03-18	Head of the Tombros McWhirter Knowledge Commons	Pennsylvania State University
2538	2011-10-27	Project Director (Learning Commons and Renovation)	George Washington University
2716	2012-4-5	Learning Commons, Reference and Instruction Librarian	University of Georgia
2853	2012-10-29	Learning Commons Supervisor	Zayed University, Abu Dhabi Campus

3047	2013-5-15	Student Engagement and Information Commons Librarian	University of Texas at San Antonio
3050	2013-6-2	Information Commons Coordinator	Armstrong Atlantic State University
3274	2014-4-11	Director of Public Services and Coordinator of the Learning Commons Partnership	Seattle University
3292	2014-5-20	Learning Commons Director	Southern Maine Community College
3330	2014-07-16	Studio Librarian	University of Tennessee at Chattanooga
3353	2014-8-18	Learning Studio Coordinator	University of Kansas
3407	2014-10-23	Commons Librarian	Providence College

ticipate actively in strategic planning, library-wide projects and in the smooth operation of the Learning Commons."

Closely aligned with overseeing daily operations was staff supervision. These positions often required some aspect of "hiring, training, directing and mentoring" those who provide services in the commons. Library staff would sometimes be listed as "paraprofessionals" or "permanent." Student employees were often mentioned, whether it was "student workers" or "graduate student assistants." Exact number of student workers might also be included. Otherwise, there was simply a reference to the size of the staff, such as "large student work force." Again, the level of specificity varied. What was expected could be simply stated or be fairly explicit. For example, one posting specified that the person filling this position "recruits, hires, trains and supervises undergraduate and graduate students as tutors, supplemental instruction leaders and other Learning Commons staff."

Several job announcements included the desired outcome, or goal, of staff supervision. One saw such aspirations as to "ensure that staff receive comprehensive training," "ensure high quality customer service," or "provide effective public service."

Surprisingly, student workers providing technical support or computer assistance were mentioned only twice. One should exercise caution when reading job announcements that do not list responsibility for a given service before concluding that it does not exist. It may not, but it may also be that it is overseen by someone else within the library or by another unit. Penn State provides a good example. It has nearly 150 students employed as information technology consultants. They provide technical support in the forty public computer labs on campus, including the Knowledge Commons. They are hired and supervised by the manager of Information Technology Services

(ITS) Lab Consulting. The head of the Knowledge Commons works closely with him and participates in the training he provides, but is not involved in the hiring or ongoing supervision of the student workers.

The ability to collaborate was usually identified as a requirement. Sometimes, it was simply stated as an ability to "collaborate with other units," "collaborate with colleagues," "build partnerships," or "work closely with librarians, faculty and students." As with staff supervision, the desired outcome of this activity was also identified. One would see goals such as "to ensure the highest quality services," "to support undergraduate student success," "development of productive relationships," or "to create an environment in which students can thrive." With whom one was expected to collaborate was also specified. This might be within the libraries, with public services staff, or with one's supervisor. The need to "develop positive relationships," "establish regular communication channels," or "strengthen collaborative relationships" might also be extended to student support services, academic departments, and ITS. There were times that announcements would include the expectation of building those relationships with groups yet to be identified, "potential partners," for example.

As part of managing the commons operations several positions requested that candidates have familiarity, experience, knowledge, and/or a demonstrated strong background in assessment. This was especially likely when the position included responsibility for assessing operations and services. Some defined the task in general terms, such as "assess, plan, and set goals," "assess effectiveness of services and programs," or "plays a key role in assessment of library services." Others specified the skills needed, such as to "define appropriate metrics" or "establish methods to receive user input into service development and their effectiveness." The importance of good assessment to change or improve services was also apparent, with such phrases as "continually assess service delivery and engage in service improvement," "ascertain student needs and provide creative solutions," or "makes recommendations for innovations and improvement based on the review and tracking of system and process data." Definitions of learning outcomes of students using the commons started to appear more frequently in later postings, and will likely become more prevalent as this is mandated at more institutions of higher education.

Although several institutions identified the person in this position as either providing assessment leadership or playing a "key role," some stated that the person would be part of a team and would be working with others (again, the importance of collaboration). Sometimes, this was simply "work with academic partners," "with library personnel," or "with partners in the Libraries" engaged in assessment activities. One specified that the person would be expected to work closely with the director of assessment.

"Provides vision, leadership and oversight" was an overriding theme in most postings. In some, leadership was described in somewhat visionary terms as "anticipating future trends," "bring[ing] fresh ideas," and being "willing to take risks and pursue new opportunities." One announcement stated that the person in this position would be expected to "enthusiastically embrace the challenge of reinventing traditional reference and information services."

Several institutions sought candidates with strong technical skills and identified expectations that the person would teach "software packages" or provide "workshops on using hardware, software, and other technologies." At a minimum, successful candidates should be able to lead the "implementation of technology tools," "ensure the Commons has a strong technological presence and infrastructure," or "pursue technological and other innovations, including software and instructional technology that will provide new opportunities for students." Technical skills received greater emphasis in the qualifications sought in candidates. Basic competency was often expressed as "having a working knowledge," "broad computer applications knowledge," or "demonstrated technology savvy." Knowledge of networks, hardware, software, and web design might include specific applications or programs. Whereas one institution sought someone with "technical adeptness and aptitude," another wanted someone who could "learn and teach new technologies quickly." "A willingness and ability to learn and teach new and appropriate technologies to staff and patrons" was a desired qualification at one institution. Several specified a desire, willingness, ability, or demonstrated experience in the use of technology to support learning outcomes, in the classroom and online. The expected understanding of social media ranged from "its use in higher education" to its usefulness as a venue for promoting library services. And frequently, there were references to candidates possessing an awareness or knowledge of "current and emerging technologies as they contribute to meeting the needs of students and researchers."

Additional responsibilities varied by institution and where the position fit within the organizational structure. An equal number of institutions identified expectations that the successful candidate would participate in library instruction and/or reference services. There were also expectations to participate, collaborate, or actively engage in public or access services. A few postings included collection development responsibilities. Two specified that the person in this position would handle copyright questions.

Finally, a very small number included the ambiguous, open-ended "other duties as assigned." Though this was rare, some job descriptions were so brief that one might assume that there would be additional responsibilities.

It was interesting to find that many announcements included expectations of professional behavior. For example, several stated that the person would be asked to serve on, and actively participate in, "library committees, task forces, and working groups" as well as "relevant University committees." There were also references to continued professional development, to "stay abreast," "stay apprised of trends and developments," "maintain currency in the field," or "keep informed on advancements and changes in the field."

Increasingly, library professionals oversee or provide leadership in programs and services supporting students, but are not expected to have direct contact with these users. True to form, only two postings directly mentioned student interaction. One indicated that the person holding this position would "work closely with students"; the other expected the applicant to be "providing services and interacting with students." More common were statements that the position occupant would "join colleagues" or "provide leadership" in "programs and initiatives aimed at supporting undergraduate student success" or "to create an environment in which students can thrive." It should not be inferred that this absence means that the person in this position would not have any direct interaction with students. Rather, it may have been tacit, not deemed worth mentioning in these pay-per-inch announcements (unlike serving on committees and continuing education).

Tenure-track positions specified the requirements to obtain tenure and promotion at their institution. "Participate in research, publication, and other professional and scholarly activities" and "provide service to the university, the community, and the profession" appeared in these positions.

It was evident that libraries expected the people filling these positions to assume a leadership role promoting their commons. In spite of the differences found in the actual duties, there were also remarkable similarities. To illustrate this, the most frequent verbs from the announcements were entered into a wordle, a web-based tool that depicts the frequency of certain words by font size (see figure 8.1). The verbs appearing most frequently highlight the expectations held of those who will fill the position of commons manager: collaborate, lead, oversee, manage, coordinate, and supervise. Presumably the qualifications sought, described below, would enable the occupant to meet these expectations.

INSTITUTIONAL DESCRIPTION

Descriptions of institutions varied. In some, one found detailed entries that included a brief history, numbers of students and faculty, and Carnegie classification. Others provided a link to their website containing this and other information. Regardless, postings often were sprinkled with descriptors that characterized the environment in which the successful candidate would work. Not surprisingly, the most frequent phrase used was "rapidly changing environment." Likewise, one might find the work setting described as everchanging, continuously changing, dynamic, fast-paced, and busy. One would

Figure 8.1.   Job Announcement Verbs Displayed in a Wordle

also find combinations such as "dynamic and collaborative academic environment" or "fast-paced and changing information environment." The library's collaborative or collegial work environment was also stressed.

QUALIFICATIONS

As previously stated, the positions reviewed were most likely to advertise for someone with a master's degree in library science from an American Library Association–accredited program (or equivalent). One institution accepted applicants with a bachelor's degree and experience that equates to a master's or a combination of education and experience. Another indicated that it would entertain someone with a PhD. Yet another stated that an "international equivalent in library or information science" was acceptable. Institutions where librarians have faculty status and are expected to publish often indicated a requirement, or preference, for an additional graduate degree.

In addition to the education requirements, job announcements specified the experience sought. "Professional library experience" was often requested and many institutions quantified it with two, three, or five years post-MLS. Many specified that this should be in an academic library or higher education. Because of the relatively recent creation of "commons," only one institution asked for "previous experience in a learning/information commons environment." Recognizing that few candidates would have this experience, another institution sought someone with expressed "enthusiasm for the concept of the Learning Commons in libraries." More likely, you would see requests for experience in customer service, public service, instructional services, or, more generally, academic support services. "Progressively responsible experience" in any of these areas was sometimes desired. In addition to the post-MLS experience, supervisory experience was the most common experience sought, and it was often qualified that this should be "substantial" or "successful."

Institutions where librarians are members of the faculty included requirements for promotion and tenure. It was specified that successful candidates would be expected to publish and present research findings and to actively participate in related professional organizations. One position asked for "evidence of, and continuing commitment to, professional growth through scholarly activity and service." Most, however, simply sought someone who "demonstrated potential for meeting university libraries faculty promotion and tenure requirements" or "demonstrated scholarly and research interests and ability to meet tenure requirements." The latter suggest that these institutions would consider librarians relatively new to the profession or those who did not hold faculty status in their current position.

The desired library experience often reflected where this position would fit within the organizational structure. Experience or "demonstrated ability" was often sought in providing reference or library instruction. Some specified that candidates should be knowledgeable of these services in an online environment, requesting experience with virtual reference or online instruction. Knowledge of web-based information resources appeared, as well as an "understanding of technology and its applications to libraries." Desired were candidates who also understood or had a wide-ranging knowledge of emerging or evolving trends in libraries, whether with public or reference services or information technologies.

A fourth requirement appearing in all positions was communication skills. These appeared in one way or another. "Written and oral communication skills" were described as needing to be strong, excellent, or outstanding. Institutions differed as to how they qualified them. Several expressed the need for the successful candidate to effectively communicate with diverse populations or a "variety of constituencies."

The ability to communicate effectively was often linked to another quality, the ability to work well with others. "Interpersonal skills" always needed to be excellent. One institution wrote that the successful candidate should show an "ability to interact effectively and work productively, collegially, cooperatively, and collaboratively with a variety of individuals and groups." In all announcements, proven success working with others was required. As one posting phrased it, they sought someone who had a "demonstrated ability to win the trust and confidence of staff and colleagues." The candidate, moreover, was often expected to build relationships and work effectively with campus colleagues and "stakeholders" across campus.

Depending on the position, the candidate might be asked to be knowledgeable of staff development issues and to actually develop effective training programs. Indeed, developing training programs was often one of the managerial skills being sought. Several positions described the need for someone with strong staff management skills, strong collaborative leadership skills, and experience.

Project management skills, or the "ability to plan, design, and implement new services," were also identified as desirable. Related was experience in strategic planning and implementation with a broad knowledge, or awareness, of issues in undergraduate and graduate education.

Of the qualities needed, one of the most prevalent was the ability to provide good customer service. This was expressed in different ways, with varying emphasis. Some identified their need for a candidate who possessed a "strong commitment to quality user services" or who had "excellent customer service skills." Others elaborated on skills, such as "strong, enthusiastic commitment" and "highly responsive customer service in all environments." One identified the importance of not only developing but sustaining "productive customer relationships."

Other qualities were sought. Acknowledging the ever-changing environment in which one works, several institutions identified the need for flexibility and the willingness not only to embrace change but to thrive on it. One institution warned candidates that they would need to be able "to deal with ambiguity." The ability to take the initiative, to direct oneself, to work independently was stressed. Strong organizational skills, including effective time management, were likewise sought, as well as the ability to handle multiple responsibilities and to "think on one's feet with energy and flexibility." Finally, creativity, resilience of character and perspective, energy, and, possibly most important, a sense of humor were frequently identified as desirable.

It is no surprise that when the adjectives found in the job announcements are put into a wordle, "collaborative" stands out (see figure 8.2). Other frequent adjectives reflect the leadership expected in these positions—innovative, visionary, and creative. Given the frequency in which the commons was described as ever-changing, it should not surprise anyone that "energetic" and "dynamic" were also mentioned often.

CONCLUSION

Although there were important differences in the candidate requirements identified in these postings, there were nevertheless several common to all.

Figure 8.2.   Job Announcement Adjectives Shown in a Wordle

These included a graduate degree in library and information science, with two to five years of professional experience, along with supervisory experience, and the ability to build a team and exercise leadership. These librarians, moreover, were expected to participate actively as members of committees and working groups in the library and larger institution. Finally, candidates were sought who possessed good communication and interpersonal skills.

At the same time, the postings reviewed demonstrated that libraries were seeking leadership abilities in those who were to oversee these innovative and highly technical learning spaces. Typically, these commons managers were expected to assess the space and its services, develop partnerships with internal and external groups, and oversee staff members in a manner that would provide the best possible service. It is not surprising therefore that the postings were designed to attract energetic and enthusiastic candidates who would thrive in these ever-changing and dynamic work environments.

Reviewing these positions, one may question the importance attributed to a graduate degree in library and information science. Do library schools better prepare their graduates to be team builders and leaders than other graduate programs? If managers of highly technical areas are needed, should they not be looking for candidates with degrees in computer science or engineering? And doesn't a doctoral program in education or one of the social sciences better prepare individuals to assess and evaluate educational services, especially in light of the increasing mandate that "measurable learning outcomes" be developed and employed when doing so? One may wonder if search committees asked similar questions. And there may be institutions that have answered them affirmatively, especially if personnel with such qualifications would complement existing staff or support other strategic objectives. Barring these exceptions, however, there remains one very good reason why libraries should continue the practice of hiring credentialed librarians to oversee their commons.

Of the qualities sought in these postings, the one that appeared repeatedly and was stressed most strongly, was a collaborative nature. It was clear that collaboration was needed both with others in the library and with external partners. The ability to bridge two worlds—that of the traditional library and that now appearing in the commons—provides a library presence and ensures that the work being done and the services provided extend the long history of libraries as the locus of the tools and resources good scholarship requires. Without such a presence, without a librarian in this leadership role, these "commons" could easily become just another campus computer lab or coffee shop. Library schools do not train librarians how to be collaborative. Library schools, however, do provide them with the history and foundation of library services. Imbued with this tradition, the librarian serving as the commons head, manager, supervisor, coordinator, or whatever the title bestowed, can keep the commons firmly planted in the library and ensure that the various specialists at work there—information technology consultants, multimedia specialists, writing tutors—understand the library resources available and that the library faculty and staff, in turn, understand the new resources available to students in the commons. It is making these connections, building bridges, being collaborative, that necessitates, indeed makes it critical, that librarians serve in these roles.

REFERENCES

Beagle, D. (1999). "Conceptualizing an Information Commons." *The Journal of Academic Librarianship* 25(2): 82–89.
Beagle, D. (2010). "The Emergent Information Commons: Philosophy, Models, and 21st Century Learning Paradigms." *Journal of Library Administration* 50(1): 7–26.
Bonnand, S., and T. Donahue. (2010). "What's in a Name? The Evolving Library Commons Concept." *College and Undergraduate Libraries* 17(2): 225–233.
Cowgill, A., J. Beam, and L. Wess. (2011) "Implementing an Information Commons in a University Library." *The Journal of Academic Librarianship* 27(6): 432–439.
Halbert, M. (2010). "The Information Commons: A Platform for Innovation." *Journal of Library Administration* 50(1): 67–74.
Leeder, C. (2009). "Surveying the Commons: Current Implementation of Information Commons Web Sites." *The Journal of Academic Librarianship* 35(6): 533–547.
Lippincott, J. K. (2010). "Information Commons: Meeting Millennials' Needs." *Journal of Library Administration* 50(1): 27–37.
Malenfant, C. (2006). "The Information Commons as a Collaborative Workspace." *Reference Services Review* 34(2): 279–286.

Ren, S., X. Sheng, H. Lin, and J. Cao. (2009). "From Information Commons to Knowledge Commons: Building a Collaborative Knowledge Sharing Environment for Innovative Communities." *The Electronic Library* 27(2): 247–257.

Chapter Nine

Beyond the Information Commons

The Evolution of the Hub

Marissa Ball and Patricia Pereira-Pujol

This chapter presents a case study of the patron-driven evolution of the Hub @ Green Library, Florida International University (FIU), a flexible learning and research environment.

Years' worth of patron feedback, user-created designs, planning, and site visits culminated in the transformation of a traditional academic library reference space into a new research and learning environment—The Hub @ Green Library. Taking advantage of student technology fee funding, the Green Library (GL) was able to improve infrastructure, technology, and space to enhance access to the collections in an environment embodying the definition of a hub as "a chief center of activity," a focal point, and a point of confluence (Gove, 1993, p. 1098). A setting "different from that of a typical library," the Hub provides seamless access to resources and services not previously available to the FIU community, and the ability to manage and produce projects, research, and assignments in one centralized location (Lippincott, 2006, p. 7.2).

The interest in and process of creating an information commons at GL had its inception in 2002. Information commons had become widespread in university libraries by the end of the 1990s and early 2000s, and had proven to be a popular success (Accardi et al., 2010, p. 311). Believing that such a facility would provide great benefits to FIU students, a site visit to Georgia Institute of Technology's Library West Commons, which had just opened in 2002, was arranged. Georgia Tech's commons provided students with an individual productivity lab, multimedia studio, and presentation rehearsal studio, and GL envisioned providing similar facilities for its students (Fox and Doshi, 2013, p. 86); however, it was not until the fall of 2013 that GL was able to finally open the Hub, its own reconceptualized information commons.

BACKGROUND

The Green Library is the sole library serving the Modesto A. Maidique Campus (MMC), the larger of two university campuses. A large urban public university located in Miami, Florida, FIU is currently ranked as the fifth largest of public universities by enrollment, currently at fifty-four thousand students (http://www.fiu.edu/about-us/rankings-facts/index.html). In 1998, enrollment at FIU was around thirty thousand students, most of whom attended the MMC (http://www.flbog.edu/resources/factbooks/factbooks.php). Due to the continuously increasing student population and expanding library collections and services, five floors were added to the original three-story building. The construction of the building was planned with further expansion in mind, allowing for the possibility of adding an additional five floors in the future. While the building currently has eight floors, GL itself occupies only seven, and most of that space is used for collections or offices. Public seating is available throughout six of the seven floors of GL, most of it located on the second floor; however, as the student population grew by 80% throughout the last sixteen years, space and infrastructure became increasingly inadequate to meet the needs of students. Recognizing these needs, FIU Libraries has always made providing adequate space and technology for students one of its main priorities.

THE INFO COMMONS EVOLUTION: HOW IT HAPPENED

In the dawning of the "information commons era" of the late 1990s and early 2000s, as with most institutions, when the Green Library began its effort to create an information commons, the initial focus was to create additional seating for students and provide a space to offer more computer access, "a combination library and computer lab" (EDUCAUSE, 2011). In 2002, the space available at GL for a facility such as an information commons was limited. While creating an information commons was considered a priority, there was reluctance to transform the spaces occupied by collections and public seating. In addition, while the structure of the building allowed for the construction of additional floors, there was no funding available for a major building project. GL did have a small space on the second floor for a dedicated computer lab, the Electronic Research Center (ERC), used to provide access to library materials available on CDs or through limited online access, as well as some productivity software. Given the low likelihood of creating a true information commons, the decision was made to make minor renovations to the ERC and expand the available technology to at least offer students some of the resources the library lacked. In the end, the upgrade consisted mostly of new, more powerful desktop computers, new hardware such as scanners, and the addition of software packages needed by students to complete projects and assignments.

While creating a more adequate information commons continued to remain a goal for Green Library, it was not until 2009 when once again the process was put in motion. A library-wide Information Commons Planning Task Force (IC Task Force) was created to develop a formal program and service plan for an information commons on the second floor of GL. The Green Library, in partnership with FIU's Center for Excellence in Writing, Media Services, and University Technology Services, wanted to develop a new model for coordinated student services. Members of the IC Task Force conducted site visits to information commons at four universities (Georgia Tech, Emory University, North Carolina State University, and Duke University), to observe firsthand what peer institutions had implemented and how the space was being used, and to gather feedback on what did and did not work for their facility and population.

By that time, the literature regarding the adoption of information and learning commons had progressed, and consisted of a holistic vision of flexible and adaptable space.

> Academic libraries have been challenged to use their physical space in different ways. The library community has responded to this challenge by creating and implementing inventive new facilities and services, so-called "social spaces," such as cafes, collaborative group study spaces and "learning commons." Major driving forces toward this movement include: a shift in pedagogy in higher education that has placed more emphasis on group projects and collaborative work and a focus on millennial students' learning and working styles. (Yoo-Lee et al., 2013, p. 498)

The IC Task Force, with this learner-centered concept in mind, recognized the importance of involving students in the project, and thus the Interior Design Graduate Department Studio Design Project was started. Running in tandem with the work being performed by the IC Task Force, and in collaboration with interior design faculty, the students in the graduate design program were asked to work in groups to develop student-centered design proposals to "promote student use of, and interaction with, [the] library services . . . [and] the spaces . . . that help them perform well academically"). As part of the project, the students conducted focus groups, surveys, and observations—including more intensive focus groups that asked participants to draw their ideal library space. Out of these activities, student groups presented four major design proposals to the IC Task Force and other library stakeholders. In the end, the Green Library gained invaluable insight into what kind of spaces and technology the students wanted and needed and what kind of environment they were seeking in GL; however, lack of funding once again prevented the implementation of any of the students' proposals.

@FIU DEAR MR. PRESIDENT, ARE THERE ANY PLANS TO EXPAND THE GREEN LIBRARY?

A hub can be defined as "a chief center of activity," a focal point, or a point of confluence (Gove, 1993). At FIU, the Green Library itself is often referred to as the hub of the MMC, evidenced by student comments about GL as their second home, their long stretches of time spent occupying study tables and group rooms, and the difficulty they have locating an empty spot or computer to work in/on. Through past surveys and studies (LibQUAL, user studies, space observations) FIU Libraries learned that students' library-use habits are not only related to their own unique proclivities, but have also developed out of GL's and FIU's distinct circumstances. In 2012, these distinct circumstances—an ever-increasing student population; limited access to study and group space; and even more limited access to computers, technology, and electrical outlets to power devices—came to a tipping point and were competing with the "library as a second home" association that FIU students had established for the Libraries.

One can imagine, given the large commuter population of the FIU student body, that parking might be a problem on campus. It is everyone's favorite thing to hate. There are countless anecdotes from students, faculty, and staff about having to arrive to campus hours early, just to drive around and hunt for parking; because of this, once students arrive on campus or at GL for the day, they do not like to leave. Unfortunately, some of the most frequently repeated comments GL receives—aside from the building being too cold— are those comparing the effort of finding an empty spot in the building to the quest for a parking spot on campus. Ouch. No wonder "at FIU finding a parking spot in the garages or a spot in the library are the two most difficult daily tasks" (https://twitter.com/ExtraEazyE/status/325012747316252675).

Statistics show that students love to borrow technology from GL, some because they do not own computers, tablets, or laptops, others because they do not want to carry them around all day and do not have dependable access to power outlets to charge them when they run out of battery life. The libraries have steadily added more laptops and other devices for students to borrow (e-readers, iPads, cameras, GPS devices, etc.). Device checkouts have been exponentially on the rise; for the academic year 2013–2014 (fall and spring), laptop and device checkouts at GL equaled 54,344 for sixteen out of the thirty-two weeks of the two semesters. Similarly, it seems GL can never supply enough desktop computers for students to use.

As with most libraries/institutions, FIU Libraries often relies on user comments from both informal and formal surveys or anecdotal feedback to gauge its success with services or operations, but most recently, it has also relied on feedback and comments received through social media—primarily Twitter—to act as a quick and easy barometer. From 2010 to 2012, as enrollment numbers increased and space and resources at GL were becoming more and more strained, the comments collected echoed the anecdotal evidence and formal survey responses. Comments about students being in love with FIU Libraries and feeling like the library is their second home were increasingly interspersed with frustration and disappointment—no space, no seats, no power, overpopulation, etc. The themes were more than obvious:

>:(It takes an hour to find a place to sit to study in the library @FIU. (https://twitter.com/ImagineGladys/status/128548069678653441)

You have a better chance of seeing a heard [*sic*] of unicorns than finding an open seat in the FIU library right now. #finalsweek (https://twitter. com/JPags90/status/458395636103385088)

Finding a spot in the Fiu library is like finding a parking spot at Fiu, #impossible! (https://twitter.com/Pablo738/status/60478400552370 176)

@FIU We need a bigger library with more study space! I can't find anywhere to sit in the quiet study floors. (https://twitter.com/ JuneHawk20/status/187592908130627584)

Just ran around the library like a maniac trying to find a place to sit and plug in my computer. Never again =(#FIUProblems (https://twitter. com/Call_Me_YaYa/status/509427093005160449)

I'm hanging out at FIU Library while I wait for my dad, and realized they need more power outlets. Every kid has a laptop here, yet no power. (https://twitter.com/brianbreslin/status/132224740927610880)

@FIU dear Mr. President, are there any plans to expand the green library? (https://twitter.com/Daniel_F_Correa/status/450719448056741888)

The idea for the Hub emerged out of Green Library's vision for an information commons that would cater to the needs of its own unique population and address their discontent. Given all of the qualitative information gathered over the years, GL had a general idea of what the Hub space needed to accomplish for its user population: it needed to be a space and an infrastructure that supported the learning and research needs of the university, and

- provided collaborative study space
- provided access to high-powered multimedia editing and computer stations
- offered easy access to laptops, e-readers, and other devices via a dedicated device checkout desk

- served as a place for on-demand research and technology assistance and support

THE BIG IDEA! (AKA THE PROPOSALS AND DESIGNS)

The frustrations being voiced by FIU Libraries users were shared by librarians and staff responsible for providing services to them. There was a general sense that the problems being cataloged and faced every day were out of their hands. It was clear that there was no money available for a major information commons addition or remodel, as had been envisioned as part of the Studio Design Project. More importantly, it was also clear that no new or additional space for GL to expand was on the horizon; however, the need for a solution was becoming increasingly urgent.

Meanwhile, FIU (along with other state universities in Florida) began collecting tuition-based technology fees from students in accordance with Florida Statutes Section 1009.24 as amended in 2007. Technology fees, as detailed in the statute, are intended to enhance instructional technology resources for students and faculty. FIU's guiding principles for utilization of technology fees seemed a natural fit for the FIU Libraries: 1) Broaden students' access to the university's technology services that are needed in support of instruction and learning; 2) enhance the quality of students' learning experience at FIU through the use of technology; 3) raise students' technology competency; and 4) promote the integration of technology into FIU's curriculum (https://techfee.fiu.edu/SitePages/Bylaws_Procedures.aspx). As a result, FIU Libraries had been very successful in submitting proposals for technology and resources that allowed it to implement a number of smaller projects in relation to improving technology; in the years leading up to the development of the Hub project, FIU Libraries had been awarded over one million dollars' worth of funding for a number of separate distinct projects that directly impacted student learning. Infrastructure and other major issues that had a much higher cost, however, had yet to be addressed. That changed during the 2011/2012 round of technology fee proposals.

As part of the annual technology fee process, FIU Libraries typically holds a series of brainstorming sessions, where faculty and staff have an opportunity to gather together and share ideas for possible projects. In 2012, several project ideas were developed that would eventually be merged to constitute the Hub proposal: postproduction multimedia development stations; more laptops and devices and the storage for them; infrastructure and electrical upgrades; the creation of movable/portable group study stations; a dedicated device/technology checkout and support area; and a "research center" (open-concept computer lab).

Providing multimedia development stations for FIU students was considered important. As multimedia became more prevalent in class projects, students and faculty had been asking for these resources more frequently, but the university offered no such facilities or resources for students to support this shift in the curricula. Bruce E. Massis (2010) concludes:

> As technology continues to evolve, the academic library has been compelled to reimagine and redesign the development and delivery of its programs and services. While the primary mission of the college library has always been to support the curriculum, the concept has been enhanced considerably given the technology needs and expectations of today's students. In an effort to address the persistent issue of relevance, the learning commons offers the student not only curriculum support, but . . . an enhanced teaching and learning experience. (p. 161)

Upgrading and increasing the number of laptops and other e-devices for checkout, as well as acquiring secure and reliable storage for them, was also important. As mentioned earlier, many students do not have access to laptops or e-devices when they are on campus, except through FIU Libraries. As much as these resources have been expanded, the demand is still higher than can be met. Upgrading the electrical infrastructure in highly used spaces was considered essential. The increasing use of electricity throughout the building had begun causing power interruptions in some areas, and the limited number of electrical outlets had led to safety issues as students blocked walking paths and fire exits in their attempt to access existing power. Furthermore, students often found themselves unable to do their work because they had no place to charge their laptops. Related to the number and storage of laptops and e-devices, the need to create a technology checkout desk separate from the regular circulation desk had become apparent. Lines and wait time at the circulation desk had become very long, due mostly to the high checkout rate of laptops and other e-devices. In addition, the checkout process for these technologies requires special procedures, care, and maintenance. Lastly, but even more importantly, more group study areas and an open-concept computer lab to be used for research and other college work were highly desired by the students.

As these separate proposal ideas were developing, and given the reality of GL's space constraints, just about all the proposed projects were targeted for one particular area of the building, the bustling second floor (also the main floor) within the general reference area and existing "computer lab" area. Following a series of meetings, it was decided that the best approach might be to combine the six separate proposal ideas and develop one "big-ticket" proposal for technology fee funding. Out of this decision, the proposal for the Research Center/Technology Hub @ Green Library was submitted and approved with a total budget of $890,082.25. The newly funded project would provide increased access to more powerful computing workstations, new multimedia editing and production stations, increased access to electrical outlets for laptops and other devices, a dedicated laptop and e-device check-out desk with staffing for device management and support, a centralized print/copy/scanning area, and increased access to technical support. Finally, after a ten-year journey, GL had all the necessary elements to successfully create its own version of the information commons that it had envisioned. The Hub @ Green Library opened in the fall of 2013, immediately receiving a positive reaction from students:

> FIU really revamped the 2nd floor in the Library!! At least 30 new desk-top Macs and furniture/style [person raising both hands in celebration].   (https://twitter.com/_Hollywood_7/status/369888160966520 832)
>
> Holy crap. The Hub on the 2nd floor is a beauty. @fiulibrarian (https://twitter.com/AMas92/status/372132484768874496)
>
> The new computers in the FIU Library are on point! (https://twitter.com/YesseniaFalla/status/421393000045236225)
>
> OMG FIU got new Mac desktops at the library I'm in love #secondhomenow lol. (https://twitter.com/kissmygips/status/372382233312509 952)

FOR THE STUDENTS BY THE STUDENTS

From the beginning, the Green Library sought to involve students throughout the process of planning and designing the space, wanting to ensure that the space met the needs of its users. At the time of the first site visit to Georgia Tech in 2002, the motivation for creating an information commons was mostly driven by the success of such facilities at other academic libraries. Librarians and staff that worked directly with students, however, provided anecdotal evidence of the students' desire for access to better study spaces and improved technology. Starting in 2003, FIU Libraries put increasing emphasis on gathering direct input from the students. LibQUAL surveys were conducted in 2003, 2005, and 2013. Focus groups and social media were used to gather feedback and comments.

As previously mentioned, students were also closely involved in the design of the space. As part of the Interior Design Graduate Department Studio Design Project, students collected space designs from students outside their department, as well as ideas as to favorite places to study, motivating study spaces, library surroundings, and available technology. All this input was integrated into the design proposals that emerged from the project. Once the Hub project was funded and the implementation began, the architect and department of Academic Space Management responsible for the space design asked their student interns to create their own designs for the space. It ultimately was one of those student designs that was chosen and implemented.

Most important of all, the project was made possible due to funding that came entirely from the students. Even the Technology Fee Advisory Council, which chooses the proposals to be funded, is heavily influenced by students, with half its membership composed of undergraduate and graduate students. To emphasize the important role that students played in making the Hub a success, GL's slogan for the project became "Your Tech Fee Dollars at Work."

NEXT STEPS

It is fitting that information commons and learning commons—and, most recently, learning spaces—have developed within libraries because "The academic library as place holds a unique position on campus. No other building can so symbolically and physically represent the academic heart of an institution." . . . In keeping with its historic role as an institution of learning, culture, and intellectual community, a library location offers "a rich, comprehensive environment of print, electronic and human information resources." (Freeman and Bennett quoted in Somerville and Collins, 2008, p. 806)

FIU Libraries values its role as the "academic heart" of FIU. It continues to face the pressures of negotiating spaces for simultaneously growing physical collections and student populations, while also working to remain a relevant and integral partner in the university's strategic goal of student success. Given these exponential demands, it has persisted in its efforts to gather feedback and input from users and has been successful in acquiring additional student tech fee funding for space redesign:

- A second phase of the Hub was awarded $102,632 to purchase additional computers.
- A student study space upgrades project has been started that will transform an existing large "study hall–type" space into a more flexible, device-friendly, collaborative learning space.
- Similar to the Hub concept, a large space and service redesign is under way at FIU's Hubert Library on the Biscayne Bay Campus. The ASK! Center FIU students, the FIU Libraries' primary stakeholders, are and will continue to be the central force for innovations in space and services.

REFERENCES

Accardi, M. T., M. Cordova, and K. Leeder. (2010). "Reviewing the Library Learning Commons: History, Models, and Perspectives." *College and Undergraduate Libraries* 17(2): 310–329. doi:10.1080/10691316.2010.481595.

Bennett, S. (2003). *Libraries Designed for Learning*. Washington, DC: Council on Library and Information Resources. www.clir.org/pubs/reports/pub122/pub122web.pdf.
EDUCAUSE. (2011). "7 things you should know about . . . the modern learning commons." EDUCAUSE learning Initiative (ELI) Publication, available at www.educause.edu/library/resources/7-things-you-should-know-about-modern-learning-commons.
Fox, R., and A. Doshi. (2013). "Longitudinal Assessment of 'User-Driven' Library Commons Spaces." *Evidence Based Library and Information Practice* 8(2): 85–95.
Freeman, G. T. (2005). "The Library as Place: Changes in Learning Patterns, Collections, Technology, and Use." In *Library as Place: Rethinking Roles, Rethinking Space*. Washington, DC: Council on Library and Information Resources. www.clir.org/pubs/reports/pub129/contents.html.
Gove, P. B., and Merriam-Webster. (1993). *Webster's Third New International Dictionary of the English Language, Unabridged*. Springfield, MA: Merriam-Webster.
King, J. (2010). "Design project for Green Library, 2nd & 4th floors" [Assignment Proposal]. Florida International University.
Lippincott, J. K. (2006). "Linking the Information Commons to Learning." In D. G. Oblinger (ed.), *Learning Spaces*, chapter 7. EDUCAUSE. E-book.
Massis, B. E. (2010). "The Academic Library Becomes the Academic Learning Commons." *New Library World* 111(3): 161–163. doi:10.1108/03074801011027664.
Somerville, M. M., and L. Collins. (2008). "Collaborative Design: A Learner-Centered Library Planning Approach." *The Electronic Library* 26(6): 803–820. doi:10.1108/02640470810921592.
Yoo-Lee, E., T. Heon Lee, and L. Velez. (2013). "Planning Library Spaces and Services for Millennials: An Evidence-Based Approach." *Library Management* 34(6): 498–511. doi:10.1108/LM-08-2012-0049.

Chapter Ten

MOOCs, Digital Badging, and Embedded Librarianship

Intersections and Advice

JJ Pionke

As a librarian at a large research institution, keeping up with patrons involves checking email on the cell phone, helping students find materials, answering questions via chat, collaborating with professors on their projects and teaching, developing initiatives to generate greater use of library resources, and building digital objects of all sorts to be sent out through email and course management systems. Today's librarian is all about focusing on assuaging needs before they arise through the use of innovative tools and engaging users where they are rather than waiting for them to come to the library.

Embedded librarianship, massive open online courses (MOOCs), and digital badging are three areas of education that intersect directly with librarianship. Sometimes, this intersection is explicit, as in the case of embedded librarianship. At other times, the place for librarianship, as in the case of MOOCs and digital badging, must be carved out by the librarians themselves. It is the aim of this chapter to focus on each of these educational modalities individually and as a whole in terms of their intersectionality and how librarians can more deeply engage patrons in these environments.

EMBEDDED LIBRARIANSHIP

What does it mean to be an embedded librarian? Ask ten librarians this question and there will be ten different answers. S. J. Schulte does an excellent job describing the evolution of embedded librarianship in "Embedded

Academic Librarianship: A Review of the Literature" (2012). She breaks down the history, definitions, and actions that librarians take as they engage in being embedded librarians. It is argued here that while there are certainly commonalities that reach across librarians engaged in embedded librarianship, ultimately, each librarian develops embedding as his or her own unique brand or blend of outreach, skills, support, and teaching.

Embedding is institutionally and situationally specific. What works at one institution might not work at another one. Case in point: At a medium-sized institution in the Midwest of the United States, embedding might mean being a part of the class and including various links to information literacy resources. At a large research institution, embedding might mean working with the professor to refine research questions and syllabi and link up resources at the point of need. These models of embedding are similar but ultimately require different approaches. Where and how librarians embed is just as important as the resources that they make available to students and professors. Elizabeth Chisholm and Heather Lamond discuss the issues related to when and where to embed at length in "Information Literacy Development at a Distance: Embedded or Reality?" A key point of their article is that placement, user buy-in (professor and student), and need all influence the level of success of an embedded librarian (2012, p. 229). It is also argued here that it is the librarians themselves that help determine success as well. A strongly motivated librarian, willing to reach out to the professor and students, as well as a librarian that is deeply engaged with the material, will go a long way toward creating a successful embedding experience in a class or research project. This level of engagement can be tremendously rewarding and is a hallmark of the embedded librarian.

> The embedded librarian becomes just as engaged in the work of the team as any other team member. As the engagement grows, the embedded librarian develops highly customized, sophisticated, and value-added contributions to the team—contributions that sometimes go far beyond the confines of traditional library reference work, and contributions that some might be surprised to find a librarian delivering. (Shumaker, 2012, p. 25)

The goal of being an embedded librarian is collaboration and integration into the fabric of the class and learning lives of students and faculty.

MOOCS

Though MOOCs have been around for only a few years, they have already made an indelible mark on the academy in all sorts of ways, educationally, politically, and financially (Mahraj, 2012, p. 362). Geoffrey Little (2013, pp. 94–95) and Robert Grossman (2013, pp. 30–33) both give good overviews of the history of MOOCs and how they got started, including some pedagogical discussion. Gillian Gremmels points out that while MOOCs are new, librarians supporting distance education is not. "Librarians have been supporting distance education for almost 30 years and are familiar with the challenges of providing resources and information literacy instruction long-distance, but always within the contexts of their own students or another institution's students" (2013, p. 242). Perhaps one of the more interesting developments around MOOCs is how librarians have endeavored to engage in them.

Librarians have been active with MOOCs through three main areas: negotiating copyright and licenses; finding open access materials; and helping professors and their graduate students learn the technology required to run a successful MOOC, especially to be in compliance with the Americans with Disabilities Act (ADA) (Rathemacher, 2014). Brandon Butler discusses the legal issue surrounding MOOCs and libraries at length in his white paper "Massive Open Online Courses: Legal and Policy Issues for Research Libraries," including a discussion that explores the ADA issues that have arisen in MOOC environments (2012). Little sums up the copyright and access to materials issues that libraries face quite eloquently when he says:

> While more and more universities are making these courses available to anyone with an internet connection, academic library collections are a series of walled gardens in large part due to license agreements signed with commercial vendors that restrict what can and cannot be done with proprietary resources. (2013, p. 95)

Because of these "walled gardens," most librarians recommend to professors that they use open access materials to negate the need for expensive licenses and the potential for copyright violations. The need for copyright information means that librarians reach out to MOOC professors in a research capacity, especially in terms of publisher and author negotiation (Courtney, 2013). These three main areas are not the only ones that are of concern to librarians in terms of MOOCs. Perhaps the most complex issue that librarians face in regard to MOOCs is how to support thousands of students in one course at varying degrees of aptitude for the material.

With sheer numbers on their side, how can a single librarian support ten thousand students? The realistic answer is that the librarian can't, and that is why libraries have focused largely on copyright and access issues. That is not to say that it can't be done. Bernd Becker provides practical advice:

> Avoid supplying a librarian's direct contact information. If using a LibGuide in a MOOC, then hide the owner's profile box and suggest an alternate mode of contact. Consider creating an FAQ page, self-paced tutorials, or even set up an e-mail account that isn't necessarily tied to one specific librarian but rather is monitored by several librarians. (2013, p. 138)

This advice is to protect the identity of the librarian for practical reasons, in terms of sheer volume of correspondence, but also for safety reasons.

DIGITAL BADGING

What exactly is digital badging? The shortest answer might be to say that digital badging is kind of like Girl Scout or Boy Scout badges that are awarded for skills that have been proven to be learned. Carla Casilli states, in her blog entry "Badge System Design," that

> badges exist as visual representations—distillations if you will—of meaning. They're sort of a shorthand for content. They can act as formalized recognitions of associations, achievements, skills and competencies, endeavors, values, etc. And on the other hand they can act as fun, playful reminders of past experiences, in-jokes, and community membership. (2012)

While digital badging can be about skill building and acquisition, it can be more than that. A badge could be earned for completing a class, learning something specific, or demonstrating a skill. Badges can be issued by authority figures, whether peers or experts in the field. The key for any digital badge is that there is proof to back up the conferral of the badge. In short:

> Badges are useful for certifying complex processes or skills that are not comprehended in our traditional grading systems. . . . What we do not grade—interpersonal skills, collaborative skills, imagination, innovati[on], initiative, independence—are most of the things employers most want in future employees. At present, education, including higher education, doesn't have a system for measuring or counting those things. (Davidson, 2011)

The fact that digital badges can be awarded by peers, at a very granular level, is something that makes the technology disruptive, especially for academia.

This disruption is perhaps best stated by Tonia Lovejoy in her blog post "Badges: The Way the New Learner Learns": "This trend of self-directed, laissez-faire learning is particularly popular in the technology industry, where skills can become outdated quickly and specialization is necessary" (2013). The typical path of higher education is to receive a liberal arts education for the first two years and then specialize for the last two years of an undergraduate degree. Badges are disruptive in part because they are removing the pieces of education that students might not be interested in, so that they can instead focus on specialization. In a traditional classroom, specialization might be seen informally in terms of peer education, when students help each other with assignments or skill acquisition to succeed.

While digital badging offers a great deal of flexibility in terms of skill acquisition, when used in large formalized learning environments such as classrooms or MOOCs, consistency across the coursework is key, as evidenced by a case study discussed by Daniel Randall, J. Buckley Harrison, and Richard West:

> We quickly found that assignments and rubrics needed to be standardized and consolidated into one location in order for our badges to have consistency and rigor. Though the instructors now have less flexibility in their schedules, assignments, and rubrics they were still heavily involved in the assignment creation process. Standardization also provided the instructors the benefit of additional time to work with students [because they could put less time into creating the aforementioned class materials]. (2013, p. 92)

When being used across a large class with many sections, the standardization was necessary for the creation of a badge that made sense. It could be argued that the standardization of skill acknowledgment is at the heart of digital badging, insofar as it creates a flexible way that skills, especially "soft skills," can be acknowledged.

INTERSECTIONS

While embedded librarianship has been around for quite some time in one form or another, and digital badging and MOOCs are new, they all have a single factor in common: education. They are all learning modalities that allow learners to actively pick and chose in many ways how they learn. MOOCs and digital badging encourage students to learn skills that they are most interested in and in ways that are most appealing to them, whether that means doing everything in one weekend, collaborating with others, working by oneself, or some combination of all of the above. More than anything, these three modalities are employing an active learning approach and librarians should be engaging students in these modalities in exactly the same way that they are learning.

One of the largest struggles in the classroom, digital or otherwise, has concerned how to create that interactive component without seeming to promote "busywork." The trend, through the use of MOOCs and digital badging, is to allow the learners themselves to figure that out by giving them tools and opportunities to engage in the material. A logical next step for MOOCs is to have digital badges for skills learned in addition to the certificate of completion, which is already offered if a student completes the course. While this might sound as if digital badging might undermine the MOOC structure, just as the MOOC structure is disrupting traditional academic institutions, the reality is far different and relates back to student motivation for going to college.

Why do students take classes? In traditional institutions of higher education, students are there to learn skills to get a piece of paper that is a doorway to a job, so that those students might lead successful and productive lives. The troubling question about diplomas is what skills do they actually represent? The skills learned at one institution will be very different in the same degree at another institution. MOOCs and digital badging offer a way to refine and develop skills as well as a way to show that those skills have been learned. Embedding a librarian into the MOOC and digital badging process will improve the quality of both.

While supplying links to materials and putting an "ask the librarian" thread in the discussion board are good ways to provide information and an outlet for student engagement, they are not necessarily actively engaging the student. The counterargument would be that librarians don't have enough time to actively engage in every class in which they are embedded. The same is true of students who are taking MOOCs or working on digital badges. At what point does the time-versus-outreach ratio tip into negative space? The answer to that question is as varied as the job descriptions of librarians. What works for one librarian will more than likely not work for another. Still, there are methods that can increase outreach and resource use. Below is some advice that could be utilized to increase connectivity between librarians and their constituent groups, especially in the face of these new disruptive technologies.

Create a Personal Relationship with Patrons

Whether the instructor is developing a MOOC, a series of digital badges, or a face-to-face class, creating a personal relationship is key to getting into his or her classes, syllabi, and students. Community organizing principles work well here. "Person-to-person contacts build organizations where people feel equally valued. When someone takes the trouble to visit you and talk with you about her or his organization, it means something" (Kahn, 1991, p. 98). This means going to the people that librarians serve and not waiting for them to come to the librarian. Librarians often lament that people aren't using the library enough. It is arguable that one of the major reasons behind this is that potential patrons don't know what it is that librarians can do for them. Long gone are the days when a library was just about books. Academic librarians will talk at length about digital resources and data management plans. Public librarians will discuss programming, community involvement (especially in times of strife), and teachable moments, from having a community fish tank to starting a book club aimed at the elderly. Creating that personal relationship, one that keeps the librarian and library on the patron's mind, allows the library to educate patrons so that they start coming to the information experts with their information problems rather than trying to do it themselves.

Among other things, Peggy Pritchard discusses how outreach to researchers and professors often takes the form of an extended reference interview and that this interview allows the librarian to guide the conversation toward current research and potential areas of need (2010, p. 381).

In terms of MOOCs, digital badging, and embedded librarianship, to be successful in any of these areas is to reach out to library constituent groups and form relationships with them. Librarians will often have to provide a lot of education for others to understand what it is that librarians actually do. For instance, in a recent hypothetical conversation with an administrator, it was clear that the administrator's view of the library was books and that the librarian was the gatekeeper to those books. The conversation started with course reserves, and after addressing the administrator's questions, the librarian quickly interjected a question about how students used the library and where they struggled. This led to a discussion that revolved around information literacy, and the librarian suggested several methods by which to reach out to students and faculty, including guest lecturing in classes, orientations, and having on-site office hours. Within minutes of the conversation revolving around a traditional topic (course reserves), the librarian was able to educate the administrator on some of the other services that the librarian could provide. By the end of the conversation, the administrator remarked that they had no idea that the library could do such things, and that their view of libraries and librarians was fundamentally altered. These are the kinds of conversations that should take place with patrons in terms of relationship building.

Play with Ideas and Perspectives

Too often people get hung up on seeing a problem or idea from one point of view. Changing perspective is important. In the film *Big Hero 6*, the main character has a eureka moment when he literally changes his view of an object (he hangs upside-down). While hanging upside-down might not be the best method for seeing alternatives, the example does illustrate the need to be creative with ideas. Drawing on a giant whiteboard to visualize connections, ideas, and what happens when things are moved around helps in moving from a textual to a visual perspective. Building things out of Legos, throwing a Koosh ball around, and baking are all great ways to become more tactile with brainstorming and perspective changing.

Playing with ideas can be particularly pertinent for digital badges, where the maker of the badge has complete control over not only what qualifies for the badge but the badge design itself. Something not working right? Have you tried inverting it? Turning it sideways? Reordering it? This technique works well with Post-it notes and walls, where you can move things around easily. Never underestimate the power of imagination or office products.

Case in point: while trying to understand why a problem was occurring, sitting down and diagramming out the relationships among people and departments in order to better understand the situation helped create a perspective change. This revealed where there were significant breakdowns, and offered a road to follow to not only complete the original project but also to start conversations with people that weren't as invested in some of the issues.

Ask the Novice Questions

In Buddhism, the idea behind having a beginner's mind is that you always approach ideas without the fetters of previous experience. "Zen practice is for people who don't mind always being at the beginning, because every moment is new, because we are not separate from the moment" (Blackstone and Josipovic, 1986, p. 17). Put another way, "Beginner's mind is unified mind. It is completely involved in whatever we are doing" (Blackstone and Josipovic, 1986, p. 16). To be a beginner is to give something one's full attention. In this technologically advanced world, where there is a constant connection to the Internet, it can be very hard to stop and give complete attention to a single thing. For librarians who don't have subject expertise in the area that they have been assigned, to have a beginner's mind is critical. Endeavoring to talk, not only to professors but to students, and to ask them basic questions about their learning, teaching, subject matter, and general experiences helps build relationships and lets them be the teacher of the librarian. They'll appreciate the librarian's enthusiasm and willingness to hear what the students have to say, and that they get to teach the librarian rather than the other way around.

Applying this to MOOCs, embedded librarianship, and digital badging is even more important, because what is obvious for the librarian might not be for the person engaged in developing a MOOC, creating a badge, or trying to get either. Look at the entire MOOC or digital badge and ask the most basic questions—is there support for those questions? If the answer is no, what support is needed? What can be created to help students, especially the most vulnerable ones, through the process? For example, in going through a job change, a librarian might be assigned an area that he or she knows little about. Two of the first questions that should be asked are: What publishers are prominent in this area of study, and what are the main research foci of the students and faculty? The publisher question helps the librarian do collection development, and the research question helps the librarian connect to his or her people and understand them and their needs. A librarian who is not a subject expert might never fully understand the subject, but he or she should strive to understand the subject with fresh eyes to better assist patrons in an interdisciplinary way.

Be Adaptable

One of the major issues in classrooms is what to do with students who are at opposite ends of the ability spectrum in that subject. Novices require a lot more time and attention, whereas students who have mastered the material are bored and want something to challenge them. Developing a multi-tiered approach, so that novices get the scaffolding that they need and advanced students have more challenging material, is useful, especially in MOOCs where thousands of students will have a wide range of ability levels. Conversations with students, or discussion board threads, will show the librarian where the student is, and after assessing where the student is, the librarian can either nudge the student toward scaffolding for learning skills, or ask a few pointed questions to guide the more advanced student toward more questions or resources.

Determining ability level can take time and effort, but it can also be streamlined a bit with decision trees, properly assembled peer support, and pretesting. The best method is to spend real time with students and see where they are in a face-to-face environment, but if that isn't possible, creating lessons that allow students to decide for themselves what skills they need to acquire can be useful. For MOOCs, this may be the only way to reach students equally. In this scenario, students who are at the high end of the ability scale might be able to test out of the lessons, whereas students at the lower and middle ends might have to complete varying degrees of lessons. This is where digital badging could come in to help determine who needs what and how much.

CONCLUSION

Embedded librarianship, MOOCs, and digital badging are constantly evolving and they are changing the way students are educated. Librarians need to be engaged in ways that push the envelope and their comfort zone in order to better support the needs of learners. Doing this is not an easy task, but one that librarians are certainly up to.

REFERENCES

Becker, B. W. (2013). "Connecting MOOCs and Library Services." *Behavioral and Social Sciences Librarian* 32(2): 135–138.

Blackstone, J., and Z. Josipovic. (1986). *Zen for Beginners*. New York: Writers and Readers Publishing.

Butler, B. (2012) "Issue Brief: Massive Open Online Courses: Legal and Policy Issues for Research Libraries." Association of Research Libraries.

Casilli, C. (2012). "Badge System Design: What We Talk About When We Talk About Validity." Blog post.https://carlacasilli.wordpress.com/2012/05/21/badge-system-design-what-we-talk-about-when-we-talk-about-validity/.

Chisholm, E., and H. M. Lamond. (2012). "Information Literacy Development at a Distance: Embedded or Reality?" *Journal of Library and Information Services in Distance Learning* 6(3/4): 224–234.

Conli, R. (producer), and D. Hall and C. Williams (directors). (2014). *Big Hero 6*. Motion picture. USA: Walt Disney Pictures.

Courtney, K. K. (2013). "The MOOC Syllabus Blues: Strategies for MOOCs and Syllabus Materials." *C&RL News* 74(10): 514–517.

Davidson, C. (2011). "Why Badges Work Better than Grades." Blog post. http://www.hastac. org/blogs/cathy-davidson/why-badges-work-better-grades.

Gremmels, G. S. (2013). "Staffing Trends in College and University Libraries." *References Services Review* 41(2): 233–252.

Grossman, R. J. (2013). "Are Massive Online Courses in Your Future?" *HR Magazine* 58(8): 30–38.

Kahn, S. (1991). *Organizing: A Guide for Grassroots Leaders*. Revised ed. Washington, DC: NASW Press.

Little, G. (2013). "Massively Open?" *The Journal of Academic Librarianship* 39: 308–309.

Lovejoy, T. (2013). "Badges: The Way the New Learner Learns." Blog post. http://dev2. guide2digitallearning.com/blog_tonia_lovejoy/badges_way_new_learner_learns.

Mahraj, K. (2012). "Using Information Expertise to Enhance Massive Open Online Courses." *Public Services Quarterly* 8: 359–368.

Pritchard, P. A. (2010) "The Embedded Science Librarian: Partner in Curriculum Design and Delivery." *Journal of Library Administration* 50(4): 373–396.

Randall, D. L., J. B. Harrison, and R. E. West. (2013). "Giving Credit Where Credit Is Due: Designing Open Badges for a Technology Integration Course." *TechTrends* 57(6): 88–95.

Rathemacher, A. J. (2014). "Developing Issues in Licensing: Text Mining, MOOCs, and More." *Serials Review* 39(3): 205–210.

Schulte, S. J. (2012). "Embedded Academic Librarianship: A Review of the Literature." *Evidence Based Library and Information Practice* 7(4): 122–138.

Shumaker, D. (2012). "The Embedded Librarians: Taking Knowledge Where It's Needed." *Online: Exploring Technology and Resources for Information Professionals* 36(4): 24–27.

Chapter Eleven

Watch Out for the Bus

Tales of Cross-Training, Teams, and Rotating Duties in an Academic Law Library

Ashley Krenelka Chase

Is your library budget shrinking? Are there fewer people to do more work? Are you terrified that a colleague, who performs daily tasks you know nothing about, will go on vacation to Tahiti and decide to move there permanently, leaving you to perform tasks that have never been a part of your position before? Welcome to the 21st-century library!

For many years, the Stetson University College of Law libraries have focused on cross-training in case the primary person gets "hit by a bus" (or moves to Tahiti). It is a humorous (though morbid) way of reminding everyone in the library how important cross-training is to the library's long-term success. Within the last eighteen months, the libraries at Stetson University College of Law combined all of the support roles in the library (technical services, circulation, copy cataloging, administrative support, and university mail services) into one Access Management and Services Team (AMST). In the beginning, AMST used a system of rotating teams to ensure that each member of the group knew how to perform each and every AMST function; they cycled through tasks on a weekly basis. Recently, however, due to loss of personnel, the library has stepped back and utilized a new cross-training method. Throughout this long and continuous process, library administration and staff have learned many lessons, many of which may prove helpful to other libraries seeking to shake things up, and hopefully become more efficient, well organized, and functional.

LITERATURE REVIEW

For years, library literature has described the trials and tribulations of cross-training, changing staffing levels, and decreased budgets. These case studies, rumors, and articles have indicated that, as library departments merge and individuals are forced to work together in new ways, things become much more complicated (Glazier and Glazier, 2004, pp. 263–274). Large-scale organizational change impacts everyone in the library, no matter how adaptable or forward-thinking they claim to be. Rhonda Glazier and Jack Glazier discovered that, as staff and librarians are forced to work together, not only are they required to overcome difficulties in learning new duties, but they must overcome all of the assumptions and preconceived notions they had about their coworkers and the abilities and responsibilities that go with those individuals. The perilous descriptions of organizational change are common throughout the literature.

In 2012, a survey was conducted in ARL libraries to determine how access services departments were being reimagined in libraries around the country. Asked about combining library services, 85% of respondents stated that the individual units within their access services departments shared duties and collaborated on products, but this sharing and collaboration was limited to public services—there was no indication that the libraries had integrated technical and public services (Wilson, 2013, p. 166). While the combining of technical and public services is not an earth-shattering concept, the execution can be difficult where buy-in has not been established throughout the organization.

Taylor Fitchett et al. (2011, pp. 91–111) notes that staff should be utilized from the beginning to assist with necessary changes and developments; these groups often identify nuanced issues, as they often see things that librarians and those in library administration do not. Staff may feel less terrified about large-scale library changes if they feel they are being included in the decision-making process for their individual jobs, the library, and the institution (Nuckolls, 2008, pp. 39–52). Among the more standout changes to libraries, Lihong Zhu (2013, pp. 127–54) notes, are substantial decreases in the number of technical services positions available, or the relocating of staff members who formerly worked exclusively in technical services to other departments in the library.

The decrease in technical services positions or reallocation of individuals who previously worked in technical services to other areas of the library has required an evolution of library workflows, training, and management. According to Marshall Breeding (2012, pp. 23–25), changing library technologies were historically used to address the same tried and true workflows that remained largely unchanged. As libraries evolved from print-centric to focusing more on electronic materials, Breeding found that libraries needed not only to keep up with the quickly changing technology, but also to evaluate their operations to rework workflows for print and electronic resources. The print to digital shift, Breeding found, may help libraries to utilize staff to evolve and increase overlapping duties for more effective cross-training.

The first step to any effective change in a library, Denise Branch found, is to identify inefficiencies and be willing and eager to change (2012, pp. 315–332). An organization that fails to identify weaknesses can't move forward, and an awareness of both strengths and weaknesses is essential to any organizational change. The Stetson University College of Law Dolly and Homer Hand Law Library followed the model set out by Mary Ann Mavrinac (2013, pp. 30–32) when discussing "future libraries"; the reorganization and change in cross-training for staff has involved collaboration and team building, all with a focus on key constituents: students, faculty, staff, and the public. With the ups and downs associated with change in mind, the Dolly and Homer Hand Law Library at Stetson University College of Law strives to be innovative, collaborative, and patron- and project-focused, both in the way staff are trained and in the way that training affects the users.

BACKGROUND

Founded in 1900, Stetson University College of Law (SUCOL) is the oldest law school in Florida. SUCOL has a student body comprising roughly nine hundred full-time students and one hundred part-time students, both JD and LLM students, who complete their programs as Florida residents (for JDs) as well as through distance education or locally (for LLMs). The law school comprises two campuses in the Tampa Bay area, one campus in Gulfport and one campus in Tampa, and the entire student body has the option of attending classes on both campuses.

These campuses are served by the Dolly and Homer Hand Law Library on the main campus in Gulfport, and the Tampa Law Center library at the school's Tampa campus. The library staff comprises six full-time employees who make up the Access Management Services Team. The library employs two part-time reference librarians (both with MLIS degrees), five dual-degreed (JD/MLIS) librarians, and a full-time, paraprofessional systems administrator. Of the five dual-degreed librarians, two are in library administration: the library director and the associate director. All of the members of the professional and paraprofessional staff work on both campuses seven days a week, along with a group of student workers.

Due to contracting campus budgets, professional librarians and library staff who have left the library in the last three years have not been replaced. Previously, the library administration comprised the library director, the assistant director/head of technical services, and the associate director/head of public services, and the library staff was divided into the traditional technical services and public services/circulation departments. Because of the retirements of the associate and assistant directors in September 2013 and January 2014, respectively, a new library administrative team of three was appointed in July 2013 to supervise and direct activities within the library. In April 2014 and April 2015, two members of that team left the library as well, and neither has been replaced. The restraints on hiring new paraprofessionals when vacancies occurred—in conjunction with the change in administrative structure—brought about a combined Access Management Services Team that handles the duties previously segmented into the technical services and public services/circulation departments. The associate director is responsible for managing access management and services, reference, outreach, emerging technologies, and collection management, and is overseen by the library director, who is also a tenured member of the faculty and SUCOL's director of electronic education.

The changes in the library's organizational structure have made cross-training within the library an absolute necessity. Unsurprisingly, the original method of cross-training, implemented after a particularly ill-fated meeting of the original technical services department, has now been abandoned in favor of a new method of continuing staff education, led by the members of AMST themselves.

LET'S START AT THE VERY BEGINNING: ORIGINAL IMPLEMENTATION OF CROSS-TRAINING TECHNIQUES

Approximately seven years ago, members of SUCOL's technical services department had a meeting, and in that meeting they discussed what happens to new or updated items that arrive in the library. The results looked a little like this:

This mass of craziness was, from that point on, known affectionately as "spaghetti bowl junction." If a map of library processes is this hard to look at, it was reasoned, something was being done incorrectly. During this meeting the library director, associate director, and technical services workroom supervisor decided that things needed to be streamlined and that some cross-training needed to occur—heaven help all of the members of the team if one of those squiggles was held up because someone was on vacation or hit by a bus!

Initially, the cross-training process was within the technical services department only. Technical services duties were broken into thirteen categories, divided into four groups: group A: journals (primary tasks related to routing), filing of advance sheets, updating the federal register; group B: filing and shelving newsletters, filing loose-leaf updates, filing pocket parts; group C:

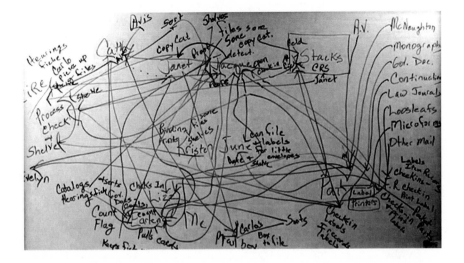

Figure 11.1. Process Mapping circa 2008

ordering for the library's temporary/contract fiction collection, mail retrieval and sorting, filing of other updates; and group D: audiovisual, acquisitions and cancelations of both continuations and monographs, and microforms (the main library is also the mail center for the campus). These groups rotated weekly, so each member of technical services knew how to do each task in every group.

The weekly rotation in the technical services department worked well. There was a designated "team lead" for the various tasks, which provided the members some ownership over the tasks they completed. This individual maintained procedures to ensure that things were done similarly by all members of the teams. No paraprofessional ever "lost" a skill because they returned to it every four weeks. There were issues with consistency, and lengthy (sometimes extremely elaborate) procedures were written out for each task, to bridge the gap between differing work styles and outputs. Because the members of technical services were accustomed to working together and doing these "back of the house" tasks, the department ran smoothly and, if a member of the team got sick or went on vacation, there was no trouble filling in when people were out of the library.

This method of cross-training worked with very few hitches until the library downsized. Loss of staff and budgetary constrictions led to the joining of circulation and technical services into one Access Management and Services Team (AMST). When these two departments, with seemingly disparate tasks and responsibilities, were joined together there was a great deal of unhappiness (some might even say hostility). Workstations were moved and, because all of the paraprofessional staff would now sit at the circulation desk, customer service skills were emphasized. In addition, every member of the paraprofessional staff had to learn new tasks that, besides being unfamiliar, were often uncomfortable. "I never wanted to work in technical services" or "I never wanted to work in public services" was a common refrain.

When the teams were joined, the breakdown of tasks was quite different. The four teams remained and, besides sitting at the circulation desk from 7 a.m. until 5 p.m., the teams were expected to complete the following tasks:

a. Mail, check-in (including preliminary processing and routing), recording of electronic resources keeps/cancelations notes, claiming of serials, shelf reading.
b. Printer and copier maintenance, library upkeep, course reserves, public computer maintenance, iPad maintenance, input of patron records into the ILS, shelving and filing.
c. Interlibrary loan, holds, on-campus deliveries, final materials processing, overdue notices, missing books, binding, archives.
d. Library administrative assistant duties, acquisitions, double-check processing, incoming Yankee Book Peddler shipment processing.

The addition of sitting at the circulation desk to the teams' circulation tasks meant there was a lot more for each group to do. Adding the circulation staff to the teams, however, meant there were more people to work on each task within the group. Much like when the tasks strictly involved technical services tasks and staff members, these teams were rotated weekly and, within each team, each task was completed by every member. Team leads were again assigned to guarantee that procedures were in place for each task and there was consistency. The rotation of duties continued to ensure that, should any member of the staff be out of the library, no task would go unfinished.

THE CIRCLE OF WORKFLOWS

Well, times change and workflows, like people, grow, and the Stetson University College of Law libraries were at an impasse: with the loss of additional paraprofessionals from the AMST, those teams were down to one or two people per team. This didn't make for much efficiency, and so the workflows were reorganized, this time into two teams. The original A and B teams were combined, as were C and D. This allowed for more AMST members in a group, which led to a much more equal division of labor within the groups and among the teams, and the team leads could still have control over the procedures in their individual areas. With the new A and B teams in place, it was determined that the teams would switch tasks every two weeks. This guaranteed more time for each member of the team to perform each task, thereby maintaining valuable skill sets, and it also allowed ample time for each team to complete their tasks during the two-week period and not leave any unfinished projects for the next team to pick up after the rotation.

In spite of what the library administration considered to be an ingenious way of cross-training, the library paraprofessional staff shrunk once again and the administration was forced to make a tough call: Go back to the way things had been (with individuals completing individual tasks and no cross-training), or try to continue a method of cross-training that caused stress, anxiety, and anger as well as breeding inconsistency and mistakes? Instead of making that decision, the members of AMST were asked to devise a scheme for ensuring that all of the tasks enumerated above were completed in an efficient way, with some cross-training involved, as shown in figure 11.2.

Each colored box in the new tasks breakdown represents a single member of SUCOL's AMST, divided into areas of specialty with tasks and priorities, chosen by them, based on skill sets and areas of interest for each member of the team (not entirely dissimilar from the team leads previously utilized for individual tasks). The boxes in the middle list backups for each set of tasks. The members of AMST chose a "continuing staff education" model, in which they must report cross-training activities to their supervisor on a monthly basis. This model continues to ensure that every task in the library is

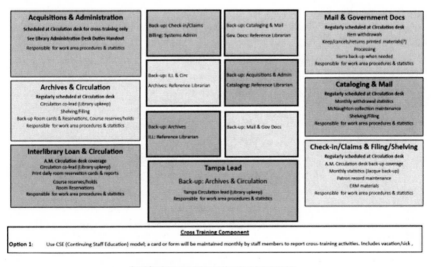

Figure 11.2. Current Task Mapping at SUCOL Libraries Courtesy of Kristen Fiato, library technical assistant, MLS student at the University of South Florida.

completed, but that ample cross-training is also completed so that, should the dreaded bus run one of the members of the team over, other team members are prepared to keep the library running with minimal downtime.

BIG CHALLENGES, BIG CHANGES, BIG LESSONS

The last six years have brought about a lot of change at the Stetson University College of Law libraries, both good and bad. In the endeavor to navigate these changes with a modicum of grace, many lessons have been learned about cross-training and dealing with budget cuts and staff shortages—some lessons easier to handle than others.

First, recognizing when change is necessary is half the battle. It would have been easy to look at "spaghetti bowl junction" (figure 11.2) and say, "Well, it's working well enough so we'll just keep doing it this way." Very few individuals were thrilled with cross-training across an entire department, as was originally implemented. When the library's administration made the tough decision to join the circulation and technical services department into AMST, it was extremely difficult. The cross-training that occurred thereafter was uncomfortable for almost every person involved; it is never easy to learn an entirely new set of tasks, let alone be required to work in an entirely different department!

The second lesson learned from all of this is that cross-training is essential, whether on a large scale or a small scale. Because the libraries at SU-COL have seen both sides of the cross-training coin, an understanding has developed as to what works and what doesn't (for SUCOL, anyway). While cross-training every member of the library paraprofessional staff to do everything within technical services (and then access management and services) seemed like a great idea at the time, the scale at which it needs to be done must be subject to change. Having four teams with four members each to complete a list of sixteen tasks is great! Having four teams with two members each to complete those same tasks, all while rotating once a week, was not great. Recognition by every member of the library that cross-training would always be essential to success helped the library to move forward.

The necessity of buy-in by everybody in the library is also an important lesson learned during this process. It is easy, as a member of the administration, to see why things must change and think that implementation should be seamless. It is another thing altogether to implement changes without disruption. When it came time to reinvent the cross-training scheme at Stetson's law libraries, the most important buy-in needed was from the members of AMST who do the work daily. When given the freedom to lay out a cross-training scheme that both worked for them *and* ensured completion of all of the work in the library, previously done by a variety of teams, everyone was much happier. In fact, the work is still being done and it is being done more efficiently and by happier library employees.

Finally, the process teaches library staff that they should not be afraid to step back and say, "Well heck, that didn't work!" The Stetson University College of Law libraries' process of moving from an isolated, workflow-silo-type arrangement, to workflows that required constant cross-training and a staff full of individuals who could do everything, but none of it all that well, and then back to individuals with individual tasks and logical cross-training was not easy. Looking at what is best for the library, however, necessitated all of these changes at the times they were implemented. It was not easy to make any of these decisions, and it was probably even harder to give up on a method when it didn't seem to work particularly well. Had the library and its staff not been adaptable, however, the library would have likely continued on a path with unhappy professionals who, while cross-trained, felt no particular desire to excel in one area, because they knew they'd be doing something else a week later.

The Stetson University College of Law libraries would affirmatively recommend their strategy to any library, academic, public, or otherwise, thinking about instituting large- or small-scale cross-training schemes. There are, of course, many ways to do things differently. The best advice would be to just get started. What the process looked like in the beginning and what it looks like eight years later are, clearly, very different. As any good librarian knows, though, it may have been easier to spend eight years trying to decide how to get the perfect process in place. Particularly in light of where the SUCOL libraries have ended up, the positives of going through this process far outweigh the negatives and, with the big picture in mind, it is easy to remember that the best way to manage the 21st-century library is with thoughtful cross-training, invested library employees, and a willingness and eagerness to try new things and to adapt.

REFERENCES

Branch, Denise. (2012). "Electronic Workflows: Taking It to the Cloud." *The Serials Librarian* 63(3–4): 315–332.

Breeding, Marshall. (2012). "New Library Collections, New Technologies: New Workflows." *Computers in Libraries* (June): 23–25.

Fitchett, Taylor, James Hambleton, Penny Hazelton, Anne Klinefelder, and Judith Wright. (2011). "Law Library Budgets in Hard Times." *Law Library Journal* 103(1): 91–111.

Glazier, Rhonda R., and Jack D. Glazier. (2004). "Merging Departments in a Small Academic Library." In Bradford Lee Eden (ed.), *Innovative Redesign and Reorganization of Library Technical Services: Paths for the Future and Case Studies*, pp. 263–274. Westport, CT: Libraries Unlimited.

Mavrinac, Mary Ann. (2013). "A Tale of Two Libraries." *Library Journal* 138(15): 30–32.

Nuckolls, Karen. (2008). "Technical Services Reorganization in Law Libraries: A Survey." In Bradford Lee Eden (ed.), *More Innovative Redesign and Reorganization of Library Technical Services*, pp. 39–52. Westport, CT: Libraries Unlimited.

Wilson, Duane. (2013). "Reenvisioning Access Services: A Survey of Access Services Departments in ARL Libraries." *Journal of Access Services* 10(3): 153–171.

Zhu, Lihong. (2013). "The Role of Paraprofessionals in Technical Services in Academic Libraries." *Library Resources and Technical Services* 56(3): 127–154.

Chapter Twelve

Surviving in a Global Environment

New Skills for Library Development

Apollo Abungu and Margaret Law

As the library and information science environment continues to change, the skills required of library staff must continue to evolve in order to support nimble and flexible libraries. The leading cause of this change is the evolution of the technological environment (Barlow, 2008; Nussbaumer, 2008; Whitmell, 2006) coupled with economic pressures. As information products and services change, the expectations of librarians also change. Traditionally, librarians worked in a print environment and were responsible for assisting users in finding the information that they wanted; they are now expected to manage, preserve, and work with material in new formats such as streaming audio and video, as well as to maintain their former expertise in the preservation and organization of print resources. Additionally, they are expected to demonstrate skills in "entrepreneurialism, creativity, project management, leadership, fundraising, competitive intelligence, 'marketing on steroids,' and risk taking" (Cawthorne et al., 2012).

The discussion about the changing skill needs of librarians is not new; in 2003 the Special Libraries Association identified "managing information organizations" as one of the four major competencies of all information professionals, including librarians (http://www.sla.org/about-sla/competencies/). In the time that has passed since the association identified this need for management skills, the LIS environment has continued to become more complex. Funders have increased expectations for outcomes and accountability; traditional funding sources have not increased to match the pace of change, requiring libraries to diversify their revenue streams; and community expectations of libraries have continued to change as information becomes both more and less accessible.

This chapter describes some particular management skills, project management, fund development, partnership building, flexibility, and teamwork by illustrating their development and use in a project to develop a public library and community center in the village of Ndwara, Kenya.

BACKGROUND ON THE PROJECT

Ndwara is a small village situated in the southwestern region of Kenya, in Siaya County. Administratively it is located in East Migwena sublocation, South Sakwa location, Nya'ngoma Division, Bondo District of Siaya County. It is approximately sixty kilometers from Kisumu, which is the third-largest city in Kenya after Nairobi and Mombasa, respectively, and seven kilometers from Bondo, a town of approximately thirty-four thousand people (2009 census), which is the nearest administrative center and the district headquarters. The people of the village are members of the Luo tribe; most of the younger people speak English as well as Kiswahili, but many of the older people still only speak DhoLuo, the tribal language. The population of Ndwara is estimated at about fifteen hundred people, with the majority being young people of school-going age. There is also a sizable group of elderly people that includes both those who never left the village and those who have returned there to live after retirement; however, there is a noticeable lack of similarity between these groups.

Ndwara is a typical African rural village with buildings made of mud walls and corrugated iron sheets. Over time, the village has moved away from the grass-thatched, round mud houses that were the traditional housing among the Luo, and shifted to the more modern homes made of iron sheets locally known as *Od mabati* (house made of iron sheets). The village is located on gently rolling ground and surrounded by seasonal rivers, with Abiero hills to the west and natural forest cover. Many former villagers of working age have moved away as economic refugees.

Like many other small rural communities in East Africa, the Ndwara community experiences the challenges of poverty, HIV/AIDS, unpredictable rainfall, reduced access to education, unemployment, alcohol abuse, and idle but educated youth, and they lack infrastructure that would help to address these issues. In particular, the lack of a library, the lack of electricity, and the lack of communication technology means that villagers are not able to access information about government or nongovernmental organization (NGO) programs that might assist them.

The decision to build a library and community resource center (referred to as the Ndwara Library) came about as a result of a meeting between two academic librarians: one from the village who shared the belief that a public library could inspire and support both economic and cultural development in the village; the other from Canada with experience in rural library development. Throughout this chapter, these individuals are referred to as the partners. The development of this library, starting with the decision to build it, is used to illustrate the discussion of new skills in this chapter.

PROJECT MANAGEMENT SKILLS

In a time when resources are limited, libraries need to determine how to best utilize those that are available in order to meet strategic goals. Project management is the process of planning, organizing, and applying resources in order to meet a specific goal. It is different from regular operational activities, in that it is a one-time activity, with a defined outcome and a defined time frame that is often constrained by the resources available. As it is not generally a process that can be learned through repetition since the project is a one-time activity, good project management involves the development of particular skills and strategies. The challenge with project management is to deliver the required outcome on time, and under budget. The key words for project management are scope, time, quality, and budget.

When the decision was made to build a library at Ndwara, the partners started with a drawing of what was wanted on a piece of paper. This was not sufficient: in order to begin the project, it was necessary to define the scope, the quality, and the budget. The timeline for construction was left until much later, as it would be driven by the ability to raise funds and the success of various funding strategies. The first step was to gain support in the village for building the library, and then to acquire a piece of suitable land for construction.

As neither of the librarians involved lived in the village, it was essential to develop a means of gaining both local input and community ownership. An interim library committee was organized made up of senior members of the community, and they took on the roles of local management of the project and of engaging members of the community by convincing them of both the benefits of the project and the likelihood of its success.

As the committee, including the two librarians, developed the scope of the project, several decisions had to be made. The first was, how big? The options were to start with something small in the hope that it would be possible to add to it later, or to build the facility as it had been conceived. With the consensus of the committee, it was decided to build the complete facility: adult and children's library, senior center, and cultural center all at once, as it would be more economical than trying to make additions afterward, and would engage all segments of the community from the beginning.

The budget was developed by the local committee, who had a good understanding both of the type of building that would be suitable and the types of materials that were available for building locally. The decision was made to use local labor as far as possible, in order to help alleviate the economic stress being felt by the community. This had the additional benefit of reducing vandalism and theft of materials during the building project; so many members of the community were involved in the construction that they maintained an informal security watch throughout.

The donation of the land made the construction possible, and a budget identified the amount of money that would be needed to purchase material and hire labor. Some of the less skilled labor was done by volunteers, which was factored into the budget. For example, the land was cleared by a group of women, working together, who wanted to contribute to the project but had no money. The budget included sources of revenue, including a membership fee, a local fundraiser, donations from Canadian well-wishers, and applications for grants.

The timeline for the project completion was very flexible, as it turned out that the speed of construction was controlled by the revenue required to purchase material. At each step of the way, goals were set for the next step of construction.

As the partners learned project management skills throughout the process, several things stood out. First of all, it is important in any project to leave enough flexibility for unexpected events. In this case, a grant that was applied for to build a fence at the start of the project was eventually granted two years later. By this time the fence was already built, but as a result of having a clear plan, it was possible to shift the funding to purchase material for the roof, thus speeding up the construction plans.

Second of all, good communication among all of the stakeholders is essential for smooth project development. In this case, communication was a challenge due to the lack of communication technology in the village, but by using all of the means possible, the members of the library committee and the partners managed to stay in touch and monitor the development of the library project.

Without an overall plan for the development of the library and good project management skills, it would have been easy to stray from the original decision. Everyone involved knew what the next step was each time, and progress was measured and celebrated at regular intervals. Photographs of the building at every stage, posted on a Facebook site, allowed funders and supporters to see that the project was on track.

Workers were recruited from unemployed and underemployed local youth. The supervisor was a village resident, who had some formal training in construction. He was also part of the library committee and was very involved in other local initiatives. His knowledge of local conditions, including the impact of weather, meant that the building plans could be altered as necessary while still progressing as planned.

TEAMWORK, COLLABORATION, AND
PARTNERSHIP BUILDING

Collaboration and partnerships are based on the belief that shared thinking, shared expertise, and shared ideas can come together to create "a new way of thinking to solve a problem" (Giesecke, 2012). Partnerships and collaboration have been identified as critical components of the future in all types of libraries (Irvine, 2011). In order for any collaborative effort to be successful, librarians need to learn the skills to support new ways of working.

The essential factors that are required for a collaborative approach to work include "trust, vision, goodwill, and a belief in the value of cooperation" (Sarjeant-Jenkins and Walker, 2014), and these will allow the development of appropriate structures and processes to move toward shared objectives. Partnership development also requires that individuals develop skills in organizing work, combining skill sets, and establishing mechanisms to balance the contribution and the benefits of each of the partners. It is necessary to create a structure that will sustain the enthusiasm of the partners without making them feel that they are losing control, and that balances organization and innovation. A partnership needs a clear enough structure to guide it forward, but not so much that it becomes bogged down in its own organization.

The Ndwara Library started as a partnership between two people, which soon evolved into a larger partnership involving the local library committee, and then developed further to encompass the two groups of supporters in Korea and Canada. The elements of this partnership included a clear understanding of the roles of each of the partners along with the development of the necessary sense of fairness, acceptance, communication, and unselfishness described by Joan Giesecke (2012). The underlying vision that tied the partnership together was the creation of a new library, a new value for the community, which could only be created together. None of the partners was able to complete the project without the contributions of the others.

For the original two partners, it was clear what each brought to the collaboration. One had a great deal of experience and background in developing rural libraries; the other had a breadth of knowledge, not only of the community, but of Kenyan culture and politics. There was, therefore, an inherent respect for each other and what each brought to the partnership.

As the partnership grew, new challenges arose. How easy would it be to develop trust and understanding between a Canadian and a group of village elders from rural Kenya? The local knowledge of the Kenyan partner helped here. After the first visit of the Canadian partner to Ndwara, it was clear that she became an adopted member of the Kenyan partner's family. In a kinship-related context, belonging to a family helps you to find your place in the community. Time spent at meals, visiting, and doing routine tasks together resulted in increased understanding and therefore a higher level of trust.

The development of the partnerships with the two groups of library supporters was based on a high level of consistent communication. Because of the distance that separated these groups from the Ndwara Library, it was essential to have a method of providing feedback to supporters. The development of a Facebook page proved to be the vital link among these partners, as it both showed the development of the library and allowed partners to communicate with each other.

Initially, the community was skeptical about the role and input of the Canadian partner. They had previous experience with development activities in the community, not all of it positive. This began to change as relationships developed in both formal and informal ways. As everyone got more familiar with each other, everyone worked more closely together and in a more relaxed fashion. The Canadian partner participated more fully in daily life with each visit, which led to increasingly trusting relationships.

The original partners also learned to be flexible with each other, and to explicitly address areas of confusion or misunderstanding. The majority of these were cultural—one partner not understanding how things were perceived by the other—and were quickly remedied.

Everyone involved in this project learned partnership skills as they went along. The two major skills that were learned to support the development of the partnership were communication and organization. First of all, it is important to be explicit and clear about expectations when working with a partner. In this case, communication was complicated by distance and by cultural differences, so learning to listen carefully and to double-check understanding proved essential to developing the level of understanding and trust necessary to work together.

The communication skills were closely tied to the second skill development, the need to be well organized. Due to the limited opportunities for working together, all of the participants learned to delegate work based on skill and ability, and to develop a level of trust in each other. This involved making sure that at each step of the way, everyone was clear about who was responsible for which activities, who needed to be consulted, when the committee could expect to hear feedback, and how challenges and problems would be dealt with as they arose. In general, this worked well, and as the members of the committee learned to work together as partners, it became increasingly clear when everyone needed to be involved in a decision, and when a decision could or should be made by the partner dealing with the situation.

Teamwork also contributed to the project at a much more practical level. By integrating the skills of many people into the construction of the library, the project became community owned. As a community-owned project, it enjoyed a higher level of security than it would have otherwise, as individuals who had contributed to building the library also voluntarily provided security, which meant that the construction was completed without the theft of material or any other vandalism.

Teamwork allows individuals with different skills to contribute in different ways. Those who volunteered to work on the construction of the library were able to contribute practical skills, which resulted in a building that was congruent with local traditions, but still brought new value to the community. The employment of some community members on the construction project provided spin-off employment; for example, women from the community made some income by selling hot meals to workers.

FUND DEVELOPMENT SKILLS

As the traditional and stable sources of funding for libraries continue to dwindle, library staff are called upon to increasingly seek and establish new sources of revenue. These can take many forms, including writing grant applications, seeking donations, undertaking fundraising activities, and developing revenue-generating services for the library. The skills required to do this have not traditionally been part of LIS education; few librarians have the relevant background to undertake this effectively and, indeed, many actively dislike it (Lorenzen, 2010). Many librarians do not see this role as part of their job, and may perceive it to be over and above their regular duties (Ercolano, 2007); however, it is increasingly becoming part of the expectations of senior librarians to secure growing portions of their resources "from outside the primary funding source" (Winston and Dunkley, 2002).

Skills required for effective fund development include not only financial skills but also good communication, both oral and written, and the ability to tell an engaging story. Fund development requires a great deal of understanding of human motivation, as well as skills in relationship building. Skills required to identify and cultivate donors have become an important factor in hiring librarians for senior positions. As the fundraising environment becomes increasingly competitive, library fundraising demands skilled librarians with a "thorough knowledge of the development process" (Winston and Dunkley, 2002). Although the need for these skills has been identified for over a decade, few if any LIS programs include any in-depth training in this area.

In the case of the Ndwara Library there was no funding source, so the librarians and the library committee had to begin from the ground up. The fundraising activities were carried out in three countries: Kenya, Canada, and Korea. In each of the countries, different fundraising approaches were undertaken to reflect the interests of the communities.

Many people questioned the advantages of fundraising in the village of Ndwara, since the majority of the community residents were living at a level of extreme poverty. Taking the advice of the library committee, which was situated in the community, the real purpose of the two fundraising activities was to increase community ownership, allowing the members of the community to feel that they were engaged in the project. Three fundraising activities were carried out.

The first was a traditional harambee. This is a Kenyan tradition of community self-help. The Kiswahili word *harambee* translates as "all pull together," and a harambee is used to bring members of the community together to support a project, in this case the construction of the library. Individuals donate cash, and all contributions are celebrated, even the smallest. In this case, children from the school sang and performed skits as part of the entertainment.

The second fundraising method used in Kenya was to ask community members to pay a membership fee. This proposal from the library committee did not sit comfortably with the two professional librarians, who were both committed to the ideal of free library service. It was made clear, however, that in the opinion of the library committee, it would be well received by the community, and individuals would see it as a way of both donating some money and publicly expressing support for the project. In fact, two of the first members to proudly pay their membership fees were elderly widows, who stated that they were doing it, not for themselves, but to ensure a better future for their grandchildren. Throughout the membership drive, it was made clear that individuals could use the library whether or not they paid as members.

The third option for fundraising in Kenya was a grant application, as described above, for building a fence around the land prior to the beginning of construction. The grant, from the Constituency Development Fund, eventually came and was used for the roof. Although it was not enough to complete the roof, the committee members felt confident enough to start an advocacy program to ask for the additional funds needed to complete it. An additional grant application was made to an NGO, but the results of that application are not yet known.

The second region for fundraising was Canada, primarily because one of the two founding partners was an active part of the library community there. There were a number of activities, some more successful than others. One of the first planned activities was a collection of loose change. This had the advantages of getting many people involved with a small initial investment and developing a list of potential future donors. It resulted in enough money to pay the legal fees to deal with the land transfer and the setting up of the library committee as a legal entity. Far more valuable, however, was that it engaged a large number of people in the success of the library.

The second activity was a sponsorship, in which the Canadian partner asked people to sponsor her for a year of not drinking coffee. Sponsors could commit to payment by the day, week, month, or year. When this was explained to the Ndwara community, they were very skeptical, unable to see why anyone would pay for such an activity. In the Canadian community, however, sponsorships are a common way to raise money, demonstrating the need for fundraising activities to be culturally appropriate.

Other activities used to raise funds in Canada included asking for funding commitment for specific activities, such as sending a box of books to Kenya; buying daily newspapers for the library; and donating a laptop for the library.

One of the essential parts of the Canadian fundraising efforts was the development of a website and a Facebook account to track the progress of the library. It turned out that the website was not as valuable as the Facebook account—individuals stated that they felt secure in making donations since they could track the growth of the library through the photographs that were posted regularly. Many of the donors stated that they liked donating to this project because they knew that 100% of their money was going to the project. The website did include a PayPal option, which continues to regularly bring in random amounts from individuals who prefer to pay that way.

The development of the fundraising activities in Korea demonstrates the need to be prepared to talk about the library's mission and its needs at all times. While on vacation in Korea, one of the partners was asked to be a visiting speaker at an expatriate club. A slideshow about the Ndwara Library, with a compelling story about the help that was needed, resulted in a variety of support projects. As in Canada, the first one was very small, intended to engage individuals and create a list of potential donors. Each interested person was asked to donate a pair of rubber sandals (about a two-dollar commitment), as many of the children using the library habitually go barefoot. Twenty-four pairs of sandals were sent to the village, and another group of donors began to follow the success of the project.

The following Christmas, a caroling event raised money that was sent to the library. This has become an annual event, along with drives for school supplies at the beginning of every new school year. One of the skills needed as part of a fundraising activity is the ability to be flexible and find different ways for people to become involved. Being able to negotiate with potential donors to find compromises that both benefit the library and engage the donor became an essential component of success. This also includes the ability to decline donations that are not aligned with the library's mission.

A frequently asked question was why the partners didn't simply seek funding from one of the many charitable organizations that build libraries in developing countries. This highlights an important factor in library fundraising. The partners and the library committee had a very clear vision of the role that the library would play as a community resource, addressing unemployment as well as information needs. For that reason, it was essential that it be built with local labor in a style that was congruent with local construction. Despite reviewing a number of options, the partners were unable to find an organization that was willing to meet the library committee's conditions, so the decision was made to not seek funding in that way.

Why were people in Korea willing to commit funds for a project that they would probably never see? The members of the Korean community that got involved were primarily young English teachers, many of whom were away from home for the first time. They were working and making good salaries, and the contrast between the conditions they were working under and the conditions in Kenya surprised many of them. They were excited to see themselves as part of a story that would have a happy ending and that, for a relatively small amount of money, would make a positive impact on the lives of young people who were close in age to them. They also became regular followers of the library's development on Facebook.

ADAPTABILITY AND COMFORT WITH CHANGE

Increasingly librarians are being asked to be flexible and adaptable to change. What does this mean in action, and how can these attributes be developed? Typically these are not attributes that can be taught formally but are developed as a result of experience. Adaptability has been identified as one of the top attributes of library leaders, along with communication, teamwork, collaboration, and integrity (McKeown and Bates, 2013).

Adaptability is a self-management skill, the ability to respond to changing situations and expectations. People who are adaptable see the positive aspects of challenge, and interpret new information or unexpected demands as opportunities rather than roadblocks. Adaptable people are often skilled at taking advantage of team problem-solving approaches in order to maximize the contributions of different perspectives.

When the Ndwara Library building project commenced, the goals were to create a library to provide access to information for the community, and as a community center to provide a place for people to gather. As community members became more involved in the project, many began to express concern that secondary school students from other villages were coming to Ndwara to use the library. There was no secondary school in Ndwara; the few children who went to secondary school were those whose families could afford to send them to boarding school.

As a result of this concern, and with the community optimism that was increasing as the library took shape, members of the community decided to build a secondary school. They approached the partners and asked if they would head up the school building as well, but both declined, pointing out that this was an opportunity to get more people involved in community development. The fundraising for the school construction started, and emboldened by the way in which the library started without a building, the school committee decided to start offering classes out of a spare space in the elementary school.

The decision to build a school, while it was congruent with the original values of the library project, introduced new challenges as it divided the attention of the partners, the library committee, and the funders. The individuals involved quickly adapted, tying the two projects together. A strategy to ensure that the schoolchildren attended the library on a regular basis, and a decision to keep donated schoolbooks in the library, meant that the two projects proceeded together rather than being competitive. One donor provided enough money each year to buy the required textbooks for the secondary school. These were also kept in the library, ensuring that both donors and users tied the two projects closely.

As the relationship between the library and the school was cemented, the library became the logical place for students to study during an unanticipated teachers' strike. Although the library development was not at a stage where it could accommodate so many students, plans were quickly implemented to borrow furniture and create a study space. Volunteers supervised the students and provided study help in the library.

CONCLUSION

All of the participants learned all of the skills discussed here as the project progressed. As skills were developed, they were shared with others, both formally and informally. This meant that more people developed these skills, and both the partners and members of the library committee are asked for advice on building other rural libraries.

What was learned:

1. Project Management Skills: These skills turned out to be essential to the success of this project. Knowing and being able to articulate what you are trying to do, in what time frame, and what resources are necessary are the keystones to many of the other activities that contribute, in particular as a basis for fundraising. Good project management adds to the credibility of any project, and provides the infrastructure for communicating regularly with supporters, and for making changes as needed.
2. Fund Development: As there was no formal basis for funding, all of the money for this project had to be raised by the participants. It turned out that there was skepticism about funding that was not antici-

pated, both on the part of donors and on the part of community members. Excellent record keeping and ongoing communication proved to be the keys to fundraising. One of the hardest skills to learn was actually asking for money directly, rather than just telling people what was needed and hoping for the best. This was an interesting skill to develop, and clearly got easier over time.

3. Teamwork and Collaboration: Teamwork was essential to the success of this project. It was made more challenging by the cultural differences of the participants, but this also added to the richness of the outcome, and personally benefited those who engaged in understanding others. Teamwork also relies on ongoing good communication, to develop trust and goodwill.

4. Adaptability: This project reinforced the knowledge that nothing ever stands still. As conditions changed and new information emerged, it was the ability to adapt that allowed everyone to continue to work together for the success of the project. The main learning here was that you need to stick to the vision, but be prepared to change the details and processes that lead to achieving the vision.

REFERENCES

Barlow, R. (2008). *Stakes in the stacks: Library buildings and librarians' professional identities* (Ph.D. dissertation).

Cawthorne, Jon E., Vivian Lewis, and Xuemao Wang. (2012). "Transforming the Research Library Workforce: A Scenarios Approach." Presentation, ARL Fall Forum, Washington, DC, October. http://www.arl.org/storage/documents/publications/ff12-cawthorne-lewis-wang.pdf.

Ercolano, Adriana. (2007). "But It's Not My Job: The Role Librarians Play in Library Development." *The Bottom Line* 20(2): 94–96.

Giesecke, Joan. (2012). "The Value of Partnerships: Building New Partnerships for Success." *Journal of Library Administration* 52(1): 36–52.

Irvine, Kate. (2011). "Collaboration as a Strategy to Accelerate Change." *Journal of Organizational Transformation and Social Change* 8(3): 313–326.

Lorenzen, Michael. (2010). "Fundraising for Academic Libraries: What Works, What Doesn't?" *Library Philosophy and Practice* (October): 1–21.

McKeown, Anthony, and Jessica Bates. (2013). "Emotional Intelligent Leadership: Findings from a Study of Public Library Branch Managers in Northern Ireland." *Library Management* 34(6/7): 462–485.

Nussbaumer, A. (2008). *The changing role of reference librarians at the university of Victoria's McPherson library* (M.A. thesis).

Sarjeant-Jenkins, Rachel, and Keith Walker. (2014). "Library Partnerships and Organizational Culture: A Case Study." *Journal of Library Administration* 54(6): 445–461.

Whitmell, V. (2006). "The future of human resources in Canadian libraries, 'the 8Rs study' considerations for the Canadian Association of Research Libraries." http://www.carl-abrc.ca/projects/scholarly_communication/pdf/8rs_v.whitmell_report_rev.pdf.

Winston, Mark D., and Lisa Dunkley. (2002). "Leadership Competencies for Academic Librarians: The Importance of Development and Fund-Raising." *College and Research Libraries* 63(2): 171–183.

Chapter Thirteen

From Communication to Collaboration

Developing the Spectrum of Activities for Effective Shared Services at the University of California

Emily S. Lin

"Why is collaboration so difficult?" a library director once asked aloud among a group of library leaders. While the keys to successful collaboration may seem elusive, it is clear that libraries in the 21st century cannot exist as islands unto themselves. If collaboration is viewed as "building a collective capacity to respond to turbulent conditions" (Gray, 1996, p. 58), such as "rapid economic and technological change," "competitive pressures," and declining organizational growth (p. 59), then it is an essential strategy for academic libraries facing a storm of factors: the exponential growth in volume of information; volatile increases in costs of information resources; shifts in information consumer practices and expectations; and "absolute declines in the dollars allocated" to library budgets (Lowry, 2013, p. 11).

Capacity building, however, is a process that requires vision and effort over the long haul and is not in itself a tangible product easily pointed to as a successful outcome of collaboration. For collaboration to be sustained, participants need to realize the value, at a personal level as well as at an organizational level (Cropper, 1996). The other challenge is identifying or forging what is "collective": while many institutions attempt to identify with peer institutions and forge reciprocal relationships with those of equivalent rank and stature, no organization exists that is a replica of another in terms of values, culture, form, and functions. Indeed, one of the benefits of collaboration is diversification of the resources and knowledge available to an organization. While it may be easier to associate with an organization with similar qualities, transformation and learning among members of an organization may be gained through engagement with one that is different.

While the University of California (UC) may be viewed as a system, each of its ten campuses distinguishes itself as a research institution in its own right. Each campus has its own library—or system of libraries, depending on the size and history of the campus—that operates independently within the context of its campus, even though the UC libraries have also had a history of working together. The ten campus university librarians and the executive director of the California Digital Library (CDL, sometimes referred to as the "eleventh library") compose a Council of University Librarians that governs system-wide library services and initiatives. Under the Council of ULs, an advisory structure of standing groups composed of leaders and experts from the ten campus libraries and the CDL work together to develop, implement, and manage shared programs and services.

In 2009, the Council of University Librarians launched the Next-Generation Technical Services (NGTS) initiative, the purpose of which was to "move technical services operations to the network level" (NGTS, 2009, p. 1). The initiative undertook a reexamination of the work required to acquire, organize, describe, preserve, and make available information resources to users, in order to make the best use of available tools and resources, as well as to respond to external pressures to demonstrate operational efficiency. Given the scale and complexity of the UC system and its libraries, the NGTS initiative offers a case study of approaches to the challenges of multi-institutional or "mega" collaboration.

BACKGROUND AND HISTORY OF UC LIBRARIES COLLABORATION

Collectively, UC serves 244,000 students, has over 200,000 faculty and staff, and has over 1.5 million living alumni. Over five hundred miles separate the northernmost campus at Davis from the southernmost at San Diego. Established over the course of more than 125 years, from the opening of the first campus at Berkeley after the signing of the state's Organic Act in 1868 to the newest campus at Merced in 2005, the UC campuses and libraries have each been shaped by their own unique history.

The 1960 California Master Plan for Higher Education designated UC as the "primary state-supported academic agency for research," as differentiated from the California State University (CSU) system and the California Community Colleges system (Coons et al., 1960, p. 3). According to the master plan, the UC system offers admission to the top one-eighth of the statewide high school graduating class. Each of the UC campuses, with the exception of UC San Francisco and its focus on medicine, are comprehensive research universities that offer baccalaureate through doctoral degrees. While all fall under the umbrella of one UC Office of the President, each of the campuses has its own chancellor, provost, academic senate, and governance structure, as well as systems and operations. All have earned Carnegie Research Very High classification, with the exception of Merced, which is on track to reach Carnegie High within its second decade. The libraries, in turn, reflect the stature of their campuses and have each developed distinction. Seven of the UC campus libraries are members of the Association of Research Libraries. The combined collections of the UC libraries represent the largest academic library in the world.

COLLABORATION: A RESPONSE TO TURBULENT CONDITIONS

While the California Master Plan represented a commitment to higher education for all of the state's residents, variability in enrollments and in the state's financial health have presented challenges to the ability of its higher education systems to fulfill those commitments. Over the last decade in particular, the University of California experienced a steady reduction in state funding support. In the four-year period between 2008 and 2012, state funding for UC dropped by nearly nine hundred million dollars, or about 27%. A 2010 report by the UC Commission on the Future laid out the challenging fiscal context under which the university operates. The commission projected an additional five billion dollars in the university's core expenditures over the next decade given inflationary cost increases; retiree pension and health benefits; the need to close competitive salary gaps; improvement and maintenance of the student-faculty ratio and quality of instruction; graduate student support; and critical investments in infrastructure. The university has pursued a range of strategies to contain costs by streamlining and pursuing "Working Smarter" initiatives, as well as seeking ways to advocate for and obtain additional funding support. In the period since 2008, campus library funding cuts averaged 20%; some of the libraries have been reduced in size by 25% and continue to face reductions over the next six years.

In times of expansion and contraction, greater attention has been paid to a "system-wide" perspective on library planning and operations. In the early 1970s, as the country experienced an economic downturn and as the census indicated slower projected enrollments than had been anticipated, the state's Department of Finance issued a report on the University of California libraries and urged that more should be done to "to improve interlibrary cooperation and coordination within the UC system," in particular in the acquisition and use of collections (as cited in Office of the Executive Director of Universitywide Library Planning, 1977, p. 19). In response, the university launched a series of system-wide library planning efforts, culminating in a 1977 report,

The University of California Libraries: A Plan for Development, produced by the Office of the Executive Director of Universitywide Library Planning (commonly referred to as the Salmon plan) and endorsed by then UC president Saxon. According to the 1977 report, one of the foundational "bases" of library planning established by an earlier task force (1974) stated that "the library holdings of all the campuses should be considered as a single University collection rather than nine separate collections" (p. 21). The Salmon plan further articulated a new approach to library development that prioritized timely access to materials based on user needs, as well as improvements to the identification, location, and delivery of library materials through implementation of a unified system of bibliographic information for the complete UC collection, over the "traditional acquisitions approach" of developing locally owned collections that were self-sufficient in addressing user needs.

In the subsequent decade, many of the recommendations of the plan were implemented, including the Melvyl electronic union catalog for UC, the establishment of the Northern and Southern Regional Library Facilities, and improvements in the delivery of interlibrary loan materials. In the mid-1990s, the University of California Digital Library Executive Working Group (1996), citing challenges of a financial crisis as well as the "compounding differential between needs and capacities" for the libraries (p. 1), presented a proposal that established the California Digital Library to manage and deliver shared digital information resources and services for the system, including licensed e-resources, archiving of digital collections generated by the campus libraries, the union catalog (Melvyl), and the interlibrary loan/document delivery management system. Each of the campuses supports CDL operations through funding models and the system as a whole realizes significant benefits from consortial negotiations on electronic resources as well as other shared services. Yet despite declarations of "One University, One Library," each of the libraries, including the CDL, asserts its own identity and distinction. In contrast to a consortium where members pool resources to form an alliance, with a governance structure and typically a central office to support the consortium, the CDL does not serve as a coordinating central office, nor does it report to the Council of University Librarians as a governing board. It was established as a "co-library" and as a unit under the UC Office of the President, and thus is subject to the directions and budgetary conditions under that office. The groups that exist are advisory and there are no fiduciary arrangements, apart from the pooling of resources to fund shared resources or operations, that make one directly accountable to another. Cooperation among the ten campus libraries is out of no formal mandate, agreement, or requirement, but out of recognition of its value and benefit.

IMPETUS FOR NEXT-GENERATION TECHNICAL SERVICES

An autonomous approach to acquiring and managing collections on the campuses, as well as challenges to integration and a more holistic approach, persisted. Three decades after the Salmon plan, the Bibliographic Services Task Force (2005), charged by the UC libraries' Systemwide Operations and Planning Advisory Group (SOPAG) to rethink bibliographic services, echoed many of the statements in the 1977 report:

> Within Library workflows and systems too much effort is going into maintaining and integrating a fragmented infrastructure. We need to look seriously at opportunities to centralize and/or better coordinate services and data, while

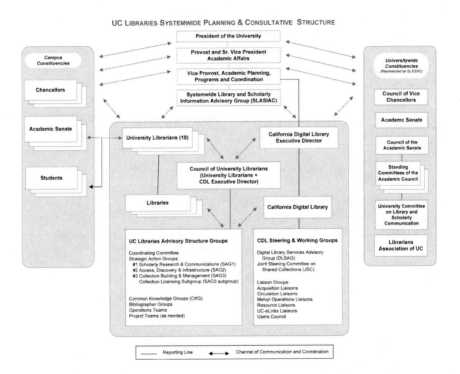

Figure 13.1.   The UC Libraries Advisory Structure in 2009 Under the Council of University Librarians (ten university librarians and the executive director of CDL), one associate UL- or deputy UL-level representative from each of the eleven libraries was selected to serve on the Systemwide Operations and Planning Advisory Group (SOPAG) to reflect diversity of expertise (public services, collections, technical services, etc.) and provide strategic planning and oversight for library operations. The all-campus groups, typically unit heads from each of the eleven, reported to and had liaison members on SOPAG.

> maintaining appropriate local control, as a way of reducing effort and com-
> plexity and of redirecting resources to focus on improving the user experience.
> (p. 2)

As a result of the task force's recommendations, the UC libraries embarked on the development of a "Next-Generation Melvyl" online public access catalog to improve the user's search and retrieval experience. The report reiterated the desirability of a single data store for bibliographic records on which discovery and presentation services could be architected. The task force recommended that "University of California cataloging should be viewed as a single enterprise" and "move beyond a practice of shared cata-loging to a practice of integrated cataloging" (p. 21). In the ensuing three years, the Next-Generation Melvyl initiative focused on the development of the front-end public access interface. In 2008, however, SOPAG prepared a discussion paper to take up once again the recommendations for an integrated approach to cataloging by considering the benefits of "Adopting UC-Wide Collaborative Approaches to Technical Services" (Declerk and Yokote, 2008). The paper pointed out the success of the Shared Acquisitions and Shared Cataloging Programs, which support consortial licensing and catalog-ing of electronic resources, in achieving reduced costs per record for cam-puses and timely delivery of records to local campus integrated library sys-tems as well as Melvyl. The group posed the question of whether collabora-tion could be expanded to technical services functions, perhaps with centers of specialization for acquisitions and cataloging of specific languages, for-mats, or subjects.

In response to the discussion paper, in January 2009, the Council of University Librarians issued the charge to develop "Next-Generation Techni-cal Services." Initially, four groups were formed with content experts from across the system to address technical service models around "broadly de-fined information resource types":

1. Commonly held content in Roman script.
2. Commonly held content in non-Roman script.
3. Unique collections.
4. Twenty-first-century emerging resources.

The teams were tasked with proposing one to three transformative models that would incorporate values and principles outlined in a scope statement, including:

- Speed up processing and eliminate redundant work.
- Free up resources to focus on unique resources.
- Start with basic description and allow for continuous improvements.

- Measure success by users' ease of access.

A governance structure consisted of 1) an executive team of three university librarians, the executive director of the CDL, and the chair of the steering committee (an associate university librarian of collection services); and 2) a five-member steering committee composed of representatives from four of the campuses and CDL who were assigned as liaisons to the teams. The charge for the steering team was to develop a framework for the next three to five years, identify areas to be addressed, and implement "low hanging fruit."

Over the course of a half year, the four teams conducted environmental scans and extensive surveys, developed a wide range of recommendations for near-term and long-term goals, and submitted these to the Next-Generation Technical Services Executive Team. Some were explicit, such as the recommendations to "implement a consortial integrated library system" and to "implement shelf-ready services systemwide" (NGTS Executive Team, 2010). Others were stated in broader terms, such as "expand technical services to support shared collections and collections management," as well as "determine what 'good enough' means for cataloging." The teams identified the need to develop coordinated management or delivery of specific types of content, such as "a systemwide government documents collection," print serials, harvested websites, and electronic theses and dissertations. The recommendations brought to the surface issues about the complexities of working with different campus financial systems and practices, and the need to facilitate intercampus transactions; questions about collocation of expertise and work; and emerging areas such as research data curation and support for born-digital materials that had yet to be addressed by system-wide strategies. Among the information gathered in this phase was the finding, based on self-reporting by campus units, of over 71,605 linear feet of collective unprocessed manuscript and archival collections.

FROM ISSUES TO ACTION

The executive team, upon review and discussion of the reports of the four teams, identified four areas of priority as "issues that must be resolved first in order to move us along" and as having the most potential to transform operations:

1. A financial infrastructure that facilitates intercampus business transactions.
2. Enterprise-level technical services and operational infrastructure.
3. New modes for access to special collections, archives, and digital formats.

4. Strategies for re-visioning collection development for the 21st century.

The NGTS Next Steps document (2010) speaks to the tension between a desire to uncover the underlying issues to be addressed for "transformation" rather than leap to specific solutions such as a consortial ILS, and the desire for specific action plans. The executive team formed three new teams, charged with addressing the first three areas in a proposal with "estimates of transition costs, timelines, an outline of points of effectiveness, and an assessment of benefits." A kick-off planning meeting was held with all three task groups along with members of the executive and steering teams participating. A consultant was engaged to lead the groups in developing a better understanding of team dynamics and approaches to managing projects, as well as an understanding of "transformational change."

In this second phase, teams grappled with the challenge of honing in on what actions would address the roots of, for example, the one-hundred-thousand-volume backlog and the thirteen-plus miles of unprocessed and inaccessible archival collections. How could increased capacity be found (or freed) to address burgeoning new areas and forms of information? What would transform practices and yet could be cast in concrete and realistic terms? Pressures to produce actionable yet "transformative" recommendations were palpable: in August 2010 the executive vice president and provost of the university charged a task force composed of UC faculty, administrators, university librarians, and external members with delivering recommended strategies for library services in response to environmental changes and fiscal constraints, with a "focus on the efficiencies that can be gained in library operations areas" (Systemwide Planning and Scholarly Information Advisory Committee Library Planning Task Force, 2011, p. 5). Campus library leadership, however, desired self-determination of any proposed changes to UC libraries operations.

Given three months' time, the three NGTS phase 2 teams delivered over twenty recommendations that addressed the libraries' financial, technical services, and digital library infrastructures and approach. Of those, the Council of University Librarians selected ten as "high priority" and "pursue now" (2010):

1. Move to a deposit account to reduce the number of recharges for shared acquisitions.
2. Implement system-wide shelf-ready recommendations.
3. Implement a "good enough" record standard for UCL.
4. Expand and adjust Shared Cataloging Program.
5. Develop a system-wide model for collections staffing.

6. Implement "More Product, Less Process" tactics for processing archival collections.
7. Support system-wide use of the Archivists' Toolkit (and transition to ArchivesSpace).
8. Systematically and efficiently digitize high-use, high-priority collections for access.
9. Implement a system-wide solution for creating and managing digital objects.
10. Using the University of California Curation Center (UC3) microservices as the foundation, develop and implement the infrastructure to manage (preserve) unique digital assets.

Some of the recommendations were identified as "immediately actionable, if not already underway," whereas others required further examination, though they were likely critical for achieving longer-term goals. Among the more radical actions that were not selected for immediate pursuit were 1) the recommendation to fund commonly held collections and technical services from a central source; 2) central funding, negotiation, and acquisition of collections-related tools and services; 3) adoption of a cloud-based system-wide ILS; 4) implementation of a single database of record; and 5) implementation of UC-wide collection services centers.

The Enterprise Collection Services report included comment that some of the recommendations would require up-front investments, but advised that such outlays be considered necessary in order to realize long-term gains in efficiency. The Council of University Librarians did not accompany its decision to move forward on selected priorities with any explicit outlay of funds or commitment of resources, and this is indicative of the challenges and constraints for collaborative initiatives. Whether due to the realities of financial pressures or budget constraints that inhibit ready allocation of funds to new purposes, or to other factors, the council placed many of the recommendations under further consideration. The council asked the Systemwide Operations and Planning Advisory Group, the group at the top of the totem in the University Librarians' advisory structure, to develop a plan for implementation and to include coordination with related processes and initiatives already under way.

IMPLEMENTATION: PRINCIPLES, PROJECT MANAGEMENT, COMMUNICATION

The transition of direct oversight of the initiative back under SOPAG was a way to bring parallel, related efforts under one umbrella and to be more explicit about coordination and consultation among existing all-campus advisory groups (groups with representation from each of the campuses, CDL, and the Librarians Association of the University of California). Under the all-campus structure, the Collection Development Committee, composed of collection development officers from each of the campuses, had issued a concept paper in 2009 that endorsed a system-wide view of the University of California library collection for the 21st century, advocating that the diverse library and archival collections of the campuses be viewed as building blocks of a cohesive, integrated, shareable collection. As a subsequent step toward realizing that vision, the committee had initiated planning for a prospective "shared monographs" program (2010). Additionally, a SOPAG "Shared Print in Place" task force (2010–2011) had developed recommendations for the actions, policies, and infrastructure required to support shared print collections, held on site at campus libraries with a commitment to retention, as a foundation for coordinated collection development. During the period that Next-Generation Technical Services had developed as an initiative, a digital library services task force, appointed by SOPAG, had delivered recommendations on the user services, technical, and organizational infrastructure needed to support digital library building for a UC digital collection. The challenge SOPAG faced was coordinating decisions about next steps and outcomes among these various initiatives.

To manage implementation, SOPAG devised a plan (2011, p. 1) with guiding principles and a structure that aimed to be both nimble and cognizant of the need for consultation and deliberate communication with stakeholders. The principles acknowledged that "transformation is an evolving, phased process, with occasional big leaps" but that "quick wins early and often are essential" for building and sustaining momentum. They underscored the focus on implementation and action over study, but also the strategic value of cost savings and cost avoidance. Finally, they laid out the importance of leveraging local experts for system-wide benefit; consistent and timely communication; and continuous vetting, assessment, and adjustments to approach.

Building upon these concepts, SOPAG explicitly incorporated project management support by tapping project management expertise identified in the system via a SOPAG Project Management Working Group, and appointed a project manager and a communications manager from within the system to the implementation initiative. The chair of the NGTS steering committee, three SOPAG members, the NGTS project manager, and the communications manager formed a new NGTS management team to oversee the implementation. The members of this management team reflected expertise from significant involvement in the preceding phases of NGTS as well as liaison relationships with the all-campus groups, including the Collection Development Committee, Heads of Public Services, Heads of Technical Services, the Library Technology Advisory Group, and the Resource Sharing Committee. The ten priorities were regrouped into seven charges:

1. Build the system-wide infrastructure to support digitized and born-digital collections.
2. Transform cataloging practices.

   • Define UC cataloging record standards.
   • Implement consortial shelf-ready program.

3. Accelerate processing of archival and manuscript collections.

   • Deploy Archivists' Toolkit system-wide.
   • Define minimal collection record specification.
   • Implement More Product Less Process practices.

4. Simplify the recharge process.
5. Maximize the effectiveness of shared cataloging.
6. Develop system-wide collections services staffing.

   • Inventory existing shared staffing agreements and projects.
   • Identify current and projected campus staffing needs.
   • Inventory existing and needed tools in support of technical services operations.
   • Eliminate current backlogs.

7. Develop a system-wide view of collections and transform collection development practices.

   • Track shared collection development commitments.
   • Recommend strategies for collecting traditional and nontraditional collections with a system-wide and multi-campus approach.
   • Redefine the roles and responsibilities of UC bibliographers.

Departing from the past practice of forming groups with representation from each of the campuses, the NGTS management team assigned a project team to each of the seven priorities; each project team comprised three members: a member of SOPAG, who served as the team's sponsor, and two domain experts from within the system. These teams were called POTs for "Power of Three" and represented the view that a small team without all-campus representation could be empowered to act in the interests of the system as a whole. The teams were further empowered to tap experts distributed throughout the system to form "lightning teams," or short-term task groups charged with tackling specific deliverables, such as gathering information, conducting pilots, or accomplishing other discrete tasks with quicker turnaround times. In addition to the three members, each of the teams was assigned a project manager who, with advice from and coordination with the other POT project managers and the overall NGTS project manager as the Project Management Working Group, assisted the team in defining and tracking tasks and deliverables; provided status reporting to the NGTS management team; assisted in addressing resource needs and risks; and inventoried project assets.

The NGTS management team defined charges for each of the Power of Three groups that explicitly outlined near-term and longer-term deliverables; set out assumptions to be tested; and expected coordination and consultation with groups that might influence the work or serve as sources of expertise. The Project Management Working Group assisted the teams in translating these charges into specific work plans with tasks, timelines, and assigned lightning teams. The communications manager developed a communications plan to provide regular reporting both up to the Council of University Librarians and outward throughout the UC libraries. In addition to a presentation outlining the framework, goals, and implementation plan for NGTS, which SOPAG members delivered on their campuses, the communications manager created a Tumblr blog with a Twitter feed as well as a monthly e-newsletter compiled from progress updates from the POTs to provide consistent communication on the progress of the initiative to the UC libraries community. The management team reframed the initiative as having four broad goals, with the work of the POTs underpinning each (NGTS Management Team, 2011, p. 1):

1. Cooperative Collection Development (POT 7): Develop a system-wide view of collections that would allow libraries to develop richer collections and to leverage selector expertise. Consider and propose actions that balance increased efficiencies of centralized collection development with more diverse multi-campus collection development.
2. Collaborative Technical Services (POT 2, 5, 6): Develop the standards, policies, and practices (addressing technical issues, human resources, and other factors) that will move UC libraries toward integrated technical services expertise and operations.
3. Collaborative Digital Initiatives (POT 1, 3): Develop policies and practices and implement the technology infrastructure to provide for collaborative UC digital services.
4. Financial and Technical Infrastructure (POT 4): Develop a fiscal framework for system-wide collaboration. Implement an integrated technical infrastructure to facilitate these collaborations.

In addition, SOPAG decided to assign three of its own members each to three additional teams, to 1) develop a framework for stable funding model(s) for shared activities (depicted as a sun shining down on the various NGTS initiatives in figure 13.2); 2) track intersections with ongoing development of Next-Generation Melvyl and its transition to a "production" service; and 3) monitor developments in the larger environment in terms of shared integrated library systems and resource management systems in order to provide information to the Council of ULs for evaluating the feasibility of pursuing one or both possibilities.

OUTCOMES

What did NGTS accomplish? The concrete outcomes include:

1. UC Cataloging Record Standards.
2. UC guidelines for efficient processing of archival and manuscript collections.

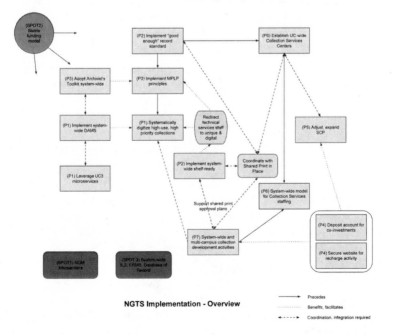

Figure 13.2. An early diagram maps out the relationships and interdependencies among the NGTS project teams.

3. Implementation of Archivists' Toolkit/ArchivesSpace archives information management system.
4. Commitment to the development of a shared digital assets management system and UC digital collection.
5. Pilot that demonstrated, with additional resource commitments, that shared cataloging workflows could be extended to another campus.
6. Pilot that demonstrated that cataloging of audio CDs at one campus could be cost-effective.
7. Assessment that a consortial shelf-ready agreement would result in minimal cost savings.
8. Articulation of the changing role of UC bibliographers and staffing models on the campuses.

One of the early wins was the adoption by all of the campuses of a common practice for financial recharges for shared acquisitions, which resulted in a reduction in the number of transactions at that level. The investigation into business practices also resulted in a common understanding that "scheduled recharges" was a more accurate term than "deposit account" in conveying the nature of the process to business officers across the campuses.

Much of the early work accomplished involved establishing a common vocabulary around technical services and shared best practices. Establishing and vetting a UC cataloging standard was viewed as a fundamental building block for other steps, such as negotiating a consortial contract for a shelf-ready approval plan, or establishing cooperative cataloging models for monographs and other formats. The *Guidelines for Efficient Archival Processing in the University of California Libraries* is an important tool for training and supporting librarians and archivists in addressing and eliminating backlogs. UC Irvine completed a project, applying the guidelines, to bring 219 previously hidden collections to the public.

In other areas, however, the teams tested assumptions and explored deeper challenges to implementing the recommended changes in practices. For example, one assumption was that stopping the distribution of records to each of the campuses by the Shared Cataloging Program for inclusion in their local catalogs and relying on the central catalog, Melvyl, alone would result in substantial efficiency. Instead, the project team found that the cost of distribution was not substantial and that the program was already a highly efficient operation. The costs were offset by the value and benefits some of the campuses held in retaining their local catalogs, including better discovery and the ability to generate ILL revenue. While expanding shared cataloging would be highly valuable, and a pilot proved that workflows could be expanded at an additional campus, doing so would require an influx of resources, and it would not be accomplished by eliminating any duplicative work or uncovering efficiencies. In the end, the recommendation to negotiate a single shelf-ready contract for the system was not deemed to produce cost savings significant enough to be worth the effort. Nearly all of the campuses had already moved to such a plan (or to demand-driven acquisition models such as at Santa Cruz) and the costs and likelihood of coordinating common shelf-ready specifications did not make a compelling case for a single vendor contract for all of the campuses.

A fundamental premise perhaps not fully recognized or considered behind the Next-Generation Technical Services initiative was that efficiencies could be realized at the campus level, which would result in benefits to the system as a whole, or vice versa. The simple assumption that stopping a particular activity or practice at the campus level would free up resources to take on new or different things as a system has not been proven. In reality, the situation is much more complicated. For example, some campuses had already made investments in infrastructure or had local resources at hand to support an archival information management system and digital asset management, and did not see value in adopting a centrally hosted system. For others, a centrally hosted system and the implementation of a shared digital asset management system have presented substantially enhanced capacity. The implementation has proceeded taking into account that the ten campuses have different needs, despite the varying levels of participation or adoption of common infrastructure.

Indeed, NGTS has demonstrated that "enhanced capacity," given the diverse, individual contexts of each of the campuses, means different things for each library. The Power of Three group charged with redefining the role of the UC bibliographer found

> considerable anecdotal evidence that, in addition and in response to the above quantifiable differences, each campus has its own strengths, needs and style. With varying library priorities, policies, practices and visions for the future[,] ten different UC library cultures have evolved. When it comes to collection building and management practices, this framework makes consensus across all campuses challenging and perhaps impossible to achieve, though multi-campus approaches and partnerships are both possible and desirable when mutually beneficial agreements can be identified, ratified, and supported. (Appel et al., 2013, p. 9)

While reduction in backlogs was established early on as one of the aims for NGTS, and while evidence gathered demonstrated there could be cost-effective ways of accomplishing this reduction, ultimately the decision whether or not to act was a local campus decision, and was not often viewed as a priority at the local level compared to other needs. Championing a system-wide view of collections is a challenge when campuses remain immediately responsive to and focus their accountability on the needs of local users. Due to the budget reductions the campus libraries have faced, many proposed actions or decision points to proceed that require an up-front investment of resources by the campuses have met with pause or no action.

Two key words used to frame the goals of NGTS were "efficiency" and "effectiveness," and many of the objectives were framed around streamlining, reducing duplicate effort, and cost avoidance. Historically, calls to collaborate and establish streamlined or integrated approaches to library collection development and management have occurred as institutions have faced crises or significant constraints. Yet this may be setting up a false expectation for the outcomes of collaboration. In *Creating Collaborative Advantage*, Chris Huxham (1996) lays out the case that "collaboration is inherently more time-consuming—and hence resource-consuming and costly—than non-collaborative activities" due to the time investments required for establishing trust and mutual understanding, the "sheer logistics" of working with members physically remote from one another, coping with accountability issues, and negotiating conflicting organizational priorities (p. 6). All of these challenges and needs have been manifest in the UC libraries' collaborative efforts, and the significant investment of time and effort required in establishing the framework, structures, relationships, and processes for communication and collaboration throughout the development of Next-Generation Technical Services is clear. Rather than expecting collaboration to result in cost avoidance or cost savings, a more realistic expectation may be of redirecting resources to new or different sets of activities.

THE COLLABORATION CONTINUUM

Collaboration has been described as a spectrum of activities or a continuum of phases, and such a framework can be useful in understanding approaches to collaboration. Arthur Himmelman (1993) has articulated four levels of engagement:

- Networking: exchanging information for mutual benefit
- Coordination: exchanging information and altering activities for mutual benefit and common purpose
- Cooperation: exchanging information, altering activities, and sharing resources for mutual benefit and common purpose
- Collaboration: exchanging information, altering activities, sharing resources, and enhancing the capacity of another for mutual benefit and common purpose

At one end of the spectrum are loose networks, or a focus on information exchange; at the other end, organizations have formed a shared vision and work together on implementing that vision. James Austin (2000) frames collaboration as a three-stage continuum: the first is philanthropic, where organizations offer resources (time, expertise, goods, etc.) with a very limited or minimal investment; the second is transactional, where organizations exchange resources through specific activities; the third is integrative, where "missions, people, and activities begin to experience more collective action and organizational integration" (p. 26). Barbara Gray (1989) identifies a general sequence of three phases in the process of forming a collaboration: 1) a problem-setting phase; 2) a direction-setting phase; and 3) an implementation phase.

Viewing collaboration in terms of stages enables one to identify the activities to promote and the steps to be taken to facilitate collaboration. If the end goal is collective action to fulfill a shared vision, then deliberate effort in laying a foundation through information exchange, dialogue, and consistent communication is needed. "Philanthropic" offers of time, expertise, or resources build goodwill and trust among members, which then allow organizations to consider what resources they may be able to offer in an exchange, in more specific, formal, or structured ways. As organizations realize mutual benefit through these activities and recognize that continued involvement is in their self-interest, they are willing to take on more risk by altering what they do and becoming more integrated with the other organization(s)—that is, giving up a level of autonomy and self-determination in order to work toward a common purpose.

The development of the Next-Generation Technical Services initiative can be roughly mapped to Gray's three stages of problem setting (stage 1), direction setting (stage 2), and implementation, although it may be argued that problem setting and direction setting were iterative or continued to recur with refinements. It may also be observed that the initiative largely focused on networking, coordination, and, to an extent, cooperation, but that it sunsetted before the "enhanced capacity" envisioned at the outset had been realized.

Yet the creation of deeper networks of information exchange is perhaps one of the most valuable outcomes of NGTS. An estimated 140 librarians out of roughly 470 in the system were involved at some point, at some level, in NGTS. As people were tapped because of their domain or functional expertise, rather than for their level in their organization, many cross-campus, cross-functional relationships were established. This approach greatly influenced the restructuring of the UC Libraries Advisory Structure that occurred in 2013. Strategic groups formed around three areas of emphasis: 1) scholarly research and communication; 2) access, discovery, and infrastructure; and 3) collection building and management. All have cross-functional representation as well as all-campus representation to provide strategic directions and operational oversight for shared services. The new structure also encourages the formation of Common Knowledge Groups to foster innovation, the generation of new services, and collaboration through information exchange. The project management and communications approaches applied through NGTS have also been incorporated in system-wide work. The lessons learned in terms of how to work together, and what is required to address the challenges of multi-institutional collaboration, have laid the groundwork for developing new partnerships and new roles ahead.

TIMELINE

2008	Discussion paper released: "Adopting UC-Wide Collaborative Approaches to Technical Services"
2009	Teams charged to address technical services models for four broad information resource types
2010	Three task groups charged to address 1) financial infrastructure; 2) enterprise-level collections management; 3) new modes of access to special collections, archives, and digital formats
2011	Implementation phase of recommendations launched with new governance • Created glossary of terms for collection services operations
2012	• Deposit system for CDL co-investments adopted; "Library Financial Data Best Practices" developed • UC Bibliographic Standards defined • Guidelines for Efficient Archival Processing in the University of California Libraries issued • Existing shared staffing agreements and projects surfaced
2013	• Launch of pilot projects to 1) investigate consortial shelf-ready contract; 2) consolidate cataloging of non-print format (audio CD); 3) extend Shared Cataloging Program workflow to UCI • Launch of UC Libraries Digital Collection implementation project • Launch of new UC Libraries Advisory Structure; NGTS management team sunsets

REFERENCES

Appel, M., C. Friedman, K. Lyons, J. Martorana, and R. Ogawa. (2013). *Responding to the Changing Collection Development and Management Landscape in the UC Libraries: The Role of the Collections Librarian.* http://libraries.universityofcalifornia.edu/groups/files/ngts/docs/pots/POT7_LT2_Report_Sept_17_2013.pdf.

Austin, J. E. (2000). *The Collaboration Challenge: How Nonprofits and Businesses Succeed through Strategic Alliances.* San Francisco: Jossey-Bass.

Austin, J. E., and M. M. Seitanidi. (2014). *Creating Value in Nonprofit-Business Collaborations.* Hoboken, NJ: Wiley.

Bibliographic Services Task Force. (2005). *Rethinking How We Provide Bibliographic Services for the University of California.* http://libraries.universityofcalifornia.edu/groups/files/bstf/docs/Final.pdf.

Collection Development Committee. *The University of California Library Collection: Content for the 21st Century and Beyond.* (2009). http://libraries.universityofcalifornia.edu/groups/files/cdc/docs/uc_collection_concept_paper_endorsed_ULs_2009.08.13.pdf.

Coons, A. G., A. D. Browne, H. A. Campion, G. S. Dumke, T. C. Holy, D. E. McHenry, H. T. Tyler, R. J. Wert, and K. Sexton. (1960). *A Master Plan for Higher Education in California, 1960–1975.* Sacramento: California State Department of Education. http://www.ucop.edu/acadinit/mastplan/MasterPlan1960.pdf.

Council of University Librarians. (2010). "Next-Generation Technical Services." Phase 2 final reports. http://libraries.universityofcalifornia.edu/groups/files/ngts/docs/CoUL_Priorities_Cover_2010.pdf.

Cropper, S. (1996). "Collaborative Working and the Issue of Sustainability." In C. Huxham (ed.), *Creating Collaborative Advantage*, pp. 80–100. London: Sage Publications.

Declerk, L., and G. Yokote. (2008). "Adopting UC-Wide Collaborative Approaches to Technical Services." SOPAG discussion paper. http://libraries.universityofcalifornia.edu/groups/files/sopag/ngts/NGTS_charge_appendix_08Dec2008.pdf.

Gray, B. (1989). *Collaborating: Finding Common Ground for Multiparty Problems.* San Francisco: Jossey-Bass.

Gray, B. (1996). "Cross-Sectoral Partners: Collaborative Alliances among Business, Government, and Communities." In C. Huxham (ed.), *Creating Collaborative Advantage*, pp. 57–79. London: Sage Publications.

Himmelman, Arthur T. (1993). *Helping Each Other Help Others: Principles and Practices of Collaboration.* Arch factsheet no. 25. http://eric.ed.gov/?id=ED364013.

Huxham, C. (ed.). (1996). *Creating Collaborative Advantage.* London: Sage Publications.

Lowry, Charles B. (2013). "ARL Library Budgets after the Great Recession, 2011–2013." *Research Library Issues* 282. http://publications.arl.org/rli282.

NGTS. *NGTS Charge.* (2009). http://libraries.universityofcalifornia.edu/groups/files/ngts/docs/NGTS_charge_22Jan2009.pdf.

NGTS Executive Team. (2010). *Next Generation Technical Services: Next Steps.* http://libraries.universityofcalifornia.edu/groups/files/ngts/docs/NGTSNextSteps100216rev100224.pdf.

NGTS Management Team. *NGTS Management Team Charge.* (2011). http://libraries.universityofcalifornia.edu/groups/files/ngts/docs/ngtsmt_charge.pdf.

Office of the Executive Director of Universitywide Library Planning. (1977). *The University of California Libraries: A Plan for Development.* Berkeley: Systemwide Administration, University of California. http://libraries.universityofcalifornia.edu/groups/files/about/docs/UC_library_plan_1977.pdf.

Systemwide Operations and Planning Advisory Group. (2011). *SOPAG: NGTS Implementation Initiative Framework.* http://libraries.universityofcalifornia.edu/groups/files/ngts/docs/ngtsframework2011.pdf.

Systemwide Planning and Scholarly Information Advisory Committee Library Planning Task Force. (2011). Final report. http://libraries.universityofcalifornia.edu/groups/files/slasiac/docs/final_LPTF_report_draft_v3_12-01-11.pdf.

Emily S. Lin

University of California Digital Library Executive Working Group. (1996). *The University of California Digital Library: A Framework for Planning and Strategic Initiatives.* http://bat8. inria.fr/~lang/hotlist/free/text/berkeley.pdf.

Chapter Fourteen

Supporting Research through Partnership

Linda O'Brien and Joanna Richardson

Disruptive technological change is transforming the world into a genuine global economy. The rise of Asia and the global financial crisis show not only how profound these changes can be, but also how globally connected the world is. Commoditization of mobile technologies, ubiquitousness of the Internet and social media, and the rise of cloud services are challenging every industry, every profession, and every organization to reconsider long-held understandings. Almost everything is now globally tradable—knowledge, goods, services, skills, and capability (Business Council of Australia, 2014, p. 3). Technology is enabling entirely new business models that can rapidly evolve to challenge established players. Tracy Schroeder (2014) describes it as a post-enterprise world, where market focus is on the consumer and on the space "above" the enterprise in highly scalable, multi-enterprise solutions.

The knowledge industry has been, and will be further, deeply impacted by these changes. The impact of digital media and the Internet on research and higher education is manifest through the rise of global competition and ranking schemes, the perturbations caused by the advent of MOOCs, the emergence of "data-led" research practice, the increased pressure from government to maximize return on investment in research, and changing publisher business models. As Niels Finnemann (2014, p. 202) notes, "the historical dynamic has reached a point where all institutions concerned with knowledge handling will have to redefine themselves." Research libraries are no exception. "The . . . library community, feeling the impact of technological progress, economic pressures, and social and political disruption, has spent the last decade thrashing about, seeking a refreshed purpose and new ways to demonstrate and create value and impact" (Neal, 2014, p. 612).

In a hyperconnected world the emphasis is shifting from provider-consumer relationships to co-creation, collaboration, and partnerships, from service provider to collaborative partner (Association of Research Libraries, 2014, p. 2), from "product to . . . process" (Lougee, 2002, p. 4). The imperative is for organizations, indeed for professions, to reinterpret and reinvent themselves through the lens of emergent business and technological possibilities.

This chapter explores how disruptive change is creating emergent business models increasingly premised upon collaboration and partnership, as evidenced in the repositioning of research libraries in the support of research. It will discuss how academic research libraries are becoming partners in the research process, building upon core capabilities, to create value and impact.

DISRUPTIVE TECHNOLOGICAL CHANGE

In his book *The Innovator's Dilemma*, Clayton Christensen (1997) uses the term "disruptive innovation" to describe a process by which a product or service is introduced at the bottom of a market and ultimately displaces established competitors. Based on the changing application of technology in the marketplace, he cites such notable examples as the mobile phone, digital photography, and online retailing. Christensen's theory has been expanded to apply more broadly to technologies that have introduced radically different behaviors into society. Rapid technological advances provide the tools with which to disrupt the market and create threats to established market players.

The Internet has created profound change in the innovation landscape, and the ways in which enterprises must operate to remain valued and valuable. Traditional business models are extremely vulnerable, with media-based industries at the forefront of the disruptive changes, and knowledge industries predicted to be most impacted in the coming decade (Economist Intelligence Unit, 2006; Dutta and Bilbao-Osorio, 2012). Consumerization of technologies has put the power into the hands of those who consume a service, allowing them to not only connect directly to content and service creators, but also to be co-creators. It allows organizations to leverage their strengths by moving from "vertical" to "virtual" integration, given the ease with which they can partner (Trimi et al., 2009), what F. Asís Martínez-Jerez (2014) describes as "adaptive strategic partnerships." Strategic alliances are better suited to dealing with a turbulent environment, providing more rapid access to knowledge and capability and greater flexibility. Companies can focus on core competencies, narrow and deepen their capability, and leverage interorganizational relationships to gain and sustain competitive advantage. Recent advances in cloud computing have served to further accelerate these changes.

Cloud computing is "an information technology service model where computing services (both hardware and software) are delivered on-demand to customers over a network in a self-service fashion, independent of device and location. The resources required to provide the requisite quality-of-service levels are shared, dynamically-scalable, rapidly-provisioned, virtualized and released with minimal service provider interaction" (Martson et al., 2011, p. 177). Cloud computing has the potential to be one of the most disruptive technologies over the next decade (Hancock, 2014; Gartner, 2013). It disrupts the roles of traditional stakeholders in the value chain and creates new roles. IT barriers to innovation are lowered and access to expertise through collaboration is enhanced (Martson et al., 2011).

Over the next three years, Gartner predicts a shift to personal clouds and to hybrid cloud and IT service models. Consumers will worry less about devices and more about services, expecting to access everything they need from any device, anywhere, at any time. Personal and external cloud services will be combined to provide a rich integrated model, totally reliant upon collaboration, shared services, and interoperability. The cloud is being driven by an ecosystem of participants, with self-empowered consumers and businesses taking the lead. Cloud services are being used to drive speed to market, agility, scalability, flexibility, and cost reduction, operating in a "boundary-less" way as businesses look to disintermediate their traditional value chains, focus on core competencies, and outsource non-core services through the cloud and thus drive competitive advantage (North Bridge, 2013, p. 1; Martson et al., 2010).

PARTNERING FOR COMPETITIVE ADVANTAGE

A partnering relationship can range from the more informal personal relationship built on mutual respect and trust to formalized contractual agreements. Within this chapter the word "partnership" includes:

- a personal and professional relationship in an area of common interest built on trust, mutual respect, mutual benefit, and shared purpose
- a strategic partnership and memorandums of understanding
- venture partnerships and shareholder relationships
- commercial partnerships built on formal negotiated agreements for services delivered

In a global economy being disrupted by technological innovation, partnerships provide a key strategy to drive competitive advantage. Organizations are seeking partners that can bring technological advantage and/or knowledge and skills acquisition, with reputation being a highly important criterion when choosing a partner (Trimi et al., 2009; Giesecke, 2012). Partnerships can drive innovation (improved product/reduced cost) through the sharing of expertise, capability, capacity, and/or resources, or by challenging existing business approaches; or they may improve market positioning by improving supply or demand, increasing agility and speed to market, and/or enhancing political gain or prestige.

In examining how companies should take a proactive approach to strategic management in the knowledge economy, Georg von Krogh et al. (2001) have developed a framework based on four key strategies. A company can leverage its existing knowledge, expand further its knowledge based on existing expertise, appropriate knowledge from partners and other organizations, and develop completely new expertise. Knowledge transfer with external partners is achieved through strategic partnerships. A specific example is given of Unilever actively developing partnerships and alliances with academia.

Martínez-Jerez (2014) refers to "adaptive strategic partnerships" to describe the new ways in which companies are collaborating effectively in a rapidly changing business environment. These partnerships are formed around bodies of work where you would normally predict vertical integration and founded on more open information exchange, more flexible contracts, and incentive systems that support innovation and partnership success, with each partner getting a larger share of overall value.

Successful partnerships can be characterized by relationships in which partners each (Mohr and Spekman, 1994; Martínez-Jerez, 2014; Giesecke, 2012):

- bring value and strength to the alliance
- share compatible goals or common purpose
- strive for mutual benefit
- jointly create processes that promote learning, innovation, coordination, commitment, trust, open communication, participation, adaptability, joint planning, and problem solving

In addition, partners must dedicate energies to "the formation and implementation of management strategies that promote and encourage the continued growth and maintenance of the partnership" (Mohr and Spekman, 1994, p. 148). Relationships need to be nurtured so as to create and strengthen mutually beneficial partnerships.

The following section explores how the process of knowledge creation and dissemination, and hence the role of research libraries, is being disrupted and why partnerships are paramount to the future success of research libraries if they are to provide value and impact.

DISRUPTION TO KNOWLEDGE CREATION AND DISSEMINATION

The process of knowledge creation and dissemination has been fundamentally altered by the rise of the Internet. This is having a profound impact on the practice of university research. According to Ikujiro Nonaka et al. (2000), knowledge creation is about continuous transfer, combination, and conversion of the different types of knowledge as users practice, interact, and learn. It lies somewhere "between order and chaos" (p. 28). Information technology now offers a virtual collaborative environment to help foster a continuous and dynamic knowledge-creating process; however, it is not only the creation of knowledge but also the actual concept of knowledge itself that is changing and thereby the nature of its relationship to scholarship.

As with scholarship, "knowledge is perpetually in motion. Today, what we call 'knowledge' is constantly being questioned, challenged, rethought, and rewritten" (Edwards et al., 2013, p. 5). Whereas traditional knowledge has been thought of as "a paper, a product, property," it can now be thought of as "a network, an infrastructure" (Wilbanks, 2007). New knowledge structures are blurring the distinction between knowledge creators and knowledge consumers. New possibilities for analysis and presentation are leading to innovative types of digital scholarship, which will contribute to research inputs for scholars. Digital scholarship is pivotal for its ability to produce discipline-based scholarship created with digital tools and presented in a digital form that transcends the current monographic format.

In their study of online communities, Julie Blakey et al. (2013) have examined how knowledge production has become increasingly interdisciplinary, multidisciplinary, and transdisciplinary. As a result, it is characterized not only by more collaboration and communication but also by more diverse and informal ways of communication. The latter encompasses blogs, wikis, various social media, and online communities. The authors, in analyzing the use of Yammer in two different instances at Griffith University, agree with Blakey's statement on page 4 that one of the benefits of this technology is "increased academic fellowship along with increased collaborative and cross-disciplinary research opportunities."

Similarly, the role of wiki technology in collaborative knowledge creation has been explored in depth by Pattarawan Prasarnphanich and Christian Wagner (2009). They particularly focus on Wikipedia, which "demonstrates the feasibility and success of this form of collaborative knowledge creation (in a broad sense) within self-organizing, open access community" (p. 33). The successful use of wikis in corporations for knowledge management has been chronicled by Joseph Meloche et al. (2009).

Such technologies have deepened opportunities for citizen science, which, as the term suggests, involves the participation of the wider community in scientific projects. Also known as public participation in scientific research (PPRS), this field of practice is growing in popularity as a method of research. It yields new knowledge by providing access to more and different observations and data than traditional science research, and is especially useful when data needs to be gathered or processed over long periods of time and/or wide geographic areas (Bonney et al., 2009, p. 15). According to the Cornell Lab of Ornithology (2014), in recent years in excess of one hundred articles have been published in peer-reviewed scientific literature that analyze and draw significant conclusions from volunteer-collected data. At the Barbara Hardy Institute, University of South Australia, public citizens have contributed information on projects involving local koala population, beach artifacts, spiders, magpies, possums, and blue-tongued lizards.

CHANGING NATURE OF UNIVERSITY RESEARCH

The rapid development and dissemination of digital technologies have helped to enable interdisciplinary research, not just in big science but also in the fast-growing field of digital humanities. Partnerships are increasingly essential in the world of research, to share expensive facilities and to work across disciplinary boundaries to solve "wicked" problems such as climate change and population health issues. Electronic networks are making it much easier for investigators from different fields to communicate and collaborate. These rapid changes are pointing toward a very different model of research practice. In the future, it appears that research will become much more open, distributed, and collaborative as it responds to even more complex problems.

According to the American Association for the Advancement of Science (Derrick et al., 2011, p. 2), the "need to accelerate the adoption of interdisciplinary approaches is even more compelling in an era with increasingly complex problems, vast data sets, and powerful research tools. Many of the most interesting and important problems in science can be answered only through collaborative efforts. The increasing complexity of science demands that concepts and methods from different disciplines be merged."

In the area of the humanities and social sciences, the Arts and Humanities Research Council in the UK regards itself as playing a greater advocacy and leadership role based in part on the view that "there will be greater need to bring arts and humanities researchers together to influence the context in which they work; to build consortia, cross-disciplinary networks and multi-funder partnerships; and to support individual researchers to forge stronger relationships with academics overseas" (2013, p. 8).

Universities are operating in an increasingly global, competitive environment at a time when collaboration and partnerships are critical to success. World university rankings proliferate as a measure of prestige, in large part influenced by measures of citation impact (Shin and Toutkoushian, 2011). This continues to fuel pressure to publish in highly ranked journals sustaining the "publish or perish" paradigm. Yet in a world where knowledge—and its application—is seen as a key to global competitiveness, where national prosperity is viewed as underpinned by knowledge innovation, there is growing pressure to make the outputs of publicly funded research openly accessible. Fundamental to innovation is the dissemination of research findings (Bowen and Graham, 2013; Chesbrough et al., 2006). The Business Council of Australia (2014, p. 6) asserts that "governments should be enabling innovation across the whole economy by fostering entrepreneurship and collaboration and thus dynamic growth and facilitating skills and capabilities." They suggest that a key building block in a proposed "innovation infrastructure" would be the alignment of Australia's research and development efforts with its competitive advantages and the fostering of cross-sector collaboration. Universities and research organizations are seen as important collaborators with industry and government.

Locking research findings in journals only read by other academics, while fostering further research and increasing citation impact, may do little to optimize the economic return on publicly funded research. The challenge is appropriately balancing the demand for improved global research rankings with the imperative to ensure research achieves social, economic, and cultural dividends.

Research outputs are no longer regarded as publications resulting from research. There is also a shift to better manage ever-increasing volumes of research data and to regard data as a first-class output of research (O'Brien and Simons, 2013). Internationally and nationally, the view is that libraries will play a key role in data access and management, particularly in relation to the vast quantities of data currently being created, and in helping researchers to manage and sift through that data (Christensen-Dalsgaard et al., 2012).

PUBLISHERS CHANGING BUSINESS MODELS

Digital content has disrupted the former relationships and roles among writers, publishers, and readers (Disabato, 2012). The traditional scholarly communication model relied upon researchers generating scholarly content, which they copyright-assigned to publishers, who arranged peer review, editing, and publication, and which the publishers then sold back to libraries at ever-increasing prices so that libraries could provide access to the material for their scholars. The Internet has enabled new models of scholarly communication, linking scholars directly with other scholars and students, and creating digital content even if in a high-ranking published journal that does not sit on a library's shelves. New publishing and pricing models are being explored for journals, scholarly monographs, textbooks, and digital materials, as stakeholders try to establish sustainable business models.

Some would argue that copyright law is no longer appropriate for a digital world where simply viewing a work is an act of copying. Developments include open access to historical content, author-funded open access to new content, and uncertainty of the future of "Big Deals," i.e., agreements or subscriptions with the large, usually expensive, publishers and use of contracts to circumvent copyright legislation.

The Internet allows individual scholars and publishers to "deal direct" on the provision of scholarly resources, bypassing the library. As funding agencies and universities enact open access (OA) mandates and publishers transition their journals from the site-license model to the gold OA model, the publishers' core business will become developing relationships with scholars, not librarians. For publishers, it makes perfect sense to cater to scholars both as authors and as readers.

In this disrupted research and publishing environment, how are libraries ensuring they continue to create value and impact in their support of research, rather than being one of the organizations that fail to grasp the opportunity?

RESEARCH LIBRARIES: CREATING VALUE AND IMPACT

As John Seely Brown notes, "The challenges we face are both fundamental and substantial. We have moved from an era of equilibrium to a new normal, an era of constant disequilibrium. Our ways of working, ways of creating value, and ways of innovating must be reframed" (Neal, 2014, p. 613).

The traditional value of a research library was often measured by the quality of its collections, and the ability of the librarian to locate and supply relevant works that were not within the collections. While librarians played a role in research, it was predominantly as collector, curator, and service provider. In a world where Google is now often the scholar's search tool of choice (Williams and Pryor, 2009; Haglund and Olsson, 2008), where the "library collection" is no longer owned by libraries or on their shelves, the value proposition must be reframed. In the future, collections—as librarians currently know them—will not exist in the same way. The focus instead will be on enhancing discoverability of "smart content," content that is semantically and richly linked and actionable, no matter where it is located (Shen, 2008). Static information products and services will have been replaced by dynamic service platforms to cater to changing ways in the consumption of information. Consumption is no longer just an object of discovery and analysis, but rather a user-driven action leading to innovation and development. Whither the librarian?

CORE CAPABILITIES

While collaboration has long been at the heart of what libraries are about (Gaetz, 2009, p. 1), it has been bounded within the more traditional notion of the library as a collection and a service provider. This capability, however, positions libraries well to develop partnerships. If they are to deliver value and impact in an environment of disruptive innovation they must seek out strategic adaptive partnerships. But in order to do so libraries must first understand the core capabilities that they bring to any partnership, those that transcend technological innovation and which add value. These provide the foundation for entering a partnership of mutual benefit. It is premised that the core librarian capabilities that can be leveraged in a digitally disrupted global knowledge environment are:

1. Knowledge of information management theory

   - from creation to destruction or preservation;
   - from discoverability to rights and ethics management; and
   - from critical evaluation to analysis and communication.

2. Demonstrated

   - structured thinking;
   - innate curiosity, self-directed learning, and evidence-based practice;
   - proactive collaboration (previously confined predominantly to library-to-library collaboration to deliver public value); and
   - ability to communicate, connect, translate, and be an honest broker (see for example Sandhu, 2013, p. 29, who describes the academic library as a "trusted partner for knowledge creation and dissemination").

3. Valuing access to knowledge for all.

With the above capabilities, librarians are well positioned to be partners in knowledge creation and dissemination—partners in the process of research. But this requires a reframing of their more traditional role as service provider to a more proactive role as partner, both within and outside universities.

In considering the characteristics of successful partnerships, it is clear that librarians can

- *bring value and strength* to the process of knowledge creation and dissemination;
- *share compatible goals or common purpose* with those of their researchers, the universities, and the national public and private bodies concerned with leveraging value from research investment;
- *strive for mutual benefit* of the partners, given their valuing of access to knowledge for all; and
- *jointly create processes that promote learning, innovation, coordination, commitment, trust, open communication, participation, adaptability, joint planning, and problem solving* given their credentials as collaborators, communicators, and honest brokers.

This aspirational role for librarians was affirmed at the May 2014 ARL membership meeting (Association of Research Libraries, 2014), which described the research library and university of 2033 as "a rich and diverse learning/research ecosystem" (p. 16), with the research library shifting from "its role as knowledge service provider within the university to become a collaborative partner that catalyzes evolution" (p. 17). The meeting predicted that research libraries would be active across institutional boundaries and heavily focused on collaborative roles (Neal, 2014, p. 613).

In examining the role of the academic research library in supporting research, Richard Luce (2008a) describes libraries as "the microcosm of the university" when it comes to expanding roles and developing new types of partnerships. He writes: "In a knowledge economy, characterized both by collaboration and competition in science, the enabling infrastructure and support systems are fundamental to competitiveness and scientific leadership" (p. 18). Digital scholarship and the challenges associated with research data offer libraries the chance to shed their "support service" label and become research collaborators (Corrall, 2013). As an integral stakeholder, the library needs to take collaboration to the next level—to become a proactive adaptive strategic partner.

THE LIBRARY AS A STRATEGIC ADAPTIVE PARTNER

A key to responding to these drivers is the formation by the library of strategic partnerships both within and beyond the university. As the main authority in the university on the ways in which knowledge is generated and transmitted (MacColl, 2010), the library should leverage its position to lead through vision and strategic initiative. At the institutional level, libraries should establish "the vital role they play in the knowledge creation process" (Tenopir et al., 2012, p. 3). In the new paradigm of collaboration and partnerships, libraries must emphasize proactive outreach and engagement by taking an active role as conveners among the different stakeholders (Luce, 2008b) as well as considering collaborative initiatives with external entities (Potter et al., 2011).

Brian Mathews (2014, p. 1) writes: "If the research library shifts from its role as a knowledge service provider within the university to become a collaborative partner then it becomes a more valuable knowledge and service partner for the university, which is, itself, becoming more distributed and more connected. And if we think about unbundling research libraries from single sites—single universities—then they can take on other roles and other partners."

Within the field of research, the library can add value and impact as both an active internal and external partner across the complete research life cycle. Many libraries are gearing up for more active roles in research, as noted by Sheila Corrall (2013) with respect to the UK; Janice Jaguszewski and Karen Williams (2013) with respect to the US; and Paul Ayris (2012) with respect to Europe.

In assessing what libraries could contribute to a successful research partnership (Mohr and Spekman, 1994; Martínez-Jerez, 2014; Giesecke, 2012), one can define their capabilities as shown in table 14.1.

If one considers the context in which libraries are operating, as outlined above, and the core capabilities libraries bring to a partnership, there are two obvious areas where libraries can create significant value and impact for research within their universities by strategically partnering:

1. Maximizing the impact of research outputs.

Table 14.1. Library Contribution to Successful Partnerships

Successful Partnership Attributes	Library Capability
Bring value and strength to the alliance	Our knowledge of information management life cycle is of critical value when considering how to manage research data as an asset or how to maximize the impact of research outputs.
Share compatible goals or common purpose	We value access to knowledge, sharing compatible goals with those of the researcher, the university, and the broader community.
Strive for mutual benefit	Refer to next point.
Jointly create processes that promote learning, innovation, coordination, commitment, trust, open communication, participation, adaptability, joint planning, and problem solving	Our collaborative nature and ability to communicate, connect, translate, and be an honest broker stand us in excellent stead to create mutual benefit through adopting positive processes.

2. Managing research outputs, particularly data, as an asset.

PARTNERSHIPS IN ACTION: MAXIMIZING THE IMPACT OF RESEARCH OUTPUTS

In a world where knowledge and its application is seen as the key to global competitiveness, the developed and developing nations have renewed their focus on knowledge innovation as a driver of national prosperity, advocating a central role for universities. As a result, governments seek to measure the quality of their universities and the contribution they make to the nation's prosperity. The impact of a university's research is a significant element of a university's contribution (O'Brien, 2010).

Governments and funding bodies also wish to maximize the economic and social returns from any public investment in research. In several Commonwealth countries, accountability is measured among universities by means of a research assessment exercise. The United Kingdom has established its Research Excellence Framework, while New Zealand universities are required to meet the requirements of the Performance-Based Research Fund. In Australia, the Excellence in Research for Australia initiative is designed to provide benchmarking data for Australian universities compared with international measures (Simons and Richardson, 2012).

In looking toward the future, the changing scholarly communication landscape is increasing the potential to enhance research impact, and also increasing the inherent complexity. From a researcher's perspective, one of the greatest challenges for disseminating research is choosing where to publish (Harley et al., 2010). With the advent of the author-pays-for-publication model, the rise of predatory publishers, and research-granting agencies requiring open access to publicly funded research outputs, the publishing landscape has become even more complex.

Increasingly, the library is taking a leadership role in partnering with researchers to ensure the outputs of their research, including publications or research data, are accessible and appropriately managed and curated. Through such partnerships, researchers can more effectively navigate the rapidly changing scholarly communication landscape to create strategic value for the university. Librarians are seeking to ensure not only that the works of scholars are captured and curated, but also that discoverability, and hence potential impact, is maximized.

One response to this challenge has been that of the University of New South Wales. In 2005 it introduced the Research Impact Measurement Service, to realign its services to support the university's goals (Drummond and Wartho, 2009). Recognizing the increasingly competitive nature of the research environment and a renewed emphasis by the university on research outcomes, the library offered a new bibliometric service providing comparative publication and citation data to schools and faculties. Knowledge gained through this process has informed collection development and training opportunities for the academy on higher-impact publishing.

At the Bernard Becker Medical Library of Washington University, librarians have worked with research investigators and clinicians to develop a more comprehensive model for the assessment of research impact than just citation analysis (Sarli et al., 2010). The proposed Becker Model has been designed to provide a more comprehensive overview of the research impact of medical investigators' study findings. Christopher Shaffer (2013) has chronicled a number of expertise systems—in which libraries are key players—that have been built to highlight the interests and accomplishments of researchers at an institution.

Within the scholarly communications ecosystem, scholarly publishers— university presses, academic societies, research institutions—are key players. They strive to fulfill the mission of "making public the fruits of scholarly research" as effectively as possible within that ecosystem (Withey et al., 2011, p. 398). While that mission has remained constant, in recent years the landscape has altered dramatically, particularly in regard to a new role for libraries. As Christine Borgman (2010, p. 13) so aptly encapsulates the shift, "The role of libraries in research institutions is evolving from a focus on reader services to a focus on author services."

A 2010 study (Harley et al.) has shown that scholars across a broad range of disciplines have a growing interest in electronic publication, and that scholars embrace the potential of linking final publications directly to data sets and/or primary source material, though most of those interviewed believed they did not have access to easy-to-use tools or to the expertise required. Publishing is seen as an emerging role for libraries as it becomes easier to implement e-press services. Karla Hahn (2008) found that in most cases, libraries were assisting scholars to move existing journals into the digital world or into open access publishing; in some cases they were publishing new titles. The overlap of expertise and demands of publishing with the knowledge and skills required by libraries has made it a natural progression.

Along with its role as co-creator in knowledge production, the academic research library has a role as infrastructure provider (Jensen et al., 2009, p. 4). In examining the changing landscape in which digital scholars find, collaborate, create, and process information and, as a result, scholarship is being transformed, Malcolm Wolski and Joanna Richardson (2014) have suggested a collaborative framework for building the necessary supporting institutional infrastructure. There is a requirement to store, deliver, and preserve the resultant outputs of digital scholarship.

The library within the institution is a logical potential source of skills and expertise in managing information and preservation. To be effective, however, will require a common approach and partnership with the IT department to a) supply the hardware infrastructure to meet the needs either provisioned locally or through the cloud; b) to leverage external services as needed, e.g., those funded by governments or specific discipline data repositories; and c) collaboration and partnering with other institutions to develop cost-effective solutions. This will also need to extend to better engagement with key stakeholders within the institution so as to have better points of intervention. (p. 11)

As a partner in knowledge, the library is ideally positioned to add value throughout the entire research life cycle. By facilitating greater access to a university's research outputs for students, researchers, and the general public, the library contributes to increased exposure for potential reuse, increased citations, higher prestige, greater public value, and greater leverage of funding.

PARTNERSHIPS IN ACTION: MANAGING RESEARCH DATA AS AN ASSET

Given that "research data is the new gold" (Simons and Richardson, 2013, p. 115), Borgman (2008) suggests that data may become the new "special collection" for libraries. She notes that strategies for data curation will require involvement from academics, the campus research office, the library, and instructional and information technology services. Clifford Lynch (2008) recommends that campuses create a support organization that can 1) reach out to scholars early in the data life cycle to assist with data management and curation/preservation strategies, involving IT professionals, librarians, and archivists; and 2) maintain a close relationship with the research and grants office. He suggests that perhaps the library could take responsibility for the long-term curation of the data at an appropriate point in the life cycle.

In 2011 the Association of College and Research Libraries surveyed a cross section of its members in the United States and Canada to provide a baseline assessment of the current state of, and future plans for, research data services in academic libraries in these countries. In the resultant report (Tenopir et al., 2012, pp. 3–4), key findings included the following:

- Only a small minority of academic libraries in the United States and Canada currently offer research data services (RDS), but a quarter to a third of all academic libraries are planning to offer some services within the next two years.
- Libraries on campuses that receive National Science Foundation funding are more likely to offer or plan to offer RDS of any type. This suggests

that funding agency requirements are driving the need for RDS. As budget decisions move toward even greater accountability, it is likely that more agencies will dictate responsible data management, so the need for RDS on campus is likely to grow. If the library is not actively involved in providing these services, some other unit is likely to be pressed into service, which can diminish the image of the library as an important partner in the research process.

- Collaboration on RDS occurs most frequently with other units on campus, most often the office of research. This collaboration is an excellent way for libraries to establish the vital role they play in the knowledge creation process and to help support the valuation of the library to the campus community.

In some universities the library collaborates with the research office and graduate research school (or its equivalent) to deliver innovative support programs. Libraries are cooperating with information technology services divisions or high-performance computing support units to provide research data management services.

The University of Michigan Library, as a specific example, has developed a model for partnering with digital humanities scholars, based on the capabilities and considerable expertise that research libraries can inherently provide (Alexander et al., 2014). The result has been win-win in that together both partners are helping to define new expressions of scholarship in an emerging field.

There is keen interest, of course, in this emerging area in other parts of the world, e.g., Australasia. In a survey of thirty-one of Australia's thirty-nine university libraries, Linda O'Brien (2011) found that just over 50% were involved in supporting their university's e-research activities through partnering both with external and internal groups. More than thirty external partnerships existed across the libraries. These were with state-based and national bodies created to support the Australian national research infrastructure agenda. Most prevalent were relationships with the Australian National Data Service (ANDS), an agency created to increase reuse of Australian research data through developing the Australian Research Data Commons (see http://ands.org.au). Arguably, the creation of this entity, along with its approach to university partnering, has accelerated support for research data within Australian university libraries at a higher rate than in the US and Canada.

Another key driver has been the Australian Code for the Responsible Conduct of Research, developed in its current format by the National Health and Medical Research Council, the Australian Research Council, and Universities Australia. It provides a guide to responsible research practice and covers a wide range of topics associated with research, including the management of research data and associated materials, and the publication and dissemination of research finding. The code assigns both researchers and their parent institutions a shared responsibility to appropriately manage research data and primary materials. Another key driver has been the expected future changes in Australian funding agency requirements in relation to research data management, following overseas trends.

In September 2014 a workshop was co-facilitated by the Council of Australian University Librarians and the ANDS for university librarians: "Open Data to Open Knowledge: The Role of the Academic Library." From this workshop it was evident that the majority of Australian university libraries represented now offer services to support research data.

One of the key workshop activities involved a panel session on different library approaches to supporting research and particularly research data management. Attendees were provided with five written university library case studies in advance of the workshop. The libraries represented were from Edith Cowan University, Griffith University, Monash University, Queensland University of Technology, and the University of Melbourne. Each of the five libraries completed a brief survey on "adding value to university research," which formed the basis for the case studies. Among the high-level categories covered were formal and informal partnerships/agreements, both internal and external to the parent organization.

Each of the libraries tended to have a combination of both informal and formal agreements with their respective research office. The library may assist with national research assessment exercises, e.g., Excellence in Research for Australia, and with drafting university policy and guidelines for areas with shared objectives, e.g., open access requirements and developments. Both elements may work together to support good practice in research data management through training, policy development and support, and compliance audits. In cases in which the respective university has a "graduate research school" to support higher research degree students and early career researchers, the library contributes to the school's programs.

The relationship with the respective university's information technology services is also a mixture of both informal and formal agreements. Areas covered may include the provision of infrastructure, a joint research data management website, and joint training and information sessions for researchers. For Monash University, a key relationship is the library's interaction with the Researcher Support Services section of the university's eSolutions (Information and Communication Technologies) Division. In the case of Griffith University, the Division of Information Services offers leadership and services through six integrated portfolio groups. Of those six, two have a predominantly library focus: Library and Learning Services, and Information Management. The university's eResearch Services and Scholarly Application

Development (eRSAD) provides access to specialist e-research technologies and library and information professionals.

The five university libraries collaborate with their respective faculties on a range of research support activities: provision of information literacy to researchers and HDRs, participation in events organized by the graduate research school, provision of skills development programs that include research data management, and support for formal funded eResearch projects. Each library also works with one or more research centers within its respective university, usually to support projects. Monash University Library collaborates with the Monash eResearch Centre (MeRC) across a number of areas. Library staff meet with MeRC staff to plan and undertake faculty engagements and partnerships. The University of Melbourne Library has a formal partnership with the faculty of arts on the Melbourne Collaborative Research Infrastructure Program–funded Social and Cultural Informatics Platform, which supports researchers from the arts, humanities, social sciences, and visual and performing arts.

In terms of library support for national services, all libraries upload data to Research Data Australia, a service offered by the Australian National Data Service (ANDS). In fact, Monash University is the lead partner in ANDS; ANDS is functionally part of the library, and the executive director reports to the university librarian. At the University of Melbourne, the library is leading a project as part of the ANDS-funded Open Data Collections Program in partnership with researchers in the Department of Genetics' Hoffmann Laboratory. Griffith University is collaborating on projects with both the Queensland Department of Environment and Heritage and the national Department of Foreign Affairs and Trade's Secretariat of the Pacific Regional Environment Programme (SPREP). In addition, thanks to library initiatives, the university is represented on the Organisation Committee and various working groups of the international Research Data Alliance.

The above examples reinforce Carol Tenopir's point that academic libraries need to demonstrate the expertise that they bring to the knowledge creation process. By actively seeking out opportunities to help drive its respective university's strategic research agenda, the library becomes an invaluable partner in the research enterprise.

CONCLUSION

It seems inevitable that disruptive innovation is the new normal, requiring new ways in which organizations must evolve if they are to create value and impact. Strategic adaptive partnerships provide a mechanism by which organizations can leverage their core capabilities, while constantly innovating and adapting to a rapidly changing environment.

Academic research libraries will continue to deliver value and impact through key partnerships with the academy, with other relevant units within their universities, and with external stakeholders who form part of the research development and dissemination landscape. Librarians, by focusing on their core capabilities in information management and on being a trusted broker, and through a commitment to knowledge for all, are well positioned for the turbulent environment ahead.

REFERENCES

Alexander, L., B. D. Case, K. E. Downing, M. Gomis, and E. Maslowski. (2014). "Librarians and Scholars: Partners in Digital Humanities." *EDUCAUSE Review Online* (June). Accessed November 13, 2014. http://www.educause.edu/ero/article/librarians-and-scholars-partners-digital-humanities.

Arts and Humanities Research Council. (2013). *The Human World: The Arts and Humanities in Our Times*. AHRC Strategy 2013–2018. Swindon, UK: AHRC.

Association of Research Libraries. (2014). *ARL Strategic Thinking and Design: A Framework for the Organization Going Forward*. Washington, DC: ARL.

Ayris, P. (2012). "Knowledge and Wisdom: The Role of Research Libraries in Supporting the European Research Agenda." 7th IGeLU Conference, Zurich, September 11–13.

Bejune, M. (2007). "Wikis in Libraries." *Information Technology and Libraries* 26(3): 26–38.

Blakey, J., M. Wolski, and J. Richardson. (2013). "Online Communities: An Ecology for Knowledge Collaboration." THETA 2013: The Higher Education Technology Agenda, Hobart, Tasmania, April 7–10. Accessed September 21, 2014. http://hdl.handle.net/10072/52202.

Bonney, R., H. Ballard, R. Jordan, E. McCallie, T. Phillips, J. Shirk, and C. C. Wilderman. (2009). *Public Participation in Scientific Research: Defining the Field and Assessing Its Potential for Informal Science Education*. CAISE Inquiry Group Report. Washington, DC: Center for Advancement of Informal Science Education.

Borgman, C. L. (2008). "Supporting the 'Scholarship' in E-scholarship." *Educause Review* 43(6): 32–33.

Borgman, C. L. (2010). "Research Data: Who Will Share What, with Whom, When, and Why?" 5th China–North America Library Conference, Beijing, September 9–10. Accessed October 10, 2014. http://works.bepress.com/borgman/238/.

Bowen, S. J., and I. D. Graham. (2013). "From Knowledge Translation to Engaged Scholarship: Promoting Research Relevance and Utilization." *Archives of Physical Medicine and Rehabilitation* 94(1): S3–S8.

Business Council of Australia. (2014). *Building Australia's Comparative Advantages*. Melbourne: The Council.

Chesbrough, H., W. Vanhaverbeke, and J. West (eds.). (2006). *Open Innovation: Researching a New Paradigm*. Oxford, UK: Oxford University Press.

Christensen, C. M. (1997). *The Innovator's Dilemma: When New Technologies Cause Great Firms to Fail*. Boston, MA: Harvard Business Review Press.

Christensen-Dalsgaard, B., M. van den Berg, R. Grim, W. Horstmann, D. Jansen, T. Pollard, and A. Roos. (2012). "Ten Recommendations for Libraries to Get Started with Research Data Management." Final report of the LIBER Working Group on E-science/Research Data Management. The Hague: LIBER Working Group on E-science/Research Data Management.

Cornell Lab of Ornithology. (2014). *What Is Citizen Science and PPSR?* Accessed November 9, 2014. http://www.birds.cornell.edu/citscitoolkit/about/defining-citizen-science/.

Corrall, S. (2013). "Designing Libraries for Research Collaboration in the Networked World." LIBER 42nd Annual Conference, Munich, June 26–29. Accessed October 10, 2014. https://www.liber2013.de/fileadmin/inhalte_redakteure/2.2_Corrall.pdf.

Derrick, E. G., H. J. Falk-Krzesinski, and M. R. Roberts (eds.). (2011). *Facilitating Interdisciplinary Research and Education: A Practical Guide*. Washington, DC: American Association for the Advancement of Science.

Disabato, N. (2012). "Publication Standards Part 1: The Fragmented Present." *A List Apart* 352. Accessed February 23, 2014. http://alistapart.com/article/publication-standards-part-1-the-fragmented-present.

Drummond, R. and R. Wartho. (2009). "RIMS: The Research Impact Measurement Service at the University of New South Wales." *Australian Academic and Research Libraries* 40(2): 76–87.

Dutta, S., and B. Bilbao-Osorio (eds.). (2012). *The Global Information Technology Report 2012: Living in a Hyperconnected World*. Geneva: World Economic Forum.

Economist Intelligence Unit. (2006). *Foresight 2020: Economic, Industry and Corporate Trends*. London: Economist Intelligence Unit.

Edwards, P. N., S. J. Jackson, M. K. Chalmers, G. C. Bowker, C. L. Borgman, D. Ribes, M. Burton, and S. Calvert. (2013). *Knowledge Infrastructures: Intellectual Frameworks and Research Challenges*. Ann Arbor, MI: Deep Blue. Accessed February 23, 2014. http://hdl.handle.net/2027.42/97552.

Finnemann, N. O. (2014). "Research Libraries and the Internet: On the Transformative Dynamic between Institutions and Digital Media." *Journal of Documentation* 70(2): 202–220.

Gaetz, I. (2009). "Collaborative Librarianship: New Light on a Brilliant Concept." *Collaborative Librarianship* 1(1): 1–12.

Gartner. (2013). "Top 10 Strategic Technology Trends for 2014." Accessed October 10, 2014. http://www.gartner.com/technology/research/top-10-technology-trends/.

Giesecke, J. (2012). "The Value of Partnerships: Building New Partnerships for Success." *Journal of Library Administration* 52(1): 36–52.

Haglund, L., and P. Olsson. (2008). "The Impact on University Libraries of Changes in Information Behavior among Academic Researchers: A Multiple Case Study." *The Journal of Academic Librarianship* 34(1): 52–59.

Hahn, K. (2008). "Publishing Services: An Emerging Role for Libraries." *Educause Review*: 16–17.

Hancock, I. (2014). "Business impacts of cloud." Sydney: KPMG. http://www.kpmg.com/AU/en/topics/cloud/Pages/default.aspx.

Harley, D., S. K. Acord, S. Earl-Novell, S. Lawrence, and C. J. King. (2010). *Assessing the Future Landscape of Scholarly Communication: An Exploration of Faculty Values and Needs in Seven Disciplines*. Berkeley: University of California Center for Studies in Higher Education.

Jaguszewski, J. M., and K. Williams. (2013). *Transforming Liaison Roles in Research Libraries*. Washington, DC: Association of Research Libraries.

Jensen, H. S., M. Volker, and D. Staunæs. (2009). *The Future of Research and the Research Library: A Report to DEFF*. Copenhagen: DEFF.

Lougee, W. P. (2002). *Diffuse Libraries: Emergent Roles for the Research Library in the Digital Age—Perspectives on the Evolving Library*. Washington, DC: Council on Library and Information Resources.

Luce, R. (2008a). "Making a Quantum Leap to E-research Support: A New World of Opportunities and Challenges for Research Libraries." Reinventing Science Librarianship: Models for the Future, Washington, DC, October 18.

Luce, R. (2008b). "The Role of Academic Research Libraries in the Digital Data Universe." CLI E-science Conference 2008: Librarians and E-science: Focusing towards 20/20, Purdue University, May 12–13.

Luce, R. E. (2008c). "A New Value Equation Challenge: The Emergence of E-research and Roles for Research Libraries." In CLIR (ed.), *No Brief Candle: Reconceiving Research Libraries for the 21st Century*, pp. 42–50. Washington, DC: Council on Library and Information Resources.

Lynch, C. (2008). "The Institutional Challenges of Cyberinfrastructure and E-research." *Educause Review* 43(6): 74–88.

MacColl, J. (2010). "Library Roles in University Research Assessment." *Liber Quarterly* 20(2): 152–168.

Martínez-Jerez, F. A. (2014). "Rewriting the Playbook for Corporate Partnerships." *MIT Sloan Management Review* 55(2): 63–70.

Martson, S., S. Bandyopadhyay, J. Zhang, and A. Ghalsasi. (2011). "Cloud Computing: The Business Perspective." *Decision Support Systems* 51(1): 176–189.

Mathews, B. (2014). "Shifting from a Knowledge Service Provider to a Collaborative Partner." *The Chronicle Blog Network* (July 7).

McCredie, J., and J. A. Pirani. (2012). "A Dozen Gurus Describe IT Collaborations That Work." *Research Bulletin*. Louisville, CO: EDUCAUSE Center for Analysis and Research.

Meloche, J. A., H. M. Hasan, D. Willis, C. Pfaff, and Y. Qi. (2009). "Co-creating Corporate Knowledge with a Wiki." *International Journal of Knowledge Management* 5(2): 33–50.

Mohr, J., and R. Spekman. (1994). "Characteristics of Partnership Success: Partnership Attributes, Communication Behavior, and Conflict Resolution Techniques." *Strategic Management Journal* 15(2): 135–152.

Monastersky, R. (2013). "Publishing Frontiers: The Library Reboot." *Nature* 495(7442), 430–432.

National Health and Medical Research Council, Australian Research Council, and Universities Australia. (2007). *Australian Code for the Responsible Conduct of Research*. Canberra, ACT: Australian Government.

Neal, J. G. (2014). "A New Age of Reason for Academic Libraries." *College and Research Libraries* 75(5), 612–615.

Nonaka, I., R. Toyama, and N. Konno. (2000). "SECI, *Ba*, and Leadership: A Unified Model of Dynamic Knowledge Creation." *Long Range Planning* 33(1): 5–34.

North Bridge. (2013). *2013 Future of Cloud Computing Survey Reveals Business Driving Cloud Adoption in Everything as a Service Era; IT Investing Heavily to Catch Up and Support Consumers Graduating from BYOD to BYOC*. Accessed October 10, 2014. http://www.northbridge.com/2013-future-cloud-computing-survey-reveals-business-driving-cloud-adoption-everything-service-era-it.

O'Brien, L. (2010). "The Changing Scholarly Information Landscape: Reinventing Information Services to Increase Research Impact." ELPUB 2010: Conference on Electronic Publishing, Helsinki, Finland, June 16–18.

O'Brien, L. (2011). "E-research Partnerships Revisited." CCA-EDUCAUSE Australasia, Sydney, April 3–6.

O'Brien, L., and N. Simons. (2013). "From Library to Research Hub: Connecting an Entire University Research Enterprise." 15th Fiesole Collection Development Retreat, Singapore, August 12–14. Accessed November 13, 2014. http://www.casalini.it/retreat/retreat_2013.html.

Potter, W. G., C. Cook, and M. Kyrillidou. (2011). *ARL Profiles: Research Libraries 2010*. Washington, DC: Association of Research Libraries. Accessed October 10, 2014. http://www.arl.org/bm~doc/arl-profiles-report-2010.pdf.

Prasarnphanich, P., and C. Wagner. (2009). "The Role of Wiki Technology and Altruism in Collaborative Knowledge Creation." *Journal of Computer Information Systems* 49(4): 33–41.

Research Information Network. (2010). *Research Support Services in UK Universities*. London: RIN.

Sandhu, G. (2013). "Building Future Capacity through Effective Digital Library Strategies to Thrive in a Rapidly Changing Information Landscape." In S. Ganguly and P. K. Bhattacharya (eds.), *International Conference on Digital Libraries (ICDL) 2013: Vision 2020—Looking Back 10 Years and Forging New Frontiers*, pp 29–39. New Delhi: TERI Press.

Sarli, C. C., E. K. Dubinsky, and K. L. Holmes. (2010). "Beyond Citation Analysis: A Model for Assessment of Research Impact." *Journal of the Medical Library Association* 98(1): 17–23.

Schroeder, T. (2014). "The IT Service Organization for a Post-Enterprise World." *EDUCAUSE Review Online* (July/August): 14–24.

Shaffer, C. J. (2013). "The Role of the Library in the Research Enterprise." *Journal of eScience Librarianship* 2(1): 8–15.

Shen, H. (2008). "Smart Content Delivery on the Internet." In A. G. Bourgeois and S. Q. Zheng (eds.), *Algorithms and Architectures for Parallel Processing*, 1. Heidelberg: Springer.

Shin, J. C., and R. K. Toutkoushian. (2011). *University Rankings: Theoretical Basis, Methodology and Impacts on Global Higher Education.* Heidelberg: Springer.

Simons, N., and J. Richardson. (2012). "New Roles, New Responsibilities: Examining Training Needs of Repository Staff." *Journal of Librarianship and Scholarly Communication* 1(2), eP1051: 1–16.

Simons, N., and J. Richardson. (2013). *New Content in Digital Repositories: The Changing Research Landscape.* Cambridge, UK: Chandos.

Tenopir, C., B. Birch, and S. Allard. (2012). *Academic Libraries and Research Data Services: Current Practices and Plans for the Future—an ACRL White Paper.* Chicago: Association of College and Research Libraries.

Trimi, S., S. Faja, and S. Rhee. (2009). "Impact of the Internet on Interorganizational Relationships." *Service Business* 3(1): 63–83.

Von Krogh, G., I. Nonaka, and M. Aben. (2001). "Making the Most of Your Company's Knowledge: A Strategic Framework." *Long Range Planning* 34(4): 421–424.

Wilbanks, J. (2007). "New Metaphors in Scientific Communication: Libraries and the Commons." *Proceedings of the IATUL Conference*, paper 32. Accessed September 21, 2014. http://docs.lib.purdue.edu/cgi/viewcontent.cgi?article=1826andcontext=iatul.

Williams, R., and G. Pryor. (2009). *Patterns of Information Use and Exchange: Case Studies of Researchers in the Life Sciences.* London: Research Information Network and the British Library.

Withey, L., S. Cohn, E. Faran, M. Jensen, G. Kiely, W. Underwood, B. Wilcox, R. Brown, P. Givler, A. Holzman, and K. Keane. (2011). "Sustaining Scholarly Publishing: New Business Models for University Presses." *Journal of Scholarly Publishing* 42(4): 397–441.

Wolski, M., and J. Richardson. (2014). "A Model for Institutional Infrastructure to Support Digital Scholarship." *Publications* 2(4): 83–99.

Index

About the Editor and Contributors

Bradford Lee Eden is dean of library services at Valparaiso University. Previous positions include associate university librarian for technical services and scholarly communication at the University of California, Santa Barbara, and head of web and digitization services and head of bibliographic and metadata services for the University of Nevada, Las Vegas Libraries. He is editor of OCLC Systems and Services: Digital Library Perspectives International ; The Bottom Line: Managing Library Finances; *Library Leadership and Management*, the journal of the Library Leadership and Management Association within the American Library Association; and *The Journal of Tolkien Research*, a new, open-access peer-reviewed journal. He is also on the editorial boards of Library Hi Tech, Advances in Library Administration and Organization, and The Journal of Film Music. He has a master's degree and PhD in musicology, as well as an MS in library science. He publishes in the areas of metadata, librarianship, medieval music and liturgy, and J. R. R. Tolkien. His two books Innovative Redesign and Reorganization of Library Technical Services: Paths for the Future and Case Studies (2004) and *More Innovative Redesign and Reorganization of Library Technical Services* (2009) are used and cited extensively in the field. He is the author of Metadata and Its Applications (2002), *3D Visualization Techniques* (2005), *Innovative Digital Projects in the Humanities* (2005), *Metadata and Its Applications: New Directions and Updates* (2005), *FRBR: Functional Requirements for Bibliographic Records* (2006), and *Information Organization Future for Libraries* (2007). His recent books include *Middle-Earth Minstrel: Essays on Music in Tolkien* (2010), *The Associate University Librarian Handbook: A Resource Guide* (2012), *Leadership in Academic Libraries: Connecting Theory to Practice* (2014), and *The Hobbit and Tolkien's Mythology: Essays on Revisions and Influences* (2014).

* * *

Apollo Abungu is currently a freelance librarian and coordinator of programs at Ndwara Community Resource Center in Bondo, Kenya. He was previously a senior librarian at the Aga Khan University in Dar es Salaam, Tanzania. He holds a master's degree in information and library studies, and has over seventeen years of experience as a practicing librarian in academic and research institutions.

Jessica Alverson is the assistant coordinator for e-learning at DePaul University. Prior to her time at DePaul she worked at Columbia College Chicago as the digital services librarian and at New York University as the librarian for journalism and media, culture, and communication. Jessica's research interests include adult learning, e-learning, and user experience.

Marissa C. Ball, emerging technologies librarian at Florida International University, devotes her time in the FIU Libraries to delving into new tactics of patron interaction and introducing new services, instruction methods, and communication tools through social networking and new and emerging technologies. Additionally, she serves as the liaison to the Center for Women's and Gender Studies, offering instruction and collection development services. Her varied responsibilities in emerging/learning technologies, social media, and women's studies are also reflected in her research interests, which include women in film, gender and technology, and technofeminism. Marissa received a BA in English (with a concentration in gender studies and a minor in women's studies) from the University of Florida, and a master of library and information science from the University of South Florida. She served as the co-project investigator and project manager for the Hub project.

Steve Brantley is the head of reference services and an associate professor in the Booth Library at Eastern Illinois University. Steve received his MLS and MA in media studies in 2000, both from Indiana University. He has published on web usability, research practices of undergraduate students, collection development and classification, fair use of library video collections by faculty, library discovery systems, and scholarly communication. Steve is active in the American Library Association and its divisions and sections related to academic librarianship. He lives in Charleston, Illinois, with his wife and two children.

Todd Bruns is the institutional repository librarian at Eastern Illinois University. Todd manages the EIU institutional repository, the Keep (http://thekeep.eiu.edu). He has an MA in library and information studies from the

University of Wisconsin–Madison (2005) and an MS in technology from EIU (2012). Todd has published on several topics related to scholarly communication, including IR management, IR metrics, digital scholarship services, and quality management. In 2014 he was an honored recipient of the Bepress Institutional Repository All-Star international award. Additionally, he chairs the EIU Booth Library Web Resources Committee, runs the annual Edible Book Festival, and has regularly presented at several national conferences. He lives in Charleston, Illinois, with his husband and two rambunctious cats.

Ashley Krenelka Chase is the associate director and an adjunct professor of law at the Hand Law Library at Stetson University College of Law. Ashley is responsible for the administration, coordination, and direction of electronic resources and web page development for the library, as well as administration, planning, management, and supervision of reference and outreach services. Ashley's scholarly interests include the evolution of student and faculty research habits and finding clever ways to incorporate emerging technologies into those habits. Ashley has a BA in English from Bradley University, a JD from the University of Dayton School of Law, and an MLIS from the University of South Florida.

Troy Davis is head of media services at Earl Gregg Swem Library at the College of William and Mary in Virginia. He promotes media literacy and creative practice across the college's curriculum. Additionally, he serves as liaison to the film and media studies program and teaches courses on remix culture and new media.

Kirstin Duffin is a reference librarian and serves as subject liaison for the departments of biological sciences, chemistry, and geology/geography at Eastern Illinois University. She earned her MA in library and information studies from the University of Wisconsin–Madison in 2010. She is currently working on her MS in biological sciences at Eastern Illinois University.

Kelly Evans is a business librarian and assistant professor at Eastern Washington University. She was previously a business librarian at Purdue University and the University of North Carolina at Charlotte. She holds an MLS from Indiana University and a BA in history from Virginia Wesleyan College. Her passion is for students to succeed in their learning. She enjoys teaching, writing, camping, and Zumba.

Joseph Fennewald has been with Penn State University Libraries since February 2000. Prior to his appointment as head of the Tombros McWhirter Knowledge Commons in January 2012, he served as the head of

Penn State's Hazleton and Worthington Scranton Libraries. He earned his MLS from the University of Missouri and has an MSW from the University of Kansas. Joe has published in leading library research journals and has given presentations at state and national library conferences. He is active with the Pennsylvania Library Association and was its 2009 president.

Margaret Law is currently director of external relations at the University of Alberta Libraries. She holds two master's degrees in library science and a doctor of business administration. Her professional career has spanned rural and urban public libraries, academic and library consortia. She is also very passionate about community development, and is a partner in the Ndwara Community Resource Center initiative in rural Kenya.

Emily Lin is currently head of digital assets at the University of California, Merced Library. She served on the management team of the University of California Next-Generation Technical Services initiative as communications manager. She has overseen the development of digital collections and digital curation services at UC Merced and has contributed to the development of plans and policies for shared services at the UC system-wide level. She managed the IMLS Leadership Grant–funded project to digitize the world-class art collection of the Ruth and Sherman Lee Institute for Japanese Art at the Clark Center for Japanese Art and Culture. The collection is available online to students, scholars, and the general public through the UC Merced website and the California Digital Library. Emily began her librarian career at the University of California, Merced in 2003. She received her MLIS from Drexel University and BA in comparative literature from Princeton University. She is a member of the 2014 cohort of UCLA Senior Fellows.

Katy Mathuews is the learning and outreach librarian at Shawnee State University's Clark Memorial Library. She also serves as an adjunct faculty member teaching microeconomics, macroeconomics, and economics of gender. Her research interests include library assessment and the role of the library in student retention and success. She holds master's degrees in applied economics and library and information science.

Kelley Minars is the web services librarian at the University of Texas Health Science Center at San Antonio and works with usability, content, and graphics. Kelley is a graduate of the University of South Florida School of Information.

Linda O'Brien is pro vice chancellor at Griffith University in Australia. She is a member of the university executive team, with responsibility for development and implementation of Griffith's information strategy and management of the university's information services, including the e-learning and e-research services; the library; university records management; and university-wide information and communication technology services, systems, and infrastructure. She has an MPA, a graduate diploma in library information science, a bachelor of education, and a corporate directors diploma. She has substantial senior university management experience, having worked in six Australian universities in a variety of roles, including vice principal of information at the University of Melbourne and vice president of university services at the University of Newcastle. She has published and presented in her field, both nationally and internationally, and contributed to a number of state and national initiatives, including as member of the eResearch Expert Working Group developing the 2011 national Strategic Roadmap for Research Infrastructure and co-principal investigator for the Australian and New Zealand Horizon Report 2012. Linda is currently a board member of the Queensland Cyber Infrastructure Foundation, chair of the Council of Australian University Librarians Research Advisory Committee, a member of the Queensland Public Records Review Committee, and founding board member of the Open Data Institute Queensland.

Patricia Pereira-Pujol has been the science and engineering librarian at Florida International University Libraries for fifteen years. After completing two years of computer science and engineering courses, Patricia changed majors and earned a BS in political science with concentrations in Latin American and women's studies from the Massachusetts Institute of Technology in 1991. She earned her MA in library and information science from the University of South Florida in 1999. Patricia was the co-project investigator and project manager for the Hub project.

JJ Pionke is the applied health sciences librarian at the University of Illinois at Urbana-Champaign. When not at work, she enjoys reading, playing video games, and riding her motorcycle.

Katherine Prentice is currently associate director for user experience and assessment at the University of Oklahoma–Tulsa Schusterman Library. She formerly was head of education and information services at the University of Texas Health Science Center at San Antonio Briscoe Library. Katie holds an MS in information studies from the University of Texas School of Information.

Joanna Richardson is library strategy advisor in the division of information services at Griffith University. Previously, she was responsible for scholarly content and discovery services including repositories, research publications, and resource discovery. Joanna has also worked as an information technology librarian in university libraries in both North America and Australia, and has been a lecturer in library and information science. Recent publications have been centered around resource discovery and research data management frameworks.

Susan Shultz is a business and social sciences librarian at DePaul University. She supports the management, psychology, and School for New Learning departments. Prior to her time at DePaul, she worked at Michigan State University as a business librarian. Her research interests include adult students, andragogy, and distance learning.

Ann Marie Stock is professor of Hispanic studies and film and media studies at the College of William and Mary in Virginia. A specialist on Cuban film and new media, she is the author of *On Location in Cuba: Street Filmmaking during Times of Transition* (2009), editor of *World Film Locations: Havana* (2014), and founding director of Cuban Cinema Classics (www. cubancinemaclassics.org), a nonprofit initiative disseminating Cuban documentaries with English subtitles. She has traveled to Cuba more than 50 times in the past 25 years and regularly curates film programs and serves on festival juries around the world.

John Weed is the head of collection resources at the University of Texas Health Science Center at San Antonio Briscoe Library and works with various consortia and licensing of electronic resources. John received his MS in information studies from the University of Texas School of Information.

Dana Whitmire is the electronic resources/serials librarian at the University of Texas Health Science Center at San Antonio Briscoe Library. Dana received her MS in library science from the University of North Texas.

Eric Willman is the library services technology manager at the Arlington Public Library. He formerly was head of library technology at the University of Texas Health Science Center at San Antonio Briscoe Library. Eric received his MIS from the University of North Texas.